Modern Japanese Cuisine

Modern Japanese Cuisine

Food, Power and National Identity

Katarzyna J. Cwiertka

REAKTION BOOKS

To Piotr and Niek

Published by Reaktion Books Ltd
33 Great Sutton Street
London EC1V 0DX, UK

www.reaktionbooks.co.uk

First published 2006

Printed and bound in Great Britain by
Cromwell Press, Trowbridge, Wiltshire

British Library Cataloguing in Publication Data
Cwiertka, Katarzyna Joanna, 1968–
Modern Japanese cuisine: food, power and national identity
1. Food habits – Japan   2. Cookery, Japanese
3. Japan – Civilization
I. Title
394.1'0952

ISBN-13: 978 1 86189 298 0
ISBN-10: 1 86189 298 5

Contents

Introduction

Multiculturalism is the defining feature of the culinary scene in contemporary Japan. It is reflected in the daily food choices of every Japanese. An average day may begin with a Western-style breakfast of toast, coffee and fried eggs, or a Japanese-style breakfast of rice, *miso* soup, pickles and grilled fish. Lunch may be either a Japanese-style *obentō* (a boxed meal of rice and several small side dishes), prepared at home or purchased at specialized *obentō* kiosks, or a quick bite at one of the ubiquitous fast-food restaurants, noodle shops or an array of other lunch establishments. Many factories and schools operate their own canteens in which indigenous fare prevails, but with strongly pronounced Chinese and Western influences. A dinner may be taken at home or enjoyed in one of many restaurants. In practically every town, a selection of Japanese, Chinese and Korean eating places, along with American restaurant chains such as Skylark and Denny's – commonly labelled 'family restaurants' (*famirii resutoran* or *famiresu* for short) – cater to diners of every age, sex and degree of affluence. Moreover, larger urban centres also offer a choice of fancy French and Italian bistros and a variety of 'ethnic' (*esunikku*) eateries that claim to serve food from such exotic places as India, Vietnam, Malaysia, Afghanistan and Ethiopia.[1]

At home, a Japanese-style dinner centred on white boiled rice accompanied by soup and side dishes, all served at the same time, still prevails. It is, however, by no means free from foreign influences. In 1997, on the occasion of the fortieth anniversary of its launch, the leading television cooking show *Kyō no ryōri* ('Dishes for Today') conducted a survey among 6,000 of its regular viewers asking them to list their most favourite side dishes appropriate to be served at a Japanese-style dinner. The top ten included (in ascending order) hamburger, fried *gyōza* dumplings, *miso* soup with *tōfu* and seaweed (*wakame*), soy-stewed chicken with vegetables

A contemporary home meal.

(*Chikuẓenni*), rice curry, *tōfu* and minced meat in spicy sauce (*mabōdōfu*), Japanese apricot pickle (*umeboshi*), sugar-simmered black beans (*kuro-mame*), home-style sushi (*chirashiẓushi*) and, as number one, soy-simmered beef, potatoes and onions (*nikujaga*).[2] Half of the dishes in this selection are of foreign origin and began to enter Japanese cuisine after the turn of the twentieth century. Other foreign-inspired mainstays in Japanese home dinners include breaded deep-fried fish (*furai*), breaded deep-fried pork cutlets (*tonkatsu*) and stir-fried vegetables.[3]

Despite the foreign origins of these side dishes, the Japanese charac-ter of the entire meal is secured by its 'rice, soup and side dishes' structure. Moreover, the side dishes are often 'Japanized' by the addition of soy sauce (*shōyu*), the most important flavouring in contemporary Japanese cooking.[4] Soy sauce is considered such a vital condiment that manufactur-ers have produced conveniently packaged travel-size bottles and sachets, so that Japanese travellers can venture forth into the world 'armed with slippers and soy sauce'.[5]

Some scholars seek the explanation for the strongly multicultural character of modern Japanese diet in the Japanese tendency to borrow from abroad, allegedly already evident in the country's ancient history.[6] This stance is neither isolated nor limited to cuisine. The capacity to adapt foreign imports successfully has often been singled out as a 'uniquely' Japanese characteristic.[7] It has been claimed that Japanese adapt foreign culture in such a way that, rather than disturbing, it merely catalyses the natural growth of the indigenous tradition; that 'alien culture is somehow invariably naturalized or Japanified at the frontier'.[8] Following Peter Dale, among others, this volume argues strongly against the idea of the timeless, adaptive nature of Japanese culture. In the course of this book, it will become evident that the multicultural character of contemporary Japanese cuisine is a result of specific circumstances in which Japan found itself during the last 150 years, and the changes that have taken place under the impact of industrialization, nation-state formation and imperialist expansion.

It is certainly true that modern Japanese cuisine is particularly abundant in foreign borrowings, especially from China, Korea, Europe and the United States. However, there is probably no cuisine that at one time or another has not relied on foreign borrowings. The recent embrace of 'ethnic food' – a term that encompasses a variety of cuisines hailing from outside the European tradition – in Europe and the United States is only one of many instances of global culinary exchanges.[9] Foreign foodstuffs, flavourings and cooking techniques have for centuries provided creative stimulation in the development of culinary cultures worldwide. Such occurrences are so plentiful in human history that one ought to view them as a norm rather than something distinctive.[10] What is more British than a Christmas dinner of turkey and roast potatoes? What tastes more Korean than pungent *kimch'i* pickle on white rice? The fact that turkey, potatoes and chilli pepper (which is a major component of Korean pickle) originated in the New World, and that rice derives from China, is of little consequence here. Since their introduction, these foodstuffs have been not only successfully accommodated into, respectively, British and Korean cuisines, but have also acquired cultural and ideological connotations of a greater importance than indigenous ingredients. A much more important question to pose seems to be what circumstances conditioned the introduction of these foodstuffs and what factors propelled their successful diffusion.

That the economic prosperity of the last few decades is largely responsible for the abundance of food choices in Japan seems quite obvious. Greater disposable income, along with the globalization of markets and information, has created opportunities for ordinary Japanese to embrace foreign tastes and global culinary trends.[11] However, the culinary multiculturalism in contemporary Japan dates further back than the economic boom of the 1960s. This volume suggests that it was part and parcel of a comprehensive dietary change that accompanied the political, economic and social transformations that the country underwent during the late nineteenth and the twentieth centuries. This web of changes was spun over decades by the joint, yet uncoordinated, efforts of the emerging Japanese state and various individuals and groups that pursued their own agendas and were motivated by specific goals. The latter, in turn, were shaped by a variety of forces, from imperialism and industrialization to nationalism and consumerism.

Multiculturalism is merely one aspect in the culinary transformation of modern Japan that can very generally be described as a persistent homogenization of local food practices and attitudes into the Japanese cuisine as we know it today. Homogenization was not a goal in itself, but rather an unintentional outcome of a variety of actions undertaken for the sake of different objectives. Tracing the trajectory of this transition, and analysing its context, constitute the core of this book.

For present-day Japanese, rice, soy sauce and fresh seafood are the ultimate symbols of 'Japaneseness', symbols more powerful than the cherry blossom or the national flag in that they satisfy visceral cravings. Yet it is only relatively recently that these three ingredients have turned into standard components of the daily meal of all Japanese. The position of rice in the Japanese diet remains ambivalent. The symbolic importance of rice in Japanese history and its role as currency in the pre-modern Japanese economy are indisputable; it was, to be sure, a preferred staple, but there was not enough of it to feed everybody. Scholars have not yet been able to reach consensus as to who ate how much rice and how often outside the urban centres, where white rice had for centuries been a daily staple.[12] It is certain, however, that soybean paste (*miso*) rather than soy sauce was the prevailing flavouring in most rural areas. Moreover, before the emergence of national brands in the early twentieth century, the taste of soy sauce varied greatly depending on the region. The consumption of seafood had also been relatively limited and confined to the areas with easy access to the sea, not to mention that the standard of freshness maintained today was simply impossible to attain before contemporary transport and preservation technologies had developed. The Japanese fishing industry's ability to exploit formerly inaccessible distant waters, along with the new technologies that revolutionized the storage and transportation of seafood, have turned octopus from the West African coast, tuna from the Atlantic, crabs from Hokkaido, Norwegian salmon and shrimp from Thailand into staples on the Japanese menus.[13] As formerly expensive and exclusive types of food became universally affordable, the daily meals of people of different social and economic status who resided in different parts of Japan have grown increasingly similar.

The following seven chapters will portray the seven most important processes in the dietary transformation of modern Japan: the embrace of the West as the model for political and economic development (chapter One), the rise of the new urban mass gastronomy (chapter Two), the modernization of military catering (chapter Three) and home cookery (chapter Four), wartime food management (chapter Five), the dietary effects of Japanese imperialism (chapter Six) and, finally, the impact of the rapid economic growth in post-war Japan (chapter Seven). The contexts and implications of each of the processes will be addressed and crucial players identified. The book concludes with a general analysis of the making of a national cuisine, and closes with a brief portrayal of the spread of Japanese food outside Japan.

I will employ the term 'cuisine' following the definition provided by Warren Belasco – a set of socially situated food behaviours comprising 'a limited number of "edible" foods (*selectivity*); a preference for particular ways of preparing food (*techniques*); a distinctive set of flavours; textual and visual characteristics (*aesthetics*); a set of rules for consuming food (*ritual*); and an organized system of producing and distributing the food (*infrastructure*)'.[14] Like Belasco's, my understanding of cuisine differs from the definitions of scholars like Priscilla Ferguson, who limits the concept to what Jack Goody would call a 'high cuisine' – an elaborated and formalized style of consumption that serves as a means of differentiating class distinctions in hierarchical societies.[15] Ferguson sees cuisine as a cultural construct that 'systematizes culinary practices and transmutes the spontaneous culinary gesture into a stable cultural code'. 'Culinary preparations' – she explains – 'become a cuisine when, and only when, the preparations are articulated and formalized, and enter the public domain'.[16] This, as Sidney Mintz astutely observed, 'is like saying that a country does not exist until someone makes a map of it'.[17] My perception of cuisine follows Mintz's approach in stressing the social embedment of cuisine rather than its intellectual and aesthetic qualities.

What makes a cuisine is not a set of recipes aggregated in a book, or a series of particular foods associated with a particular setting, but something more. I think a cuisine requires a population that eats that cuisine with sufficient frequency to consider themselves experts on it. They all believe, and *care* that they believe, that they know what it consists of, how it is made, and how it should taste. In short, a genuine cuisine has common social roots, it is the food of a community – albeit often a very large community.[18]

I see 'cuisine' as an expression of culinary activity characteristic of a particular community, which entails *selecting* foodstuffs, *transforming* them according to specific techniques and flavouring principles, and *consuming* them according to particular rules.[19] While a classic idea of a cuisine implies a local and often class-specific scope, the concept of a 'national cuisine' stands for an imagined national identity and cultural homogeneity.[20] Thus, the making of a national cuisine entails the replacement of diversified, community-tied local practices with a cuisine that is the same for all.

All Japanese words in this book have been indicated in italics, except for personal, geographical and institutional names, as well as words that have by now entered the English language, such as 'samurai' and 'sushi'. Diacriticals have been omitted in the names of main Japanese cities and the four main islands. Food-related Japanese terms have been briefly explained in the text and in more detail in the Glossary. Japanese names are presented following the Japanese convention in which the family name precedes the given name, except for authors who have published in English.

In order to provide suggestions for further reading, I refer to English-language, rather than Japanese-language, publications and sources, whenever they are available.

One
Western Food, Politics and Fashion

'Restoring' the Imperial Rule

On 4 November 1871 distinguished foreign officials residing in Japan gathered for a dinner party commemorating the birthday of Emperor Meiji (1852–1912) the day before. The banquet was prepared by Hôtel des Colonies (also known as Tsukiji Hotel or Yedo Hotel), the only Western-style hotel in the city of Tokyo at the time. It was managed by Monsieur Ruel and was renowned for its exquisite French cuisine prepared under the supervision of the French chef Bégeux. Following the nineteenth-century conventions of diplomatic dining, the menu of the banquet was in French:[1]

POTAGE

Purée de crevettes à la Bisque

RELEVÉ

Bouchées Saumon á la Genevoise

HORS D'OEUVRE

Bouchées à la Béchamel

ENTRÉES

Roast-beef au madère

Tendrons de chevreuil à la Poivrade

Canetons de volaille au Suprême

LÉGUMES

Petits pois à l'Anglaise

Céleri au Jus

ROTIS

Pâté de gibier Truffé

Galantine en belle vue

Gigot de mouton Rôti

Chapous Truffés

13

ENTREMETS
Pudding à la Diplomate
Macédoine de fruit au kirch
Nougat Monté
DESSERT ASSORTI

Three years before the banquet took place, in November 1868, the emperor moved from Kyoto – for centuries the imperial residence and the capital of Japan – to the city of Edo, which two months earlier had been renamed Tokyo (meaning 'Eastern Capital') and was soon to become the capital of the country.[2] Since the emperor's arrival in Tokyo, the Tsukiji Hotel had been entrusted with the task of furnishing European-style imperial banquets. The hotel opened for business in summer 1868 and for more than three years, before vanishing in flames with 5,000 other buildings in the neighbourhood, it maintained the most exclusive Western-style restaurant in Tokyo.[3] The city belonged to the most populous and most built-up conurbations of the pre-modern world, and fires were regular affairs in this largely wooden metropolis. Historians estimate that on average there was a major conflagration once every six years.[4]

The custom of inviting foreign diplomats to celebrate the emperor's birthday with food and drink began in 1869. Before the new Imperial Palace in Tokyo with Western-style banquet halls was completed in 1888, these receptions were usually held at Enryōkan, a Western-style house in the grounds of the Hama Detached Palace on the edge of Tokyo Bay constructed especially to house the Duke of Edinburgh during his visit in 1869.[5] In 1872 Tsukiji Seiyōken Hotel took over the responsibility of furnishing imperial banquets. It was the first high-class Western-style hotel in Japan that was owned and managed by a Japanese. Its proprietor, Katamura Shigetake, who had been a steward of Iwakura Tomomi (1825–1883), the court noble and influential politician, was explicitly entrusted with the mission of setting up the hotel by his master. Until the establishment of the Imperial Hotel in 1890, Seiyōken enjoyed the reputation of running the best Western restaurant in the capital.[6]

The dinner party on 4 November 1871 commemorating the emperor's birthday was by no means the first European-style banquet organized by Japanese authorities to entertain Western diplomats,[7] but it clearly signified the two important functions that Western food would play in the political scene of late nineteenth-century Japan. First, the adoption of Western-style dining for formal diplomatic occasions and state ceremonies became an integral component of the power politics of the new regime.

Tsukiji Seiyōken
Hotel in Tokyo,
c. 1910s.

Officially designated for state ceremonies in 1873, Western-style banquets were designed to impress foreign dignitaries with Japan's ability to succeed in imitating Western conventions and to strengthen the authority of the government in the domestic arena through its association with the 'West'.[8] Second, the year 1871 marked the beginning of a carefully orchestrated series of measures that aimed at turning the young emperor into a modern monarch and the Japanese into a modern nation.[9] Designating the Emperor's Birthday (*Tenchōsetsu*) as an official national holiday and celebrating it with a Western-style banquet were the first signs of the important roles that both the emperor and Western food would play in Japan during the following decades.

The celebration of the emperor's birthday in November 1871 took place against the background of one of the most dramatic political shifts in Japanese history. At the beginning of 1868 a coalition of middle-ranking samurai from the south-western domains initiated a *coup d'état* by taking control of the Imperial Palace in Kyoto and the sixteen-year-old emperor, who had only acceded to the throne the previous year. The regime change proceeded relatively peacefully; the 'restoration' of imperial rule was soon announced and Meiji (meaning 'enlightened rule') proclaimed the name of the new era.[10]

It needs to be clarified at this point that the political status quo of the Tokugawa period (1600–1867) rested upon the complex structure of the warrior government (*bakufu*), which was detached from the imperial court and headed by the *shōgun* or military regent, who resided in the city of Edo (today's Tokyo). Officially, the *shōgun* ruled under the reigning emperor, who resided in Kyoto, the formal capital. In reality, however, Edo functioned as de facto capital of the country and the *shōgun* effectively controlled the emperor. The only strength that the emperor retained was his potential power as a symbolic head of state, deriving from the unbroken hereditary line of the imperial family, which could be traced back to the sixth century AD. The executors of the *coup d'état* of 1868 utilized this potency fully. By claiming to 'restore' the emperor to power, they legitimized the drastic actions of abolishing the warrior government and the *shōgun* – institutions that had been central in the political system of Japan since the twelfth century. While fully exploiting the historical authority of the imperial institution, however, the Meiji politicians fortified it tremendously by creating a modern image of the emperor modelled on constitutional monarchies of nineteenth-century Europe. The major driving force behind these measures was the fear of Western domination and the national humiliation brought about by the 'unequal treaties' of 1858.

In the past, the foreign policy of Tokugawa Japan was often explained as 'self-imposed isolation'. Today, however, historians agree that it would be misleading to characterize the foreign relations of the Tokugawa government as such in view of Japan's continuous interaction with Asia during the pre-modern period.[11] The main reason for emphasizing its 'seclusion' was the inability of Western countries to conduct 'free trade' in Japan. A series of edicts issued during the 1630s banned all Westerners from the country, except for a handful of Dutch who were allowed to take residence on a tiny outpost of Deshima (or Dejima) in Nagasaki Bay, in the far western corner of the country. Only officially sanctioned trade and travel were tolerated by the authorities, which gave the latter full control and authority. The missionary activities of the Portuguese and Spanish between the 1540s and 1620s and a potential threat that the spread of Christianity among Japanese posed for the *bakufu* were the main motives behind the decision to break off ties with the 'West' in the early seventeenth century.

There is no doubt that the foreign policy of the Tokugawa regime protected Japan from Western powers, whose quest for profit and territory in Asia became increasingly pronounced in the late eighteenth century. In 1854, however, Japan's resistance to Western encroachment was broken. Under a threat of the use of military power, a fleet of nine American ships under the command of Commodore Matthew Perry was allowed to dock in Edo bay. In 1858 the *bakufu* was forced to sign the infamous 'unequal treaties' with the Five Nations (the United States, Great Britain, France, Russia and the Netherlands), which in the following years were extended to include other European countries. The treaties came into effect the following year and remained in force for four decades.[12] Their 'unequal' nature derived from the fact that they imposed a semi-colonial status on Japan, since they included extra-territoriality by which nationals residing in Japan came under the legal jurisdiction of their own countries' consuls. The treaties also provided for the establishment of designated settlements for foreigners in the so-called treaty ports (Hakodate, Nagasaki, Kanagawa, Niigata and Hyōgo), in which they could engage in international trade under the privileged tariffs specified by the treaties. The national humiliation brought about by the treaties became the driving force behind the political activism that ultimately led to the Meiji Restoration of 1868. The global reach of Western imperialism continued to play a central role in the course of Japanese history for the remaining part of the century – it provided 'the context in which the Meiji leaders acted and a model for them to follow'.[13]

The defeat of China by the British in the First Opium War (1839–42) and the shock of the forced 'opening' of Japan by Perry made many progressive Japanese intellectuals realize that China was no longer the leading force in Asia, but was replaced by the technologically and militarily advanced Western powers. The Iwakura Mission (1871–3), a large diplomatic mission sent to Europe and the United States to renegotiate the 'unequal treaties', further convinced the Meiji leaders that Japan still had far to go before it would be in a position to negotiate with Western powers on equal terms. The chief aim of the mission failed, but its members were able to see with their own eyes the technological advancement behind global Western domination.

Two conclusions were drawn from these experiences. First, Japan was to avoid being confused with China or Asia in Western eyes and instead elevate its status in the international arena through extensive Westernization. Second, the country was to be modernized by reforming its legal and political system and industrializing its economy based on Western models. To achieve this, an ambitious agenda of wide-ranging, radical reforms that were jointly coined under the term 'civilization and enlightenment' (*bunmei kaika*) was generated. Western-style dining became an integral part of the project.

Eating for 'Civilization and Enlightenment'

Although Western-style banquets were initially held exclusively for the purpose of entertaining foreign diplomats, in the summer of 1871 Western cuisine was for the first time served at court to Japanese officials without foreigners being present at all.[14] The idea was to help them to become acquainted with Western ways, including Western food and Western dining etiquette. As the occasions of Japanese and Westerners socializing in each other's company steadily increased, these qualities were required from every member of the Japanese elite. Along with personal advice from the members of the Western diplomatic community, manuals that described the details of Western-style dining were consulted. The first book that introduced this aspect of Western civilization to the Japanese public was published in 1867, and was written by Fukuzawa Yukichi (1835–1901), a leading thinker and educator of modern Japan, under the title *Seiyō ishokujū* ('Western Clothing, Food and Homes'). This richly illustrated, detailed guide to Western customs and manners taught the 'bewildered readers how to eat, dress, and even urinate in proper Western style'.[15]

Sensitivity to Western opinion and approval was very strong in the motivation to recreate Western ways in minute detail. In 1887 Ottmar von Mohl, who had previously been in the service of Empress Augusta and Emperor Wilhelm in Berlin, arrived in Japan with his wife on a two-year contract. Von Mohl's appointment aimed to advise the Japanese on the matter of etiquette and to modernize the court along the lines of European royalty. It was on his recommendation, for example, that a Belgian steward named Dewette, who had been in the service of the Russian consul in Tokyo, was engaged to train the emperor's staff.[16] The timing of von Mohl's appointment coincided with the completion of the new Imperial Palace, which was to elevate the Japanese imperial court to the European standards. These efforts proved effective, as is confirmed by an entry of 1894 in the diary of Mary Crawford Fraser (1851–1922), the wife of the British consul in Japan. She attended a dinner party for 800 held at the palace to celebrate the Silver Wedding of the imperial couple and remarked on the following:

> The dinner was admirably served – no small triumph when you remember that European methods, with all that they entail of utensils, glass, porcelain, silver, and linen, do not enter into

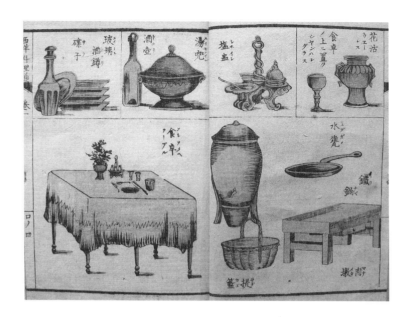

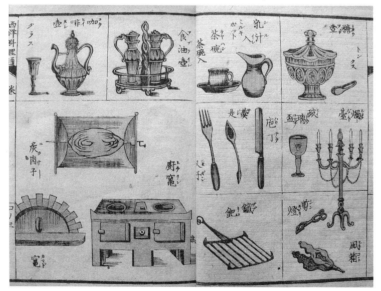

Detailed description of Western dining equipment, from *Seiyō ryōri tsū* (1872)

the daily life of the Palace at all. The service was perfect – a footman to every two guests; and all this crowd of men did not get in each other's way, attended quietly to one's wants, and made, in their dark liveries of crimson and black and gold, an effective background to the long rows of guests, where the women were almost all in white, relieved with gold or silver and covered with jewels, the men with hardly an exception in all the glory of smart uniforms.[17]

A slightly different account of the same evening was given by Ella M. Hart Bennett, who recalled that 'the little Japanese Admiral, who spoke no English, tried to entertain me by making all sorts of figures out of his bread. At each course he asked for a fresh roll, and, by the end of dinner, we had an array of minute bread soldiers, ladies and animals on the table before us, really most cleverly contrived.'[18] English conversation skills notwithstanding, it seems that by the 1890s the Japanese elite had became fully acquainted with Western-style dining.

This was by no means an easy task, considering the fact that practically every aspect of Western-style dining revolutionized the existing Japanese conventions. Not only did the form and taste of the food differ greatly from native fare, but also the eating utensils and dining furniture contradicted Japanese customs. Sitting on chairs and handling cutlery were already tortures for novice Japanese diners, not to mention the challenging flavours of butter, beef and wine. On the top of that, a Western-style banquet required its participants to be dressed in Western style, which at the time was in itself an adventure for many members of the Japanese upper class. In short, the introduction of Western food into the lives of the Japanese elite meant much more than simply a change of the menu.

The policies of *bunmei kaika* divided the life of the Japanese elite into two separate spheres – the Western sphere (represented by the ideogram *yō*) and the Japanese sphere (ideogram *wa*).[19] Western-style cuisine (*yōshoku*) was served in a Western-style room (*yōma*) and the diners were dressed in Western-style clothes (*yōfuku*). Since the intimate aspects of the lives of aristocrats, intellectuals and government officials of the Meiji period (1868–1912) remained predominantly in the Japanese sphere, the Western sphere became strongly associated with official state ceremonies. In time, the practical meaning of what was Western and what Japanese became less clear-cut, shifting across the social territories of Japan. Ultimately, the Westernized, official culture fostered by the state would merge with native class- and community-based practices and conventions.[20]

The division of the lives of the Meiji elite into the dual Japanese and Western spheres inspired the development of the category of 'Japanese cuisine' (*washoku*). The term began to be used in Japan in reference to native food only in response to the proliferation of the term *yōshoku*, which represented the food of the most powerful 'other'. The formation of the dual, Japanese and Western, styles of dining among the Meiji elite initiated the construction of the Japanese-Western-Chinese tripod, which by the mid-twentieth century was to become the fundamental structure within modern Japanese cuisine (see chapter Six).

The ideological origins of the tripod can be traced back to a treatise on food and drink published by Noguchi Hokugen in 1880 in the new magazine *Fūzoku gahō* ('Manners and Customs Illustrated'). The treatise dealt generally with the differences in food preparation among different cultures, focusing on three sets of cuisine: the Japanese, Western and Chinese. Its author emphasized the aesthetic value of Japanese cuisine and praised Western cooking for its nutritious qualities, yet regarded it as inferior to the former in terms of taste and appearance. Chinese cuisine was described as a crossbreed between the two. In his conclusion, Noguchi stressed that if only the Japanese managed to improve the nutritional value of their dishes by adopting items from China and Western countries, Japanese eating habits would certainly become superior to all.[21] The construction of a hybrid Japanese-Western cuisine indeed took place in the following decades and will be discussed later in this book. An important point to make here, however, is that the consequences of the premeditated adoption of Western cuisine in the elite circles of Meiji Japan went beyond the intended goals of expressing the autonomy and legitimacy of the new government to the political opponents at home and to validate and empower it in the eyes of foreign dignitaries.

As the nineteenth century approached its end, Western food and drink were successfully accommodated in the households of the Japanese aristocracy.[22] Mary Fraser observed soon after her arrival in Japan in 1889 that government officials were fully accustomed to Western food and drink, regardless of their inability to speak Western languages.

> One does not learn much of Japanese life at these feasts, which are, as far as their appointments go, for all the world like official dinner parties in Rome or Paris or Vienna; but it is startling to find oneself between the host and some other big official neither of whom will admit that he can speak a word of any European language . . . But the silence does not bore me.

The new faces, the old historical names, the remembered biography of some hero who perhaps sits opposite to me in gold-laced uniform calmly enjoying the *foies-gras* and champagne as if there were never a blood-stained page in his country's history – all this appeals strongly to one's dramatic appreciations.[23]

As I mentioned earlier, Western-style banquets were not only designed to impress foreign dignitaries with Japan's ability to become 'civilized', but were also used to strengthen the authority of the new political leadership in the domestic arena. Cultural conformity with the 'West' maintained by the Japanese aristocracy and government officials was a method of acquiring authority through the use of the powerful Western image. Members of the elite became the creators of fashions, confirming their superior position within Japanese society.

Based on the fashion theory of Kon Wajirō (1888–1973), the cultural historian Kumakura Isao argues that the creators of fashions in premodern Japan were not those closely associated with political power, but wealthy urbanites with relatively low social status. New trends were created

Progressive Japanese at a Western table, from *Seiyō ryōri seitsū* (1901).

22

by social deviants in the atmosphere of free urban culture, unrestrained by the strict conventions of feudal society.[24] This differed from the situation in Europe, where the ruling elites deliberately created new fashions as a means of social display and authorization of power – by imitating them the wider society acknowledged the superiority of their creators. Through a deliberate adoption of Western-style dining, members of the Meiji elite converted themselves into creators of fashions. This association with the highest circles of Japanese society attributed Western cuisine with an important advantage over Chinese food, which began to spread later through different channels (see chapter Six). From the Meiji period onwards, familiarity with things Western and, by extension, dining in Western style came to be regarded as a sign of sophistication and signified social prestige. This aspect played an important role in the rapid adoption of Western food in Japan down the social ladder.

Certainly, it took several decades before dining in Western style, or rather hybrid Japanese-Western style, became attainable to a wider section of the Japanese population. The exclusive image of Western food, however, and its association with elite culture facilitated the diffusion of certain types of Western food that were within the financial reach of urban population, such as beer and biscuits. Middle and even working classes were attracted by Western-style food precisely because it had attained a function of status marker through its association with the upper classes.

The conversion of the political elite into propagators of fashion was in line with the growing importance of cultural statecraft in nineteenth-century politics. Nation states gained a large part of their legitimacy from the promotion of a distinctive *national* culture.[25] In Meiji Japan, the emperor – elevated to the symbol of the nation – was to pave the way in embracing an official culture of the state that was heavily dependent on Western models. The task assumed a particular importance in view of the fact that the emperor's father had been well known for his hatred of foreigners and his wholehearted rejection of Western civilization. Every aspect of Emperor Meiji's life was thus used to prove the true devotion of Japan's new leadership to modernity and change. In 1872 the emperor's traditional clothes were replaced by what would become his most typical costume – a swallow-tail uniform fastened with hooks. The following year, his hair was cut and he grew a beard and moustache.[26]

The common people in nineteenth-century Japan had neither a strong sense of national identity nor a clear image of the emperor as the Japanese nation's central symbol. Customs, beliefs and practices were localized and diverse, with little national uniformity. Imperial pageantry was to become the crucial strategy employed by the state with the aim of reconstituting the Japanese people into modern subject-citizens united under the leadership of the emperor.[27] Beef was to play an important role in this project.

The West, the Emperor and the Meat-Eating Taboo

In January 1872 it was publicly announced that Emperor Meiji partook of beef and mutton on a regular basis, breaking a centuries-old official ban on meat eating.[28] This announcement placed the emperor at the centre of the newly emerging meat-eating fashion.

The issue of meat eating is one of the most contentious aspects in Japanese food history. The standard explanation declares that the Japanese stopped eating meat in the seventh century because of a religious taboo that sprang from the Buddhist precept against the taking of life. The consumption of animal flesh remained very low and limited to game (especially venison and wild boar) until the Meiji period, when it was encouraged by the new government in order to bolster the physique of the Japanese population.[29]

In essence, this account is by no means incorrect. Nevertheless, it needs to be nuanced at least in three respects: the motivation behind the introduction of the official ban was only loosely connected to Buddhism; the taboo did not become widespread before the sixteenth century; and the consumption of game remained common, though sporadic, until the Meiji period.

The first decree prohibiting meat eating in Japan was issued in AD 675. Its main provision was to ban certain types of hunting and fishing traps that were designed to catch indiscriminately, and to prohibit the eating of beef, horse, dog, monkey and chicken from late spring until early autumn. Based on the extensive study by another scholar of Japanese dietary history, Harada Nobuo, the leading Japanese food historian, Ishige Naomichi, explains that the decree 'was prompted by the spread of what had once been a purely ritual practice of eating cattle and horse meat into the sphere of private enjoyment among the peasantry; and which was motivated by fear of a decline in the already sparse number of animals'.[30] It needs to be clarified that pigs were introduced from China in the seventeenth century, and before the twentieth century the custom of raising them for food did not spread beyond the south-western island of Kyushu.[31]

Ploughing a rice field with an ox, a photograph by Kusakabe Kimbei (1841–1934), c. 1890s.

The main purpose of the ban was to prohibit the eating of beef and horse meat and protect the livestock population, as well as to prevent drought, insect damage and famine. Moreover, it was limited to the spring and summer months which constitute the paddy farming season. The additional provisions against indiscriminate trapping of animals and fish may be interpreted as reflecting the Buddhist principle of preventing needless bloodshed.[32]

Buddhism has gradually become associated with the prohibition of meat eating, despite the fact that it did not initially constitute the major motive behind it. At first, the execution of the law did not seem to meet with adequate understanding, since the authorities issued similar edicts in subsequent centuries.[33] The strength of the taboo was bolstered when meat eating began to be considered defilement also according to Shinto – Japan's aboriginal religion – deriving from the impurity of slaughtering. Yet Susan Hanley, the renowned scholar of the material culture of pre-modern Japan, insists that concerns other than religious motivated the bolstering of the taboo. She declares that the decrees banning the killing of cattle issued by the Tokugawa government were motivated chiefly by the concern 'to preserve draft animals in order to maintain and increase agricultural production'.[34]

All in all, by the late sixteenth century the eating of the meat of domesticated animals acquired a status of a taboo in Japan.[35] This situation is clearly reflected in the account of João Rodrigues (*c.* 1561–1633), a Portuguese Jesuit missionary and pioneer scholar of the Japanese language and culture, in his recollection of his lengthy residence in the country, stretching from 1577 to 1610:

> The more solemn the banquet among the Japanese, and also in China, the greater number of different broths and *shiru* provided for each guest. Each of these is made from different things; some are made from high-quality fish, others from the meat of birds which they prize, such as the crane, which ranks in the first place, the swan in the second, and wild duck in the third. This is still true even today, for on no account will they use anything but wild game and never the domestic animals and birds which they rear. They will not eat the latter and in this they differ from the Chinese, who esteem the flesh of the ass more than that of the horse, the latter more than the cow; they have an even higher regard for pork, lard and bacon, as well as domestic duck, hens and geese, while lowly persons eat dogmeat and other things. In keeping with their customs the Japanese abominate all this, for on no account whatsoever will they eat ass, horse, cow, much less pig (except boars), duck, or hens, and they are naturally averse to lard. They eat only wild game at banquets and their ordinary meals, for they regard a householder who slaughters an animal reared in his house as cruel and unclean; on the other hand, they do not show this compassion toward human beings because they kill them with greater ease and enjoyment than they would an animal. This is despite the fact that some people, especially the traders who have had dealings with the Portuguese since their arrival in Japan, now eat cow, pig and hens, but such things are not eaten at solemn banquets or, for that matter, anywhere in the entire kingdom.[36]

Rodrigues' testimony raises the point of slaughtering animals reared within one's household. Some scholars argue that the spread of the meat-eating taboo in Japan went hand in hand with the diffusion of the concept of *uchi* (inside, private domain), which represented a moral attachment to, and responsibility for, the members of one's household, including the animals. This attitude was reflected in the custom of exchanging chickens between households before their slaughter in order to avoid killing those that were raised within one's own *uchi*.[37]

An account of Rodrigues' contemporary Rodrigo de Vivero y Velasco (1564–1636), who was shipwrecked off the coast of Japan in 1609, points out that trade in game was a recognized and common activity in early seventeenth-century Japan, and that an abundant supply was available in the city of Edo. He noted that there were 'special districts and streets with shops selling game, such as partridges, geese, wild duck, cranes, hens and an abundance of every kind of bird' and on another street 'rabbits, hares, wild boars and deer without number' could be found.[38] However, as woods and open fields increasingly gave way to cropland to feed the growing population, a gradual decline of the importance of game in the Japanese diet was inevitable. Except for *Ryōri Monogatari* ('The Cooking Story') published in 1643, game recipes appeared very sparingly in cookbooks of the Tokugawa period.[39] We may conclude that over-hunting on the one hand and the spread of the meat-eating taboo on the other had largely removed game from daily life in the cities, along the coastline and on highly populated plains. We may presume, however, that game remained an important source of food in the mountainous areas.

At any rate, the practice of eating meat for medicinal purposes did not disappear. The concept of meat as medicine was long-standing in Japan. Eighth-century aristocrats generally followed Buddhist teachings, refraining from the consumption of meat, but several times a year they engaged in the so-called *yakurō* ('medicinal hunting'), a ceremonial hunt concluding with the consumption of the caught game.[40] This practice was supposed to strengthen their bodies, which were deprived of meat on a daily basis. The nourishing properties of beef began to be emphasized as a result of encounters with Europeans in the sixteenth and seventeenth centuries. Although generally the beef-eating habit was perceived as barbarous, the physical strength of Westerners was admired and associated with their diet. From the late eighteenth century onwards, under the influence of Dutch Learning (*rangaku*) – the study of Western science based on publications in Dutch – occasional consumption of meat was considered beneficial for one's health. Generally referred to as *kusurigui* ('medicinal eating'), eating meat was practised, especially in winter, either in private homes or at specialist establishments known under the name *momonjiya* ('beast restaurant'). The fact that euphemisms were used when referring to various types of meat indicates that the aura of defilement was associated with the game stew served there. *Sakura* (cherry) signified horsemeat, *momiji* (maple) venison and *botan* (peony) wild boar, the last also being known as 'mountain whale' (*yamakujira*).[41]

While a fresh supply of game was available, good quality beef was very scarce. Records of preserved beef being sent as a gift to the *bakufu* officials by the vassals of the Hikone domain, where cattle were raised, indicate that the Tokugawa elite occasionally consumed it despite the official prohibition and that this health-booster was very precious.[42] An entry of 1839 in *Kuwana nikki*, a diary of a lower ranking samurai from the Kuwana domain, suggests that beef was regarded as a treat by members of his class – stewed beef is recorded to have been served to the grandson of the diary's author on the occasion of his birthday.[43] At the same time, beef of dubious quality and origin ended up in the lowest type of 'beast restaurants', as is admitted by Fukuzawa Yukichi in the recollection of his beef-eating experiences in Osaka in the mid-1850s:

> Our way of drinking was very crude. When we did not have much money, we would be contented to buy three or five *gō* of wine and have it in the dormitory. When we felt rich – which meant we had as much as one or two *shu* to spend – we would go to a restaurant for a carouse. That was a great luxury which did not happen often. More frequently we went to the chicken-restaurants. Still oftener we went to the cheapest place – the beef-stand.
>
> There were only two places where they served beef; one was near Naniwa Bridge, and the other near the prostitute quarters of Shinmachi – the lowest sort of eating places. No ordinary men ever entered them. All their customers were *gorotsuki*, or city bullies, who exhibited their fully tattooed torsos, and the students of Ogata's school. Where the meat came from and whether it was a cow that was killed or that had died, we did not care. They served plenty of boiled beef with wine and rice for a hundred and fifty *mon*. Certainly this meat was often tough and smelled strong.[44]

To sum up, at the point when it was officially proclaimed that beef and mutton had just entered the emperor's daily diet, the position of meat eating in Japan was very ambiguous. On the one hand, it was considered defiling by most Japanese, and those who engaged in it undertook measures to disengage this act from the regular daily practice. In the countryside, neither the central hearth of the house nor the regular pans were used when meat was cooked for private consumption.[45] In and around cities, 'beast restaurants' were usually located in specially marked areas where 'marginalized people engaged in their stigmatized occupations'.[46] On the other hand, meat was considered beneficial for one's health and its taste was occasionally enjoyed.

The announcement that the emperor had embarked on meat eating in 1872 put an end to this ambiguity. Although resistance towards meat remained pronounced until the end of the nineteenth century,[47] and its consumption remained relatively low in Japan for another hundred years, the year 1872 considerably elevated the status of meat in Japanese eyes and provided an important stimulus to its spread. While there is no doubt that the emperor played a critical role in transforming the consumption practices of the Japanese population, Western residents of the treaty ports should be given credit for setting the stage for this transformation.

Westerners living in colonial and semi-colonial enclaves throughout the Far East generally retained a strong preference for their native food, although hybrid mixtures like the Anglo-Indian cuisine of the British Raj did emerge.[48] Shortage of meat supply was felt as a most severe inconvenience by the Western communities in nineteenth-century Japan, in particular by the Americans and the British, who relied heavily on meat for their daily subsistence.[49] It goes without saying that meat was a crucial indicator of the standard of living and only the middle and upper classes had the means to maintain meat-centred diets. However, it was exactly members of these classes who comprised the majority of the treaty ports' residents.

Due to the lack of domestic sources of meat except for game during the first decade of their residence in Japan, Westerners had to rely on imports, mainly from Shanghai. Since the technologies of refrigeration and canning were not yet well developed, the animals were transported alive and slaughtered in Japan. By 1868 Yokohama counted seven firms that imported and sold meat.[50] From the mid-1860s beef cattle for consumption by foreigners were also raised in the Santan area and shipped to Yokohama from the nearby port of Kobe. Over the years this meat acquired the name of 'Kobe beef'.[51]

Westerners slaughtering animals and handling meat were often depicted in popular publications that described Westerners and their lifestyle. The intense curiosity and interest of common Japanese in the novel appearance and customs of the Five Nations (British, Americans, French, Germans and Dutch) represented in the treaty ports inspired the

Westerners slaughtering and butchering animals, from *Seiyō ryōri tsū* (1872).

A Japanese dining on meat at a Western household, from *Seiyō ryōri tsū* (1872).

publication of a large number of woodblock prints, booklets, novels and articles, which brought the exotic 'other' closer to the Japanese public.[52] Despite the contempt with which meat eating had been regarded in Japan, the association with Westerners began to bolster its image. As the volume of international trade increased, the number of Japanese who socialized with Western traders rose and with it the opportunities for them to taste Western (meat) dishes.

These circumstances propelled the rise of a beef-eating fashion among progressive Japanese, a fashion that drew inspiration from the Western dietary habits, but relied heavily on the tradition of 'beast restaurants'. The new trend emerged in the mid-1860s and took a form of *gyūnabe*, a beef stew that was prepared in a similar manner to the way game used to be cooked – stewed with *miso* or soy sauce. Like many other fashions of pre-modern Japan, *gyūnabe* emerged as an expression of the free spirit of urban culture, embraced at first by 'disagreeable ruffians of the type who liked to brag that they had eaten meat'.[53]

In 1871 the playwright Kanagaki Robun (1829–1894) published an illustrated book of monologues entitled *Aguranabe* ('Sitting around the Stewpan'), a satirical portrayal of the new fashion. In his analysis of *Aguranabe* John Mertz explains that to eat beef meant 'to momentarily set outside of the realm of social significations that had infused life in "Edo", and to participate in the new *cosmopolitan* sphere of "Tokyo"'.[54] Following Mertz's argument, we may claim that meat eating played a role in breaking up the hierarchical social structure of the Tokugawa period and in constructing a modern world-view among the Japanese masses. One of the personages, 'a young man fond of the West', declares the following:

> Excuse me, but beef is certainly a most delicious thing, isn't it? Once you get accustomed to its taste, you can never go back to deer or wild boar again. I wonder why we in Japan haven't eaten such a clean thing before? . . . We really should be grateful that even people like ourselves can now eat beef, thanks to the fact that Japan is steadily becoming a truly civilized country. Of course, there are some unenlightened boors who cling to their barbaric superstitions and say that eating meat defiles you so much that you can't pray any more before the Buddha and the gods. Such nonsense shows they simply don't understand natural philosophy. . . . In the West, they're free of superstition. There it's the custom to do everything scientifically, and

Japanese enjoying beef stew, from Kanagaki Robun's *Aguranabe* (1871).

that's why they've invented amazing things like the steamship and the steam engine.[55]

The *gyūnabe* fashion rested on the foundation of the 'medicinal eating' that claimed meat consumption was beneficial for one's health. The association with Western cuisine, in view of the rising interest in Western civilization and its achievements, attributed meat eating with an aura of novelty and excitement. The consumption of beef by the emperor, in turn, elevated it into the symbol of Japan's transformation into a modern nation. The meat-eating fashion translated the reforms of 'civilization and enlightenment' into a language that could be understood easily by the common man. As a result the *gyūnabe* fashion thrived; the daily consumption of meat in the Tokyo area increased from one-and-a-half cows in 1868 to twenty cows five years later.[56] By the late 1870s Tokyo counted several hundred establishments that were serving beef stew.[57]

The Meiji government was closely involved in propagating meat eating through the encouragement of a domestic cattle industry and attempts to regulate the import, slaughter and trade of cattle in Japan.[58] In terms of ideological support, the government was aided by intellectuals such as Fukuzawa Yukichi, who devoted themselves to the propagation of meat eating. They argued that the lavish consumption of meat by the Westerners was responsible for their superior physique, and they tried to convince the Japanese public that by adopting Western dietary habits Japanese bodies would be bolstered as well. Meiji intellectuals often adopted the opinions expressed in Western scientific publications of the time that perceived meat as an ideal food essential to growth, health and strength.[59] Under the influence of social Darwinism, the discourse took on a tone of racial debate, in which the strong constitution of the Westerners came to be considered a sign of racial superiority.[60] In this respect, Meiji intellectuals were also inspired by the Western opinion that perceived meat not only as the basis of physical strength but also as a significant source of intellectual and moral capacity. Edwin Lankester, for example, a leading British scientific publicist, stated in one of his lectures of 1860 that 'those races who have partaken of animal food are the most vigorous, most moral, and most intellectual races of mankind'. Similarly, an American cookery writer, Sarah Hale, argued that the British dominance of India proved the fact that meat-eaters dominated world politics.[61]

Such views were widely shared by statesmen and social reformers of the time and it does not seem surprising that the issue of meat eating assumed such an important role in Meiji politics. Furthermore, the abolishment of the meat-eating taboo fitted perfectly with the principles outlined in the Charter Oath, a blueprint of the new regime proclaimed in the name of the emperor a few months after the overthrow of the Tokugawa government. The two last points of the Oath declared that 'evil customs of the past shall be broken off' and that 'knowledge shall be sought throughout the world' to strengthen the empire.[62]

The emperor's adoption of meat eating, like his birthday party, proved a deed of great symbolic potential. It represented the beginning of Japan's transformation into a world power on a par with Western countries and launched the emperor as a progressive ruler who would lead the nation through this journey. Eating for 'civilization and enlightenment' during the first half of the Meiji period should be viewed in the first place as symbolic; the amounts of beef consumed by the Meiji Japanese were negligible and fundamental changes in their consumption practices began to take place after the turn of the twentieth century. However, the international and domestic politics of the new government undoubtedly played a very important role in setting the stage for this transformation.

Two
The Road to Multicultural Gastronomy

Life in the Treaty Ports

The 'unequal' treaties of 1858 stipulated that several Japanese ports would be opened for Western residence and trade. The harbour of Shimoda on the Izu Peninsula (south-west of Tokyo) and the port of Hakodate in the northernmost island of Hokkaido had already accommodated Western ships since 1854. After 1859, however, the port of Yokohama in Tokyo Bay and Nagasaki at the westernmost tip of the country took the lead as the centres of international trade. The harbour of Shimoda was closed and the opening of the ports of Hyōgo (today's Kobe) and Niigata (at the Sea of Japan coast) was postponed to 1868 because of rising anti-foreign sentiments.[1]

A large proportion of the Westerners who settled in Japan did not come directly from Europe or America. Instead, major Western trading firms operating in China, such as Jardine, Matheson & Co., Dent & Co. and Fletcher & Co., set up agencies in Japan and relocated their employees from Amoy (today's Xiamen), Ningpo (today's Ningbo), Shanghai and other treaty ports on the China coast. The same held for diplomatic personnel. For example, the first two British consuls in Japan, Sir Rutherford Alcock (1809–1897) and Sir Harry Parkes (1828–1885), served as consuls in China prior to their appointment in Japan.[2] Western enclaves similar to those operating in China soon asserted themselves in Hakodate, Nagasaki and Yokohama. Within a few years, Yokohama outshined the other two as the centre of trade and the chief place of foreign residence, soon followed by Kobe, newly opened in 1868.

Estimates indicate that the Western community in Japan grew roughly from a few hundred in the 1860s to approximately 5,000 three decades later. The British constituted a majority in the ports; as early as 1861, 55 out of 126 Westerners residing in Yokohama were British citizens. Twenty-five years later, Kobe counted 228 Britons out of 390 Western

Foreign settlement house in Yokohama, a woodblock print by Utagawa Yoshikazu (1861).

residents.[3] This British dominance was by no means surprising in view of their overwhelming presence in China at the time.[4]

The British residents of China treaty ports were almost unanimous in their dismissal of local culture. They made utmost efforts to recreate their European way of life, with 'newspapers, local municipal councils, chambers of commerce and other trappings of the mid-Victorian world recognized as civilization'.[5] There was a strong reluctance to consume Chinese food; the cuisine that was served in Western households, messes and hotels was predominantly European, grander ones following the London fashion for French-style dining. Increasing use over the years was made of imported tinned food, which was convenient and protected Westerners from the danger of food contagion. A menu of a 'metallic' dinner served in Shantou in the 1870s was recorded by a contemporary as follows: 'Tinned soup, tinned fish, tinned meat, tinned vegetables and Christmas tinned plum pudding . . . Tinned sausages were the great stand-by in those days, served with green peas (also from a tin).'[6]

Westerners in Japan held a similarly defensive attitude towards local food. Basil Hall Chamberlain (1850–1935), one of the most important Western scholars and interpreters of Japan, expressed this standpoint very delicately in *Handbook for Travellers in Japan*: 'Many who view Japanese food hopefully from a distance, have found their spirits sink and their tempers embittered when brought face to face with its unsatisfying actuality.'[7] Major Henry Knollys (1840–1930), who visited Japan in the mid-1880s, proved much blunter in his disapproval of Japanese fare:

Nothing short of actual starvation would induce a European to face the forbidding native food. The country is absolutely without any supplies of meat, bread, milk, or coffee, and Japanese tea is exceedingly insipid, and even distasteful to English people. I have, however, come provided with the main elements of my meals in the shape of tinned provisions: the only local additions are eggs, rice, pears which look like jargonels but which on being tasted prove considerably inferior to inferior turnips, and sometimes an exceedingly tough chicken, chiefly made up of legs as long and as thick as miniature stilts.[8]

Perhaps the most well known is the characterization of Japanese food by Isabella Bird (1831–1904), who travelled in the interior of Japan a decade earlier than Knollys:

> The fact is that, except at a few hotels in popular resorts which are got up for foreigners, bread, butter, meat, milk, poultry, coffee, wine, and beer, are unattainable, that fresh fish is rare, and that unless one can live on rice, tea, and eggs, with the addition now and then of some tasteless fresh vegetables, food must be taken, as the fishy and vegetable abominations known as 'Japanese food' can only be swallowed and digested by a few, and that after long practice.[9]

In a footnote to this statement, Miss Bird advised travellers in Japan to equip themselves with Liebig's extract of meat, a product developed recently by the founding father of the modern science of nutrition, the German chemist Justus von Liebig (1803–1873). Incidentally, Miss Bird found the Chinese food she encountered on her later travels on the continent much more palatable.[10]

Western residents and travellers in nineteenth-century Japan were very much attached to their native food habits. The first US consul general for Japan, Townsend Harris (1804–1878), who resided in Shimoda from 1856 to 1858, despaired when he ran out of his provisions. The following is a fragment from his diary, marked 23 June 1857:

> I am now more than ten months in Japan . . . I have been out of flour, bread, butter, lard, bacon, hams, sweet oil, and in fact out of every kind of foreign supply for more than two months. I am living on rice, fish and very poor poultry, as no game of any kind has been brought to me for the last three months.

My health is miserable, my appetite is gone, and I am so shrunk away that I look as though a 'Vice-Consul had been cut out of me.'[11]

Finally, in September, a foreign ship docked in Shimoda and Harris's dietary hardships were over:

I cannot find words to express my thanks to Captain Foote and the officers of the *Portsmouth* for the generous manner in which they have divided their own private stores to help me in my distressed situation. Captain Foote supplied me with a quarter box of superior tea, two jars of lard, and a bag of prepared hominy. From the ward room I received half a dozen fine Virginia hams and five smoked tongues. I had nothing to give them in return but barren thanks.[12]

The situation improved greatly once the Western community in the treaty ports grew larger after 1859, with regular supplies of provisions and the equipment necessary to maintain Western cuisine secured. Inns and hotels were among the first businesses that emerged in Yokohama and

Americans baking bread, a woodblock print by Utagawa Yoshikazu (1861).
Foreigners engaged in cooking, a woodblock print by Utagawa Yoshikazu (1860).

Nagasaki after Westerners began to settle there. As of 1865 three hotels operated in the Nagasaki Foreign Settlement: Commercial House (soon renamed Royal House) run by Caroline Wicks from San Francisco, Oriental Hotel run by an American, Michael Broderick, and Bellevue Hotel managed by a British woman named Mary E. Green, who would later expand her activities to Yokohama and Kobe.[13] The first hotel in Yokohama was Yokuhama Hotel, as the establishment was generally referred to by Westerners at the time. It opened for business in February 1860 and its proprietor was a former captain of the ship *Nassau*, the Dutchman C. J. Huffnagel. Two employees of this pioneering hotel soon set up their own businesses – J. B. Macauly began to run the Royal British Hotel in 1862 and James Mixter the Tycoon Hotel in 1864. The Anglo-Saxon Hotel was established by John Thomas, a former steward aboard the ship *Leemoon*, in 1863. The Grand Hotel, which by the end of the century became the best establishment in the port and one of the best in the country, opened in 1873 at the initiative of a well-known photographer, Felice Beato (*c.* 1825– *c.* 1908), and a group of investors.[14]

Dining-room of the Grand Hotel in Yokohama, c. 1910.

It must be clarified at this point that nineteenth-century inns and hotels in the treaty ports, following the European example, provided meal service for their guests and often operated restaurants that catered for customers who did not stay for the night. Increasingly, the hotels' reputation depended on the quality of meals served in their dining-rooms as much as on other facilities and services.[15] Praise of the Oriental Hotel in Kobe and its proprietor, Monsieur Begeux, by one of his guests serves as a case in point:

> His is a house where you can dine. He does not merely feed
> you. His coffee is the coffee of the beautiful France. For tea he
> gives you Peliti cakes (but better) and the *vin ordinaire* which
> is *compris*, is good. Excellent Monsieur and Madame Begeux! If
> the *Pioneer* were a medium for puffs, I would write a leading
> article upon your potato salad, your beefsteaks, your fried
> fish, and your staff of highly trained Japanese servants in
> blue tights . . . [16]

By the 1870s establishments that provided the comforts of a Western diet for the treaty-port residents were thriving. Clubs, taverns, restaurants, bakeries, grocers, breweries, butchers and dairies were set up and managed by fellow Westerners. Adventurers who risked a journey to a far land to earn a fortune were among them, but most consisted of experienced entre-preneurs who followed diplomats and traders from China treaty ports and other Western enclaves in Asia. Hotel managers and chefs that were recruited to run new establishments in Japan not infrequently left success-ful careers in the grand hotels of Shanghai or Hong Kong behind them.[17] It is possible, but hardly plausible, that they exchanged comfortable life in the ingrained treaty ports for the hardships of the Japanese frontier for the sake of adventure. It seems more likely, however, that their resolve was motivated by a promise of considerable economic gain.

Many nationalities were represented in the treaty ports. For example, a bakery run in Nagasaki by a Frenchman named Charles Thomas was taken over after his death by a Canadian named Jean Couder. Next door, an Italian, P. Bernardi, traded in wine and an Englishman, James Gye, managed an establishment called the 'Medical Hall', which, as well as pro-viding medical supplies, was engaged in the production of lemonade, ginger ale and soda water.[18] The British and Americans dominated, while the French prevailed in prestigious hotels and restaurants.

The Japanese were at first employed as unskilled labour at Western households and enterprises. However, as the number of Western residents grew steadily and the demand for domestic staff and professional waiters and cooks increased, the knowledge and experience acquired on the job soon proved a valuable asset. This was so particularly during the 1870s and '80s, when Western-style dining became very fashionable among the Japanese elite, who, inspired by the spirit of 'civilization and enlight-enment', began to mimic Western lifestyle. For example, the diary of Hozumi Utako includes accounts of Western cooking being performed at the turn of the century by the family maid, Fusa, who must have acquired these skills with her previous employers. The Hozumi were a typical elite household; Utako was the daughter of Shibusawa Eiichi (1840–1931), a prominent Meiji entrepreneur, and the wife of a well-known jurist – both members of the House of Peers. While the gentlemen had frequent occa-sions to sample Western cooking in the government circles and Utako occasionally accompanied them to Western-style restaurants, the family dined Japanese style at home most of the time. Western-style food appar-ently provided a diversion in the daily routine, however, since the results of Fusa's cooking are recorded in the diary: on 22 February 1903 she baked an apple pie and on 10 September the same year she cooked stuffed chicken and stew for the children. The family also employed a cook who is recorded to have produced on 12 January 1902 a dinner of duck, croquettes and plum pudding.[19]

William Gray Dixon (1854–1928), who came to teach at the Imperial College of Engineering in Tokyo in the 1870s, has left us with a description of his Japanese cook, which unveils the relatively high status enjoyed by the domestic servants of a Westerner in late nineteenth-century Japan. Dixon writes that the cook 'rejoiced in the possession of more than one suit of European clothes, and might, on important occasions, be seen in a velvet coat and striped trousers, and with a gilt watch-chain and seals hanging from his breast and a cigarette in his mouth . . . His skill in cooking was great, and his ambition still greater.'[20] Determined young people like Dixon's cook were the ones responsible for constructing the foundations of Western-style gastronomy in Japan.

Aiming at their own comfort and mostly unconscious of the long-term implications that their presence entailed, Western residents of Hakodate, Nagasaki, Yokohama and Kobe did their utmost to replicate in Japan the living conditions at home. By doing so, they created a multiplicity of channels that facilitated the future diffusion of Western food among wider sections of the Japanese population. Handing over the knowledge and skills of Western cookery to native Japanese constituted one of the most important channels.

Domesticating Yōshoku

A characteristic feature of pre-modern Japanese cities was a full-blown and differentiated gastronomy. Restaurant culture had flourished since the late seventeenth century, with the city of Edo, with a population exceeding one million, clearly taking the lead as the culinary capital.[21] The variety and refinement of eating-out facilities in the pre-modern cities were reflected in the abundance of restaurant guides and other culinary publications that appeared during the eighteenth and nineteenth centuries, often issued as marketing devices by the restaurateurs themselves.[22] Exclusive restaurants developed under the patronage of wealthy merchants and the samurai class, while cheap eateries and food stalls catered for all-comers. The eating establishments were usually classified according to the type of food they served, for example, a *sobaya* served buckwheat noodles (*soba*), a *tenpuraya* deep-fried fish in batter (*tenpura*) and a *sushiya*, sushi.[23] However, foreign cuisine was entirely lacking. Nagasaki – the Japanese merchant enclave that since the seventeenth century had held state monopoly on international trade – was an exception; eating places that specialized in catering for Dutch traders and restaurants serving hybrid Japanese-

THE FUJIYA HOTEL, NATURAL HOT SPRING, MIYANOSHITA, JAPAN.

Fujiya Hotel in Miyanoshita, c. 1909.

Chinese cuisine (*shippoku ryōri*) operated there as well. Yet the latter became fashionable outside the enclave only very briefly.[24]

Before the 1870s no restaurants serving foreign cuisine were to be found in Japan outside the treaty ports. Since foreigners were not allowed to expand their commercial activities beyond the treaty ports, foreign-managed hotels and restaurants were confined to those areas.[25] From the late 1870s Japanese owners of inns and tea houses in tourist spots and spas gradually realized that Westerners were potentially a great business opportunity and began to provide beds, chairs and Western food for their convenience. New (semi-)European-style hotels and restaurants also emerged in the spots frequented by foreigners. Fujiya Hotel in Miyanoshita – established in 1878 – counted as a pioneering European-style establishment in the area of the Hakone mountains (in the proximity of Mt Fuji), which became a favoured resort for the Yokohama foreign community. By the end of the century, similar establishments could be found in tourist destinations, such as Nikkō, Kamakura, Kyoto and Shizuoka. Nevertheless, guidebooks recommended to foreign tourists who knew little Japanese that they 'may feel themselves more their own masters by hiring a man-servant, or "boy," also able to cook, and having neither objection to performing menial functions, nor opinions of his own as to the route which it will be best to take'.[26]

Kusano Jōkichi (*c*. 1840–*c*. 1886), who is credited with being the first Japanese to set up a Western-style restaurant in Japan, had learned to cook in the service of the Dutch in Nagasaki. The restaurant Irabayashitei, which he opened in 1863, may have been preceded a few years by a similar establishment that operated in Hakodate, but records proving its existence have not survived.[27] Irabayashitei was later renamed Jiyūtei and it is under this name that it is now remembered as the first Japanese-owned Western-style restaurant in Japan. Judging from his background, Kusano's cooking must have been heavily influenced by Dutch cuisine and differed considerably from the menus served in the treaty ports dominated by the British and Americans. However, since his customers were Japanese without prior knowledge of Western cuisine, the business thrived. By the late 1860s Jiyūtei branched out to Kyoto, Osaka and Kobe. Kusano was also indirectly involved in setting up restaurants serving Western food in the provincial towns of western Japan, such as Nara, Kōchi, Tokushima, Okayama, Hiroshima, Fukuoka, Kagoshima and Kumamoto. Yō Maenobō, who meticulously traced the early history of Western-style restaurants in Japan, confirms that the culinary connection with Nagasaki (and Kusano) stretched even to Yokohama, and from there to Tokyo. For example, Mikawaya – the very first Western-style restaurant in the capital – was relocated from Yokohama in 1867.[28] The impact of Yokohama was critical for the transition of pre-modern Edo into modern Tokyo. On the one hand, the proximity of the gateway for foreign influence stimulated public interest in Western practices and culture. On the other, however, the 20 miles that separated Yokohama from Edo-Tokyo served as 'a sort of cultural and political buffer between the capital and the West'.[29]

Despite Kusano's indisputable influence on the pioneering Western-style restaurants, the Dutch twist in the food he served was soon overshadowed by the French and Anglo-Saxon touch. The former took over the prestigious establishments and the latter permeated eating places targeted at less privileged clientele.

As we have observed in the previous chapter, diplomatic dining in Meiji Japan was entirely dominated by French food. This was determined by the supremacy of French cuisine in nineteenth-century Europe and the United States. As Stephen Mennell explains, the nineteenth century

> saw the full establishment of a French international culinary hegemony, not merely over England but over much of the rest of Europe and, by the end of the century, North America too. . . . French dishes were to be found not only at the tables of a few of the richest aristocrats and gentry, but also setting the style in London clubs, hotels and restaurants. French hegemony meant in particular hegemony within the cooking profession.[30]

In view of these circumstances it seems more than obvious that the cooks employed at high-class Western-style hotels in Japan, such as the Grand Hotel in Yokohama and the Tsukiji Hotel in Tokyo, were French. Katamura Shigetake, the proprietor of Seiyōken Hotel, followed this convention and served French menus as well:

Déjeuner:
Pain
Hors d'oeuvre (cold meat)
Poisson (deep-fried fish)
Entrée (stewed poultry)
Entrée (stewed meat)
Chateaubriand (fried beef)
Sweets, fruits, coffee, cheeses etc.

Dîner:
Pain
Potage (soup)
Poisson (baked or deep-fried fish)
Entrée (stewed poultry)
Entrée (stewed meat)
Légumes (vegetables)
Au rôti [?] (meat or poultry casserole)
Sweets or *crème glace*[31]

It was the intention of the exclusive restaurants to recreate French dining in minute detail. The food was served with a full set of china, glass and cutlery, and it was considered appropriate for Japanese men to put on a Western suit for the occasion, rather than to appear in native attire (kimono). Customarily, three ranks of set menus were served – ordinary, middle and top. The most expensive version was usually twice the price of the ordinary one (see overleaf).

At the time, one could have a bowl of noodles for 1–3 *sen* and a sushi meal for under 10 *sen*; 100 grams of beef were sold for 3.6 *sen*, 1.8 litres of soy sauce for 9 *sen*, 1 kilograms of sugar for 14 *sen* and 10 kilograms of rice for 67 *sen*.[32] It goes without saying that only the very top of the Japanese society could afford to dine at these select restaurants – cultural conformity with the 'West' was expensive and functioned as a marker of social prestige.

The Hozumi family mentioned earlier occasionally patronized Seiyōken Hotel and the Fujimiken restaurant – the two best French

Prices of set menus at top Western-style restaurants in Tokyo c. 1890.[33]

RESTAURANT	TOP	MIDDLE	ORDINARY
Tōyōken	75 *sen*	50 *sen*	35 *sen*
Azumatei	75 *sen*	50 *sen*	35 *sen*
Shin-azuma	75 *sen*	50 *sen*	35 *sen*
Sanrakutei	75 *sen*	50 *sen*	35 *sen*
Seishinken	60 *sen*	40 *sen*	35 *sen*
Fūgetsudō	100 *sen*	75 *sen*	50 *sen*
Sanentei	65 *sen*	50 *sen*	35 *sen*
Seifūken	75 *sen*	50 *sen*	35 *sen*
Yōkitei	75 *sen*	50 *sen*	35 *sen*
Banriken	75 *sen*	50 *sen*	35 *sen*

1 *sen* = 0.01 yen

restaurants in the capital.[34] They also dined frequently at the Imperial Hotel, since Utako's father, Shibusawa Eiichi, was one of its owners. The Imperial opened in 1890 and, like Seiyōken, its founding was backed up by a top government official, this time Japan's foreign minister, Inoue Kaoru (1836–1915). The hotel was to become the most luxurious establishment in the country and a principal site of state banquets and receptions.

Around the time when the Imperial Hotel opened for business, new eating places for the general public were mushrooming all over Japan. Basil Hall Chamberlain reported on this phenomenon in a rather unenthusiastic manner:

> Most Japanese towns of any size now boast what is called a *seiyo-ryori*, which, being interpreted, means a foreign restaurant. Unfortunately, third-rate Anglo-Saxon influence has had the upper hand here, with the result that the central idea of the Japano-European cuisine takes consistency in slabs of tough beefsteak anointed with mustard and spurious Worcestershire sauce. This culminating point is reached after several courses – one of watery soup, another of fish fried in rancid butter, a third of chickens' drumsticks stewed also in rancid butter; and the feast not infrequently terminates with what a local cookery book terms a 'sweat omelette'.[35]

Celebrations of Emperor's Birthday at the Imperial Hotel in Tokyo, from *Shokudōraku, Aki no maki* (1903).

Despite Chamberlain's censure, the Japanese public welcomed these new eating places with joy and excitement. Takahashi Kichitarō recalls his father, who was an apothecary in Chinese medicine, taking him, a young boy at the time, to such a restaurant for dinner in 1910. He was then treated to a three-course meal that started with soup, followed by beef cutlet and an omelette, and he never forgot the experience.[36]

The reliance on Anglo-Saxon dishes rather than French cuisine was determined by two factors. First of all, it represented the British and American supremacy in the life of Western communities in the treaty ports. Since these new restaurants were being set up and run by former employees of Western households or restaurants that were patronized by the overwhelmingly British and American Western community, they featured food that had been prevalent there. A typical (breakfast) bill of fare served in a Yokohama hotel in the early 1890s included the following items:

Porridge
Fried fish
Boiled eggs
Bacon and eggs
Ham and eggs

Poached eggs
Omelettes
Beefsteak
Cold Roast Beef
Cold Corned Round Beef
Cold Tongue
Fruit[37]

The second reason behind the prevalence of Anglo-Saxon rather than French cookery in cheap Western-style restaurants in Japan was the fact that English and American dishes were much less complex and therefore easier to prepare. Furthermore, they were relatively inexpensive, since they did not require ingredients that were extremely rare, such as the truffles and *foies gras* that featured regularly in French haute cuisine. As Stephen Mennell pointedly observed, the prestige that French cookery enjoyed in the higher social circles in England resulted in the 'decapitation' of English cookery: 'English-style cookery was deprived of elite models of its own to copy, and this probably contributed to the mediocrity which both contemporary and subsequent observers remarked on in English cookery in the Victorian era.'[38] A Japanese culinary reformer, Tetsuka Kaneko, hit the nail right on its head when in 1911 she characterized Anglo-Saxon cookery in one of her home economics lectures, in which she advocated the incorporation of foreign dishes in the Japanese home meals: 'As democratic as American homes are, and as unsophisticated as the English homes are, so extremely simple is their food, and easily adaptable for Japanese homes. Therefore, I find them most suitable.'[39]

Fried fish, roast beef, roast chicken, beefsteak, veal cutlet, croquette, beef curry, beef stew, soup and omelette dominated the menus of the cheap Western-style restaurants that began to mushroom in Japan during the 1890s.[40] Their characteristic feature was the focus on meat and fat – the two ingredients that were hitherto lacking in the Japanese diet. Of course, the fact that Victorian Britons took a dim view of vegetables, which they believed had no nutritional value and fermented in the stomach, contributed to the lack of vegetable dishes on the menus of the new restaurants, except for the popular potato croquettes.[41]

Dishes were not served – as was the general practice at exclusive French restaurants in Japan – as set menus consisting of several courses. Instead, food was to be ordered à la carte and accompanied by Japanese-style boiled rice. Worcestershire sauce was used on almost anything, for the urban Japanese took it as the Western equivalent of their own universal flavouring – soy sauce.[42] The pan-frying technique required by many recipes was changed into deep-frying, a method with which Japanese customers and cooks were much more familiar because of the (by then) domesticated and well-known *tenpura*. All these modifications made the dishes appear and taste less foreign, and they were also more suited to the budget of the Japanese public. The following list shows average prices around 1907:

Soup	12 *sen*
Fried fish	15 *sen*
Croquettes	15 *sen*
Beef cutlet	15 *sen*
Beefsteak	15 *sen*
Roast beef	15 *sen*
Rolled cabbage	15 *sen*
Ham salad	15 *sen*
Rice curry	15 *sen*
Omelette	15 *sen*
Ham and eggs	20 *sen*
Chicken cutlet	20 *sen*
Roast chicken	20 *sen*
Stew	20 *sen*[43]

Ishige reports that by the turn of the century the city of Tokyo counted 1,500–1,600 cheap Western-style restaurants, and they gradually became ubiquitous in cities and towns all over Japan.[44] Although each establishment had its own name, they were generally known as *yōshokuya* (a *yōshoku* restaurant). The term *yōshoku*, which originally – like the term *seiyō ryōri* – was used neutrally to refer to Western cuisine, gradually began to signify the food featured on the menus of these cheap restaurants: domesticated versions of selected British and American dishes served with rice. In time, *yōshoku* began to be perceived as a category within Japanese cuisine, exerting a powerful homogenizing effect on Japanese diet.

The popularity of *yōshokuya* was due to several factors, among which ideology and cultural values were far from negligible. The allure of prestige that swirled around things of Western origin had a critical impact. With its strong upper-class cachet, *yōshoku* was eagerly emulated as a means of elevating social status. Contrary to the meat-eating fashion described in the previous chapter, however, this time the West offered not only an inspiration for the new food fad, but actually provided the building blocks for the new dining style. *Yōshokuya* supplied an entirely new dining framework represented by the Western chair and tables (instead of cushions and trays called for by the native habit) and an entirely new menu. In other words, *yōshokuya* created a new space where a cultural context of modern Japan was to be conceived. The 'West' provided vocabulary for this new culinary language, but the syntax, the accent and the meaning were all negotiated by the proprietors, employees and customers of these new establishments.

Multicultural Catering for the Urban Masses

Yōshokuya and its menus served as a blueprint for the modern mass gastronomy that began to emerge in Japan after the turn of the century. It was a time when large department stores started to dominate the commercial, architectural and cultural landscape of Japanese cities. The so-called *hyakka shōten* (hundred-goods sales store) or *hyakkaten* (hundred goods store), such as Mitsukoshi, Shirokiya, Takashimaya and Matsuya, focused on upper- and upper-middle-class customers in their commercial strategies, emphasizing high quality, exclusiveness and fashion. Conversely, department stores that were founded somewhat later by railway companies – the so-called *teruminaru depāto* such as Hanshin, Hankyū, Tōkyū and Odakyū – focused on the mass market, selling modernity in the form of mass-produced merchandise at the lowest possible prices. By the 1930s

Matsuya department store in Tokyo, c. 1930s.

Palatial Dining Room, 6th floor, Matsuya, Tokyo.

Matsuya department store dining-room, c. 1930s.

the differences between the old and new style of department stores began to disappear, and together they led the way to the full-blown development of Japanese mass culture.[45]

In many respects, the Japanese department store resembled similar establishments in Paris, London and New York. Mass merchandising was directly linked to the mass production, transportation, information systems and new financial instruments that were capable of supporting this mass retailing.[46] One of the characteristic features of Japanese department stores, however, was a particular abundance of dining establishments. The first store to set up a refreshment room was Shirokiya in 1904, followed by Mitsukoshi in 1907, both located in the centre of Tokyo. In 1911, after a great renovation of the store was completed, Shirokiya opened a grander restaurant where a selection of Western as well as Japanese dishes was offered: sandwiches, sushi, Western- and Japanese-style confectionery, tea and coffee.[47] By the 1920s practically every department store hosted at least two restaurants and a teashop.

The fact that these restaurants not only served food to nourish the body but also provided entertainment in the form of unfamiliar interior decorations and unfamiliar food constituted an important added value. The interior was usually Western in style with waitresses dressed in Western-style uniforms and wearing high-heeled shoes. The modern character of the restaurant's management, which followed the capitalist

Lunch room at the Takashimaya department store in Osaka, from *Nihon hyakkaten shokudō yōran* (1937).

strategies applied by the department stores themselves, was reflected in a particular attention to hygiene and quick service.[48] The kitchen was technologically advanced, most of the equipment being imported. Along with Japanese dishes, Western-style sandwiches and ice cream, as well as a selection of *yōshoku*, were available in department store restaurants.[49] For example, in 1925 the dining hall on the sixth floor of the exclusive Mitsukoshi department store in Tokyo served the following menu:

Beefsteak (with rice)	50 *sen*
Ham salad (with bread)	50 *sen*
Curry rice	30 *sen*
Sandwich	30 *sen*
Western-style confectionery	15 *sen*
Japanese confectionery	15 *sen*
Jelly	15 *sen*
Children's bread	10 *sen*
Chilled *amazake*	10 *sen*
Watermelon	10 *sen*
Fruits	10 *sen*

Calpis sherbet	15 *sen*
Ice cream	15 *sen*
Iced coffee	10 *sen*
Iced tea	10 *sen*
Calpis	10 *sen*[50]

It needs to be pointed out that 15 *sen* was worth much less in 1925 than thirty years earlier. The price of a sushi meal had risen by then to 20 *sen* and that of noodles to 10–40 *sen*; 100 grams beef was sold for 21 *sen*, 1.8 litres of soy sauce for 86 *sen*, 1 kilogram of sugar for 49 *sen* and 10 kilograms of rice for 3 yen 20 *sen*.[51] It needs to be kept in mind that the dining halls of Mitsukoshi were relatively expensive, which implies that the same food was available for less. For example, department store menus were recreated at cheap dining halls managed by municipal governments. Certain *yōshoku* items also began to be served by noodle shops, street stalls and other native eating places.[52]

   The gastronomic stage of urban Japan began to transform during the 1920s and '30s; big corporations with grand capital, such as railways, trading companies and department stores, increasingly replaced individual entrepreneurs in the dining business. Before, most eating-out establishments were run on a small scale, and were often owned by the cook himself. Restaurants, cafeterias and teashops in department stores clearly represented the mass catering of the future – advertising was handled in close cooperation with the store's general marketing department and ingredients were supplied directly by the stores' own food departments, often produced under the store's brand name. The shift towards an increased

The kitchen of the Hankyū department store in Osaka. It served 30,000 customers daily. From *Nihon hyakkaten shokudō yōran* (1937).

interconnectedness between food-processing industries, distribution networks and the restaurant business was emblematic for the transformation that urban gastronomy underwent in interwar Japan.

The restaurant Chūōtei is a telling example of this new trend. Watanabe Kamakichi, Chūōtei's founder, had learnt to cook Western style as a servant in a Western household, just like many of his contemporaries. By the 1880s he was a well-established chef, preparing exclusive diplomatic dinners and elite banquets. In 1907 he opened Chūōtei – a posh Western-style restaurant catering for politicians and business leaders. However, as a result of the tight competition that arose between the by then numerous exclusive Western-style restaurants in Tokyo, Chūōtei was on the verge of bankruptcy merely a decade after its opening. In 1918 the restaurant was taken over by the trading company Meidi-ya, Chūōtei's main supplier of Western liquor and ingredients. Turned into a stock company, Chūōtei Co. Ltd was to become an advertising medium for Meidi-ya's products. The restaurant was then reshaped from a high-class establishment into a middle-class popular chain – an up-to-date version of *yōshokuya*. By the end of 1926 Chūōtei was operating nine outlets: five in Tokyo, two in Osaka, one in Nagoya and one in Kobe.[53]

The proliferation of *yōshoku* as a popular food for the masses took off at full speed through restaurants set up by railway companies at their newly constructed terminals. For example, in 1920 Minoo Arima Railway opened a restaurant at Umeda Station in Osaka that served commuters with beefsteak, omelette, ham salad, potato croquettes and curry. By 1927 an average of nearly 5,000 people dined there daily.[54] That year, another railway company, Tokyo Yokohama Dentetsu, set up a similar restaurant at Shibuya Station in Tokyo.[55] They constituted direct competition to the boxed lunch (*ekiben*) sold at train stations by independent pedlars.[56] Bolstered by big capital, *yōshoku* persistently acquired a growing share of the catering market.

By the 1930s restaurants serving multicultural menus to the urban masses and controlled by big corporations such as department stores, the food industry and railway companies became ubiquitous. They gradually replaced independent *yōshokuya* as the main vehicles for shifting meanings and values ascribed to Western food. By then, *yōshoku* had lost its association with the West and came to represent the new, urban mass gastronomy of modern Japan with a strong, multicultural character.

Two factors were crucial in the road towards multicultural Japanese gastronomy – the fashion for Western food that had been effectively launched by a political elite half a century earlier, and the potential of

Food vendors at a railway station, 1927.

economic gain that cooking and serving Western food in late nineteenth and early twentieth century Japan entailed. Pioneering endeavours of people like Kusano Jōkichi and Watanabe Kamakichi, but also Caroline Wicks, C. J. Huffnagel and Monsieur and Madame Begeux, were indispensable in this process. While we may presume that these individuals were highly passionate about their vocation and trade, their activities were in the first place a means of earning a living and often a way of making a fortune.

Politics and profit were the crucial lubricants that set the emergence of multicultural Japanese gastronomy into motion. This, in turn, was the first step towards the construction of the homogenized, national cuisine.

Three
Strengthening the Military

Farmer-Entrepreneur Kanie Ichitarō

The transfer of cooking skills from the Westerners in the treaty ports to their Japanese employees went hand in hand with the development of an infrastructure of suppliers of the necessary ingredients. Along with the inspiration to emulate Western-style dining by the Japanese elite discussed in chapter One, this was the third important channel that facilitated the diffusion of Western food among wider sections of the Japanese population. The demand created by Westerners was, at the early stage, a critical stimulant for the production of hitherto unknown foodstuffs, as we have observed earlier with the example of beef. However, meat supply was not the only problem. In the early years, onions for use in the treaty ports were imported from Bombay and potatoes from America.[1]

The use of vegetables in Japanese kitchens during the Edo period was very diverse, depending on the region. Various types of radishes (*daikon*, *kabu*), tubers (*gobō*, *satoimo*), gourds (*yūgao*, *tōgan*) and leeks were cultivated, and numerous kinds of wild greens, bamboo shoots and mushrooms were collected.[2] Sweet potatoes and squash were also available, but not the vegetables that were widely used in Western-style cooking, such as cabbage, carrots, onions, tomato, beetroot, celery, asparagus, cauliflower, string beans, green peas, parsley, etc. Some of them, like white potatoes, had been introduced during the Tokugawa period, but failed to spread on a wide scale.

These vegetables began to be grown in Japan soon after the establishment of the first Western communities in the 1860s.[3] New varieties of the vegetables that had been known in Japan, such as carrots and eggplants, were also introduced during the Meiji period and gradually replaced or crossed with the Japanese varieties. The new food plants were all labelled *seiyō yasai* (Western vegetables), including the Chinese cabbage that was carried to Japan by the Chinese servants and clerks who accompanied the

A vegetable stand, c. 1880s–1890s, from *Souvenirs from Japan* (1991).

Westerners (see chapter Six). Initially, Western households and Western-style hotels set up vegetable gardens around their residences in order to meet their needs. However, as the number of Western households and restaurants serving Western-style food increased steadily over the decades and demand rose, growing Western vegetables was gradually taken over by Japanese peasants whose land was situated in the proximity of foreign settlements and larger towns. Lured by the lucrative new occupation of market gardeners, they abandoned grain-centred agriculture.[4]

Onions, cabbage, carrots, beetroots, celery and potatoes were in greatest demand – not surprisingly, when one considers their central role in European and American cuisines – and their production increased most rapidly. Between 1874 and 1876 alone, the share of onions in the entire vegetable production in Japan rose from 0.06 to 0.3 per cent.[5] Onions, cabbage, carrots and potatoes were easier to grow and more robust than, for example, lettuce, cauliflower and asparagus. These attributes determined their lower price once the production in Japan began. For example, in 1906 the price of Western onions equalled that of indigenous taros, and potatoes sold for almost half the price of squash, which had been popular since the Edo period.[6] The fact that vegetables such as lettuce, asparagus and cauliflower, were not widely used in Anglo-Saxon cookery further inhibited their diffusion. The spectacular growth in demand for onions, cabbage and potatoes coincided with the rising popularity of *yōshoku*. Once these vegetables became widely available and inexpensive, they began to be used in Japanese cooking as well and their consumption increased considerably. For example, the acreage occupied by the white potato crop expanded more than tenfold between 1880 and 1930.[7]

During the first twenty years of the Meiji period, the Japanese government was very actively involved in the popularization of Western vegetables. The Agricultural Experiment Stations set up throughout the country became responsible for cultivating seeds of new vegetables and developing new varieties of already known ones. They were to encourage agricultural innovation, distributed the seeds to the prospective producers and provided them with help in starting up businesses.[8] It was at such a station that Kanie Ichitarō (1875–1971) learned how to grow Western vegetables. Kanie was born into a peasant family settled near the city of Nagoya, approximately halfway between Tokyo and Kyoto. Like other peasant boys in late nineteenth-century Japan, he experienced the hardships of the farming existence, but his life was already affected by the early reforms of

Kanie Ichitarō shortly before his departure to the front in 1904.

the Meiji government – he acquired three years of elementary education and at the age of 20 was drafted into the army.

Along with the policies of 'civilization and enlightenment', which aimed to bolster Japan's image in the eyes of Westerners, the ambitions of the new government were conveyed by the slogan *fukoku kyōhei* ('rich country, strong army'), with the 'strong army' component increasingly taking precedence. The chief objectives of the Meiji leadership were to establish modern armed forces of the strength equal to those of the Western powers and to put in place the infrastructure of a capitalist industrial economy comparable to the ones found in Europe and the United States. In order to support the two projects, the Japanese people had to be moulded into loyal subject-citizens, and this goal was to be achieved through mass compulsory education and universal conscription. In 1872 the legal basis for the system of elementary schooling for all children was created, and the following year the conscription law that obliged all males of 20 years of age and older (except those eligible for exemption) to give three years of active service was stipulated.[9]

A year before being conscripted, Ichitarō got married and moved to the nearby village. He married well, into a family more prosperous than his own. Since his wife was an only child, following the established practice Ichitarō was adopted into her family, and after the death of her father was to become the head of the Kanie household. His father-in-law was an enterprising farmer who grew mulberry as a cash crop. In view of the growing export of silk, mulberry, which was used to feed silk worms, constituted an important supplementary income for many farmers in nineteenth-century Japan.[10]

In 1895 Ichitarō was drafted to the 6th foot regiment of the 3rd Nagoya division of the Imperial Japanese Army, and his encounter with First Lieutenant Nishiyama during the third year of service inspired him to take up the market gardening of Western vegetables. Nishiyama tried to convince young farmers in his regiment that growing rice and barley was the thing of the past and that modern times called for an entrepreneurial spirit in the Japanese peasants. Propelled by the rising popularity of dining Western style, the demand for Western vegetables was constantly growing, but their production was still limited.

Since the mulberry fields of the Kanie family had been troubled by diseases for a few years in a row, upon his return in 1898 Ichitarō managed to persuade his father-in-law to devote part of the mulberry land to growing Western vegetables. Cabbage, lettuce, parsley, carrots and onions sold well during the following years, but tomatoes proved less saleable. With the hope of increasing sales, Ichitarō attempted to process the tomatoes into tomato purée. He was aided in this endeavour by cooks from Western-style restaurants in Nagoya, to whom he supplied his vegetables. In 1903 the first batch of tomato purée packed in empty beer bottles sold like hot cakes. In view of this success, mulberry fields were abandoned altogether, and growing and processing tomatoes was turned into the main activity of the Kanie family.[11]

The following year the Russo-Japanese War (1904–5) broke out and Ichitarō, being a reservist of the Nagoya regiment, was drafted again. This bloody war, in which Japan suffered nearly a 100,000 casualties, proved lucky for Kanie. He not only managed to escape injury but was awarded with 180 yen for his brave conduct on the battlefield. The money was invested in the construction of a tomato-processing factory and the enterprise began to thrive. In 1908 Kanie started to develop two products that would become emblematic for his business – tomato ketchup and the so-called *sōsu* (deriving from the English word 'sauce'), a domestic product that replaced imported Worcestershire sauce used copiously on most items on the *yōshokuya* menu. In 1912 the ketchup and *sōsu* constituted 91 per cent of sales of all of the Kanies' produce, including rice and barley that the family still continued to grow.[12]

A glimpse into Kanie Ichitarō's life provides a perfect starting point for the analysis of the role that the Japanese armed forces played in the construction of Japanese national cuisine. The conscription experience

The Kanie family manufacturing tomato purée, c. 1910

Peasants working in a rice field, c. 1900s.

broadened the horizons of young farmers such as Kanie and confronted them with objects, practices, tastes and opinions that they would otherwise have had little opportunity to encounter. In the army peasants not only became accustomed to the exotic taste of beer, meat and *yōshoku*, but also turned into regular consumers of rice and soy sauce – the two basic elements of the urban diet consumed in farm households only sporadically. Furthermore, the demand for processed food created by army and navy orders was crucial to the survival of pioneering canneries and other food-processing enterprises in Japan, which in the future would provide the Japanese public with its daily supplies. Thus, in the long run, the 'strong army' policies of the Meiji government had a significant, homogenizing effect on the consumption practices of the Japanese population.

Food Processing and the Armed Forces

The very first Japanese canned product was manufactured in Nagasaki in 1871. Matsuda Masanori (1832–1895) succeeded in canning sardines in oil using the method he had learnt from the Frenchman Leon Dury. Matsuda was not the only pioneer who embarked on experimental food processing in Meiji Japan. Yanagisawa Sakichi and Ōfuji Matsugorō, both returnees from a study trip in the United States, were the first to can peaches and tomatoes. Their canning tests were conducted at the Interior Ministry's Laboratory for the Promotion of Agriculture in Shinjuku, Tokyo. The laboratory not only worked on the mastering of the canning process itself, but also put effort in replicating canning machinery that the Japanese bureaucrats had purchased in Europe and the United States.[13]

The first commercial canneries began to operate in Hokkaido, the northernmost of Japan's four main islands. In 1877 a salmon cannery in Ishikari was set up and a year later another one in Bekkai, both under the supervision of Ulysses S. Treat, a prominent canner from Eastport, Maine. Treat was included in the team of experts that Horace Capron (1804–1885) brought with him upon his appointment in 1871 as the chief foreign advisor to the Kaitakushi, a governmental agency responsible for developing Japan's northern frontier of Hokkaido. Russian demand for a delineation of the northern boundary between the two countries compelled the new government to embark quickly on the 'civilizing mission' of the island. Although salmon prevailed, venison was also canned in Hokkaido, and since 1880 the canneries began to function as training centres for prospective canners. Apprentices from all over the country flocked to Hokkaido eager to become acquainted with the new technology.[14]

Two reasons lay behind governmental support for the canning industry. First of all, the widespread use of canned food in the United States convinced the Japanese policy makers that, along with telegraph, rail and other technological innovations, canning was an attribute of progress and modernity.[15] The second reason was related to the Japanese trade imbalance. Since the investment required for setting up a canning

Canned salmon produced by commercial canneries in Hokkaido, c. 1880s.

business was minimal and fresh aquatic and agricultural resources widely available, the authorities hoped that canned products would join rice, tea and silk as the Japanese export articles. It was not before the 1910s, however, that Japanese cans were able to meet these expectations and compete with American and European products on the global market.[16]

Canned food did not succeed in becoming fashionable in Japan, unlike beef stew or *yōshoku*, because of its relatively high price. The Western community, top-end hotels and restaurants, and the Japanese elites who could meet the expense, preferred reliable imported brands to Japanese products of inferior quality.[17] Fortunately, the infant industry could rely on the principal patron of canning – war. Warfare and imperialism had from the very outset played a prominent role in the development of the canning industry in Europe and propelled the production and consumption of canned food in various times and locations.[18] Canning technology provided Western armies and navies with long-life and easy-to-transport food that could be securely eaten out of place and out of season. It enabled expatriate Western communities in remote corners of the world to retain their distinctive food patterns and protected them from the potential danger of contagion.[19]

Canned food appealed to the Japanese military authorities for the same reasons as their counterparts elsewhere – it made the armed forces less vulnerable and more independent of local food supplies. Experts in the West believed that standardized rations could improve military planning and preparedness, and facilitate the expansion of Western economic power into non-Western areas.[20] In view of the Meiji rhetoric on meat eating, canned beef received particular attention in Japanese military circles – beef was considered critical for bolstering the disastrous physical condition of conscripts. Many drafted men were in fact excused from duty after the physical examination, simply because they could not fulfil the minimum height requirement of 151.5 centimetres; by the end of the nineteenth century such cases constituted 16.7 per cent of all conscripts (see overleaf).[21]

For the sake of comparison, it should be mentioned that the average height of Dutch conscripts at the time was 165 centimetres, and this was comparable to young males in other parts of western Europe.[22] The critical eye of Major Henry Knollys of the British Royal Artillery, who inspected the Japanese army in the mid-1880s, did not fail to notice the poor constitution of Japanese soldiers:

As regards physique, they strike one as conspicuously

dwarfish – too small, in fact, for their weapons – and no won-
der, inasmuch as their average height barely exceeds five feet.
Moreover, they appear deficient in what I may call muscular
solidarity – probably owing to their youth – as though they
might be broken up and bowled over with greater facility than
is in accordance with the generally received ideas of military
coherence.[23]

Canned beef and ship's biscuits were introduced in the Japanese
Imperial Army in 1877 on the occasion of the Satsuma Rebellion – the first
test for the new conscript army. Their introduction was motivated by convenient portability as field rations. Moreover, beef was believed to have
strengthening properties for the troops. By 1916, along with soy sauce
extract and *fukujinzuke* pickle (various vegetables thinly sliced and pickled
in soy sauce and *mirin*), ship's biscuits and canned beef constituted the
chief four items in the field rations of the Imperial Japanese Army. The so-
called *Yamatoni* (beef simmered in soy sauce with ginger and sugar) soon
became the mainstay in military menus. For example, *Yamatoni* constituted
99.98 per cent of all canned beef purchased for the troops during the
Sino-Japanese War (1894–5), the first modern war that Japan was to fight.
The army spent a total of 2,517,380 yen on canned food during that war,
of which approximately two million went on canned beef. Imports from
the United States accounted for merely one fourth of this amount; the rest
was produced domestically – quite an achievement when one considers that
both canning and beef were relatively new additions to the food production
system in Japan.[24]

By the time of the Russo-Japanese War (1904–5), which broke out
ten years later, the total value of canned products contracted by the military

Anthropometric measures for 20-year-old males based
on Military Conscription Examination Data, 1900–1940.[25]

PERIOD/YEAR	% SMALL (150 cm or less)	% TALL (170 cm or more)	AVERAGE HEIGHT (cm)	AVERAGE WEIGHT (kg)
1900	16.7	1.3	not available	not available
1901–10	14.2	1.7	not available	not available
1911–20	11.4	2.4	160.1	51.9
1921–30	7.2	3.6	159.5	52.3
1931–40	3.8	4.7	160.3	53.0

had increased ninefold in comparison to the Sino-Japanese War. This time, following the successful incorporation of canned beef, the use of canned seafood increased remarkably.[26] The share of imported cans became negligible and ship's biscuits used as field rations were also by then produced domestically.[27]

Mori Rintarō (1862–1922), military surgeon and an influential reformer of military catering, warned of the dangers of Japanese armed forces becoming too dependent on Western products. Since he was already concerned at the way Europe exploited Japan as a market for manufactured goods, he argued strongly against any large importation of Western foodstuffs, something that 'no Japanese patriot would ever desire'.[28] Dependence on Western imports had at first been inevitable, since the modern Japanese military was modelled on the Western example. Practically every piece of equipment, from weapons to beds and uniforms, had to be imported, not to mention the expensive instructors who were hired to train Japanese units according to Western standards. The collaboration between the food-processing industry and the military proved beneficial for both parties. Military orders were crucial for the survival of the pioneering Japanese enterprises at a time when the domestic civilian market had not yet emerged and the export opportunities remained limited. The armed forces, on the other hand, secured a reliable source of provisions for the troops, marking the first steps towards self-sufficient food supply, which would assume an increasingly important role during the 1920s and '30s.

Fighting Beriberi

Setting up a modern military was considered a priority by the Meiji government. The Military Affairs Ministry was set up in 1869; a decree ordering all domains to adopt the French model for their land forces and the English model for their naval forces was issued in 1870; the formation of the Imperial Guards, the first military force directly under the control of the central government, took place in 1871; and the separate army and navy ministries were established in 1872. The emergence of a modern national military is conventionally dated either from the formation of the Imperial Guards or from the Conscript Edict of 1873.[29]

The birth of modern military catering goes back to 1871, when it was proclaimed that the responsibility for feeding soldiers would from now on rest on the military itself. This decision revolutionized the existing status quo, by discarding the prevailing practice of purchasing food for the troops from contracted cook shops, inns and pedlars. The introduction of a system of military catering marked a radical change that required the development of an entirely new structure of distributing and preparing food within the armed forces.[30]

The Conscript Edict of 1873 stipulated a daily ration per soldier at 6 *gō* (approximately 840 grams) of white rice and an allowance of 6 *sen* and 6 *rin* (0.066 yen) for the remaining provisions.[31] The 6 *gō* quota was higher than an average of the contemporary civilian consumption, which oscillated between 3.9 and 4.4 *gō* and still translated into the huge amount of three to five helpings of rice according to today's standards.[32] Major Henry Knollys was astonished, along with the simplicity of the Japanese military diet, at the mass of consumed rice. 'The Japanese soldier' – he wrote – 'is perfectly satisfied with an enormous bowl of plain, snow-white rice as a staple, with little pieces of pickle as a relish.'[33]

The ability to maintain a rice-based diet on a daily basis was a marker of status in nineteenth-century Japan, similar to meat consumption as a status marker in Europe. According to government surveys conducted during the 1880s, the proportion of rice among staples consumed by the Japanese population constituted approximately 50 per cent. Barley, wheat, sweet potatoes and millet were recorded to have comprised the remaining half.[34] It is obvious that there was not enough rice to sustain the entire population, but it is practically impossible to determine precisely who ate how much rice when, and how often. This depended not only on social class, income and the region one lived in, but also on harvest conditions that varied from year to year.[35] It seems certain that the elite classes and the majority of the urban population relied on rice as their staple, never mixing it with other grains.[36] Still, scholars' opinions vary concerning the consumption of rice among the farming population, which in the late nineteenth century constituted over 80 per cent of all Japanese. Persistent peasant protests and village disturbances demanding rice are often used in favour of the argument that rice was an integral part of peasant diet.[37] On the other hand, historical records, such as the following fragment from 1721, indicate that rice was only sporadically consumed by farmers in pre-modern Japan:

> Peasants who reside in the areas with rice paddies may sometimes eat rice, but only in combination with other edibles. Many of those who live in the mountains or areas with dry fields cannot even eat rice for the three festive days of the new year. Even

Clearly undernourished peasants pounding New Year's rice cakes. Woodblock print, name of artist and date unknown.

when cooking millet, Deccan grass, or wheat, they mix in so many greens, turnips, potato leaves, bean leaves, or other leaves that one can hardly see the grain.[38]

While keeping in mind the complexities of the issue of rice as the Japanese staple, it seems reasonable to conclude that in nineteenth-century Japan, except for certain areas particularly abundant in rice, peasants resorted to staples other than rice, or sustained on rice extended with other grains. In the westernmost part of Japan, people ate a higher proportion of wheat, barley and sweet potatoes, while millet and Deccan grass were consumed more often in mountainous areas.[39] Pure rice was reserved in peasant households for special occasions, such as New Year. Despite the rising standard of living during the late nineteenth and early twentieth centuries, peasant diet still fell considerably below urban standards. *Katemeshi*, a dish consisting of rice, millet and barley cooked with chopped radish, and *hagate*, the same dish made of radish leaves instead of roots, remained a staple in many rural households during the 1920s and '30s.[40] For many drafted men, having white rice at each meal day after day was a luxury that they had never experienced before being conscripted.

Still, the rice-based daily meals, consumed either in urban or in rural Japan, were very simple. Allowing for regional variation, a standard meal usually consisted of a bowl of rice with pickled vegetables, supplemented by *miso* soup for breakfast and a fish or, more often, a vegetable or a *tōfu* dish for lunch and dinner; in the Kyoto–Osaka area the soup was served for lunch. Simmering ingredients in stock, with the addition of soy sauce and sometimes sugar or sweet rice wine (*mirin*) – the so-called *nimono* – was the most common cooking technique. Grilled fish was not an ordinary dish; it was customarily served for lunch on the first and the fifteenth day of the month.[41] On a daily basis, even high-ranking samurai followed this austere meal pattern.[42] However, the principle did not apply to meals taken by affluent classes outside the home, or at celebratory occasions. Restaurant menus and festive banquets were distinguished by their great number of dishes, which often required very complex preparation and were meticulously decorated. As elsewhere, a strong contrast between the austerity of home meals and the opulence of professional cookery was pronounced in pre-modern Japan.[43]

The rice-centred meal pattern of the urban population and the samurai class became increasingly unhealthy as rice-polishing technology improved and the preference for white, highly polished rice developed. Before the eighteenth century people who could afford rice ate it partially polished, retaining part of the bran, which is a rich source of vitamin B1 (thiamine). A diet centred on white rice, with a limited supply of vitamins from side dishes, will eventually lead to beriberi, while a comparable diet centred on brown rice, barley or other grains will not. The disease may affect the muscles, nerves and digestive system, and may even cause heart failure. It was not until the early twentieth century, however, that thiamine deficiency became known as a cause of these symptoms. Beriberi had been known in the Tokugawa period as 'Edo affliction', because it occurred mainly in big cities such as Edo, where by the eighteenth century white, polished rice had become a conventional staple, as opposed to the brown, partly unpolished rice and other grains prevailing in the countryside.[44] People who became ill while working as servants in Edo are reported to have improved soon after returning to the country.[45]

A reliance on white rice proved to have catastrophic results for the health of the troops in the modern Japanese military. Thousands of soldiers and sailors suffered from beriberi before the cause of the disease was found and the dispute over what constituted the most efficient remedy against it finally ended. In 1883 the conditions in the navy were so alarming – 120 out of every 1,000 sailors suffered from beriberi – that the Beriberi Research Committee was established in order to fight the disease.[46] One of the individuals involved in the work of the committee was

Takagi Kanehiro (1849–1920), director of the Tokyo Naval Hospital and head of the Bureau of Medical Affairs of the Navy. Takagi, who had studied anatomy and clinical medicine at St Thomas's Hospital Medical College in London, drew attention to the fact that beriberi was a typically 'Asian' disease, rarely occurring among Westerners. Presuming that the illness was a result of a very low protein intake, Takagi suggested that a diet comparable to that of Western navies might be a remedy. In 1884, to prove this theory, meals comparable to that served in the British Navy – bread, ship biscuits, salted meat and beans – replaced the rice-based meals on the experimental ship *Tsukuba*. The ship reached the destination of Hawai'i with no beriberi patient on board. Since the concept of vitamins had not yet been discovered, Takagi was unable to determine precisely the cause of the disease, but he was correct to link it with nutrition.[47] The effectiveness of Takagi's measures convinced the naval leadership that he had found a solution to the beriberi problem and ordered the entire fleet to shift to a Western-style diet of ship's biscuits, dried beans and canned beef.[48]

In the long run, the measures Takagi suggested proved too costly for the navy's budget. The solution developed in the army was much cheaper and convenient. In 1884 Horiuchi Toshikuni managed to reduce beriberi cases in the Osaka division by mixing rice with barley, and by 1891 the practice of serving the rice-and-barley mixture instead of white rice was diffused in many army units.[49] The measure was not very welcome, though, since white rice was a preferred staple.[50]

A scientific explanation for beriberi could not be found without the concept of vitamin, which did not become properly understood until the 1920s. The military physician Mori Rintarō, better known under his literary pseudonym Mori Ōgai, shared the belief widespread in the scientific world that beriberi was an infectious disease. Upon Mori's appointment as Surgeon General of the Imperial Japanese Army in 1907, the practice of serving the rice-barley mixture instead of white rice in army units was discontinued. He was also a severe critic of measures introduced in the navy under Takagi's recommendation. In 1909 the Army Ministry appointed the Board of Inquiry into the Prevention of Beriberi with Mori as its chairman.[51] The following year Suzuki Umetarō (1874–1943) of Tokyo University, who was involved in the work of the committee, succeeded in demonstrating the link between vitamin B deficiency and beriberi. After 1925, the mixture of rice and barley in the proportion 7 to 3 became officially the standard staple in the Japanese military.[52]

Modernizing Military Catering

Beriberi was perhaps the most severe, but not the only food problem in the military; logistical difficulties troubled the Imperial Japanese Army throughout its history. The fact that most Japanese soldiers who lost their lives in the Pacific War (1937–45) died not on the battlefield but of malnutrition-related diseases or starvation is telling enough.[53] Ishiguro Tadanori (1845–1941), the first General Surgeon of the Japanese army, who was responsible for the introduction of the system of military catering in 1871, did not fully apprehend the range of measures that were necessary for a proper functioning of such a system. Catering fell under the joint responsibility of the accountant and the military surgeon of each division, and no institution that was to coordinate the distribution of provisions or to advise on issues related to feeding soldiers was formed within the army organization. The lack of coordination, disunity and inefficiency represented the general state of the nineteenth-century Japanese army; it was 'unshaped in form and function, and suffered from widespread draft avoidance, low morale, and a confused soldiery'.[54]

The first establishment to coordinate the allocation of provisions to the front was prompted by the outbreak of the Sino-Japanese War in 1894, and its functioning left much to be desired. So in March 1897 the army authorities set up the Central Provisions Depot, which was to operate in both wartime and peacetime. Until 1945, when the Imperial Japanese Army was dissolved, the depot was chiefly responsible for conducting research and coordinating production and distribution of military rations and catering equipment, and at times of war for provisioning the front.[55] The operational structure of the depot was continuously reformed, and the number of personnel fluctuated. For example, between 1907 and 1911 the number of employees doubled, reaching 95; it shrank to 65 by 1937, but swelled up again during the following years to reach the all-time maximum of 571 in 1944. The depot operated through its main bureau in Tokyo and regional bureaux and local branches. In 1940, three regional bureaux – in Osaka, Ujina (now part of Hiroshima) and Hōten (now Shenyang, China) – were in operation, supported by local branches in Nagareyama, Sendai, Niigata, Nagoya, Moji (now part of Kitakyūshū), Dairen (now Dalian, China) and Rashin (now Najin, North Korea).[56]

Until the 1920s, the activities of the depot were primarily logistical, and only marginally concerned with other aspects of military catering. Issues related to the health of the troops, such as the decision whether to serve white rice or a rice-barley mixture to the soldiers, were left entirely

Cooking on board
ship in 1942.

to the discretion of the Military Medical College and the Surgeon General's
office. The Army Accounting College, in turn, was responsible for educating
paymasters who coordinated catering in each division. In 1920 the responsibility for reforming army catering was finally placed under a central
coordination of the Army Provisions Depot.[57]

The situation was very different in the navy, where a system of central food control had been in operation since 1890. The introduction of
such a system was necessary in order to implement the reforms aimed at
fighting beriberi. As mentioned earlier, Takagi's Westernized diet proved
too costly in the long run, but the measures revolutionized navy catering.
After 1890 provisions were distributed centrally by the Munitions Bureau
of the Naval Ministry, instead of the hitherto prevalent local procuring
by paymasters.[58] This made the navy much less vulnerable to the local

availability of foodstuffs. Moreover, the rations became standardized, with the amount of calories, protein, fat and other nutrients to be provided to all marines specified by the central authorities and the guidelines distributed to the paymaster of each ship. The central authorities determined in detail the kinds and amounts of food that each sailor was to consume regardless of location, even suggesting how the food was to be cooked.

Wartime menu, composition of navy rations (1904).[59]

TYPE OF FOOD	MINIMUM AMOUNT IN GRAMS
Bread	187.5
Preserved meat	150
Dry provisions	75
Sugar	22.3
White rice	375
Broken barley	131.3
Tea	1.8
Fish	150
Roasted barley flour	3.8

Suggested menu:
Breakfast: a boiled mixture of white rice, broken barley
   and roasted wheat, dried fish and aubergine simmered in
   miso, pickles
Lunch: bread, beef stew with potatoes and onions
Dinner: a boiled mixture of white rice, broken barley and
   roasted barley flour, simmered beef and taros, pickles
Additional: sweet *azuki* bean soup

The very nature of seafaring already required more careful provisioning than was the case with land forces, which could (at least in theory) always procure food locally. The introduction of a central food-control system further reinforced the commitment to good quality catering in the navy. The following statement included in the cookbook published by the Navy Educational Division in 1918 reflects this attitude:

It can be said that the quality of the military cookery and the
adequacy of the menus directly influence soldiers' nourishment,

Baking bread aboard the catering vessel *Mamiya* in 1934.

fighting spirit and combat strength. Moreover, food gives us mental comfort, and sharing meals harmonizes hearts and raises affection. In other words, peace and harmony on the ship demonstrate themselves at the table.[60]

By the late 1930s specialized catering vessels were accompanying Japanese navy convoys. For example, the state-of-the-art catering ship *Mamiya* carried a 350-man staff engaged in full-time food processing for the fleet.[61] *Mamiya* could produce daily 1,000 kilograms of noodles, 14,000 bottles of lemonade, 2,000 portions of ice cream and fresh-baked bread for 7,500 sailors. Still, bread was not a daily staple in the navy. Food strikes that took place in response to the introduction after 1890 of meals centred on bread and ship's biscuits, to which the young men were utterly unaccustomed, ultimately led to a return to rice and barley as the staple in the navy.[62] This experience, however, convinced the navy authorities of the importance of the taste of served food, and prompted the introduction of a variety of measures in order to satisfy the sailors' taste preferences. For example, in 1935 the accounting division of the second squadron conducted a dietary survey that included all Japanese battleships. Nearly 500 recipes – the most popular – were recorded and distributed among all accounting units.[63] A selection from this collection is listed here:

Fried rice
Boiled rice and barley shallow-fried with finely chopped beef, flavoured with salt, pepper, oyster sauce and soy sauce with *mirin*.

Curry rice
Rice, barley and pieces of sweet potatoes simmered until done in a sauce made of minced beef, carrots, onions fried in butter or lard and seasoned with curry powder, salt and pepper.

'Parent and child' bowl
Chicken simmered with onions, mushrooms and green peas, with an egg added at the end. Served on the mixture of rice and barley.

Grated yam soup
Soup made of fish stock flavoured with soy sauce, and grated yam (with a very slippery texture) added to it.

Miso soup with clams
Miso soup with onions, taros and canned surf clams cut into pieces.

Beef stew with *miso*
Stew made of beef, carrots, potatoes and onions, thickened with lard and flour. Flavoured with tomato purée, soy sauce, *sake*, salt and *miso*.

Pork simmered 'cultured' style
Deep-fried balls made of minced pork mixed with finely chopped onions and ginger, simmered in soy sauce with sugar.

Potatoes in sour *miso* dressing
Boiled potatoes in pieces dressed in a mixture of mustard, sugar, *miso* and vinegar.

Potato croquettes
Mashed potatoes mixed with yolk, shaped into small ovals, coated with breadcrumbs and deep-fried.

Fried ship's biscuits
Ship's biscuits deep-fried in sesame oil, served with sugar.

A characteristic feature of most dishes included in the 1935 navy collection of recipes was the prevalence of meat (beef and pork), lard, potatoes, onions and canned ingredients. By the late 1930s army menus would also follow this trend, but the innovation of army meals proceeded less smoothly than in the navy. Generally speaking, since the anti-beriberi measures of 1890, the navy continued to assign a larger budget for food than the army.[64] Furthermore, because army catering involved many more mouths to feed, coordinating it was much more complex. For example, the total number of navy personnel in the late 1930s remained fewer than 200,000 men, while the total strength of the army exceeded a million.[65]

Except for canned beef and ship's biscuits, which were used for field rations, the army accounting records from the Sino-Japanese War could pass for a shopping list of a pre-modern urban household. Along with rice, they show foodstuffs such as soybeans, fish, eggs, *tōfu*, dried guard strips, wheat gluten, *miso*, sweet potatoes, leeks, devil's tongue jelly (*konnyaku*), burdock root, carrots, lotus root, *sake*, soy sauce and sugar.[66] These provisions were more elaborate than, but not essentially different from, the food secured for the Taiwan expedition twenty years earlier – the first time that Japanese troops were dispatched abroad – which included devil's tongue, dried fish, pickled and dried vegetables and *miso*.[67] At the time of the Russo-Japanese War, pork and Chinese cabbage dominated the menus of the troops fighting in China, most probably because these ingredients

Menu served to the 2nd battalion of the 7th regiment of the 9th infantry division between 21 and 29 February 1905.[68]

DATE	DINNER	BREAKFAST	LUNCH
21 February 1905	pork, Chinese cabbage, leeks	*fukujinzuke* pickles	pork, Chinese cabbage
22 February 1905	egg, Chinese cabbage	*fukujinzuke* pickles	salted yellowtail
23 February 1905	pork, Chinese cabbage, leeks	*fukujinzuke* pickles	dried sardines
24 February 1905	beef, Chinese cabbage, potatoes	*fukujinzuke* pickles	salted Pacific saury
25 February 1905	salted yellowtail	*fukujinzuke* pickles	egg, Chinese cabbage, leeks
26 February 1905	pork, leeks, Chinese cabbage	*fukujinzuke* pickles	salted yellowtail
27 February 1905	chicken, leeks, Chinese cabbage	*fukujinzuke* pickles	pork, Chinese cabbage
28 February 1905	canned beef	*fukujinzuke* pickles	canned beef

were easiest to procure on location. However, *yōshoku* items such as curry stew and cutlets could also be found, along with potatoes, in army menus from the last decade of the nineteenth century.[69]

Menu served in the 1st regiment of the
9th company to the soldiers of the 6th pay level,
between 25 and 30 June 1900.[70]

DATE	BREAKFAST	LUNCH	DINNER
25 June 1900	thin-sliced deep-fried *tōfu*, *miso* soup with greens	simmered fish, potatoes, *daikon*, greens, *takuan* pickles	salted sardines, grated *daikon*, greens, *takuan* pickles
26 June 1900	potatoes, *miso* soup with greens	*tsukudani* preserve	herring, seaweed (*konbu*), wheat gluten
27 June 1900	pickles	cutlet, potatoes, broad beans, greens	potatoes, *daikon*, *miso* soup with carrots
28 June 1900	potatoes, *miso* soup with greens	salted sardines, raw horse mackerel, grated *daikon*, greens	potatoes, greens, cowpeas
29 June 1900	thin-sliced deep-fried *tōfu*, *miso* soup with greens	potatoes, cowpeas, deep-fried *tōfu* dumplings	simmered bonito, potatoes
30 June 1900	pickles	simmered bonito, omelette, cowpeas simmered in sugar, greens, *takuan* pickles	potatoes, *miso* soup with burdock root and *daikon*

At that time, the army began to pay greater attention to cooking the ingredients, instead of focusing only on the logistics of provisioning. On the occasion of the Boxer Rebellion (1899–1901), in response to which an international military force was gathered around Beijing, the Japanese troops were stationed along with American, British, Russian and German armies. This gave the accounting divisions an opportunity to observe the catering systems of the Western armies and made them realize that issues beyond the distribution of foodstuffs were at stake.[71] The change of attitude towards military catering became apparent in the publication in 1910 of the first army cookbook, with the following remark in the introduction:

> In the military it is necessary not to be concerned with outside beauty and luxury when preparing meals. However, if people in charge of cooking do not study cookery at all and every day repeat monotonous and tasteless menus, then even with a high sum for provisions and good quality, fresh ingredients they will never reach the aim of military upbringing. The purpose of this book, by compiling an outline of Japanese and Western cooking techniques, is to become a helpful reference for military men responsible for cooking. It should be strictly avoided to compete in vain in cooking skills or in extravagant menus. One must never forget the hardships of the battlefield.[72]

The cookbook contained 146 recipes, including several for *yōshoku*, such as rice curry, cutlet, stew and potato-and-beef croquettes; three recipes for baking bread are also found.[73] These efforts were not sufficient, however, to bolster the quality of meals served in the Japanese army. As well as lack of guidance and coordination, cooking was held in low esteem as a duty to be performed by a soldier.[74] Fragmentation of responsibilities and missing links between the accounting divisions and the Provisions Depot further contributed to the chaos in the army kitchens. The Siberian expedition of 1918 provides a case in point. The accounting divisions anticipated that rice would not be easily procured on location and provided catering divisions with portable ovens, designed by the Provisions Depot, to bake bread. For the majority of soldiers, however, this was the first encounter with bread, and, as was the case in the navy a few decades earlier, they rejected the unknown staple en masse.[75] The fact that no such drastic reactions to the Western- and Chinese-style dishes were reported suggests the particularly important position that rice assumed in the military diet.

Regardless of the shortcomings of the army catering system, in the early twentieth century military diet was far above the national average. As indicated earlier, a soldier consumed considerably more rice than an urban civilian, not to mention that few peasants could afford rice on a daily basis. Furthermore, by the 1910s the average quantity of beef consumed per soldier was approximately 13 kilograms a year, while the average per head of the population was roughly 1 kilogram. The quantity of fish served in the military was also far above civilian consumption.[76] This gap increased further during the 1920s, due to the economic recession that hit Japan on the one hand and the reorganization of army catering on the other.

The European experiences of World War One demonstrated that successful management of food resources, both at the home front and at the battlefield, could be decisive in modern warfare.[77] Influenced by this lesson, the new generation of policy makers in the Japanese army realized that efficiently prepared, good-quality, tasty food was of vital significance for the combat strength and fighting spirit of the troops. In 1920 the Army Provisions Depot was entrusted with a wide-ranging reorganization of army catering, and within a decade the mission was accomplished. The innovations involved the introduction of modern cooking equipment that allowed economizing on human labour, such as meat grinders, vegetable cutters and dishwashers. The launch of a wide-ranging educational pro-gramme for army cooks began with the publication in 1924 of *Guntai chōri sankōsho* ('Military Catering Reference Manual'), the first army cookbook that clearly stood apart from civilian publications of this sort. *Guntai ryōrihō* ('Military Cookery'), published fourteen years earlier, followed the model of civilian cookbooks, which were rather vague and did not even specify the amounts of ingredients needed for each recipe. Instructions in the cooking manuals that were issued by the Army Provisions Depot dur-ing the 1920s, '30s and '40s were written in a very clear, crisp style and each recipe was divided into an 'ingredients' and 'preparation' section, with

An army kitchen, c. 1930s.

additional information included in the 'remarks' segment. The energy value of one serving of each dish was specified, and after the late 1930s this was supplemented with the calculations of the protein content. The cookbooks were constantly improved and republished, so that even catering personnel with limited culinary training and experience was capable of achieving good results.[78]

Under the Depot's supervision, instructors were sent to advise divisions throughout the country on dietary matters, and experienced cooks were dispatched to supervise cooking in the units stationed in Korea, Manchuria, Siberia and Sakhalin.[79] The Army Provisions Depot also launched a series of cooking courses for catering personnel. For example, the second Military Catering Course took place in Tokyo in early 1928 and lasted 45 days. Next to practical training in cooking, 40 theoretical lectures were delivered: 5 on the basics of nutrition, 15 on provisions, 18 on cookery, 4 on catering management and 1 on the menu construction.[80] The practical implementation of the disseminated knowledge was constantly monitored. For example, a record from January 1927 specifies how frequently which dishes were in reality cooked in which units (see overleaf). By the 1930s the army was providing a model of efficient mass catering, with specialized equipment, motivated and well-educated personnel, and exciting menus.

Moulding the National Taste

The reforms of the 1920s in military catering largely contributed to the moulding of a nationally homogenous taste. They turned *yōshoku* items, such as cutlet, stew and rice curry, into the hallmarks of military menus to accompany the 2 *gō* of rice-and-barley mixture served at each meal. These dishes had been already tried and tested, and adjusted to the preferences of the urban masses. This reduced the risk of them being rejected by the soldiers, as was the case with bread. After 1923 army reformers also began to incorporate Chinese dishes, inspired by the recent popularity of cheap Chinese eateries in Japanese cities (see chapter Six).[81] The introduction of Chinese food proved particularly successful because it was flavoured with soy sauce.

Soy sauce was very extensively used in the military. Following the established pattern of the urban pre-modern diet, it functioned as an all-purpose flavouring in army and navy kitchens. Like rice, soy sauce constituted the daily component of meals in urban and elite households, but was more sparingly used in rural areas. Unlike rice, the taste of soy sauce in

A selection of side dishes served in the Imperial Japanese Army in January 1927.[82]

DIVISION (and its location)	DEEP-FRIED, BREADED FISH OR MEAT	*MISO* SOUP WITH PORK, VEGETABLES AND SWEET POTATOES	STEW	RICE CURRY	SIMMERED (canned) FISH OR MEAT WITH VEGETABLES
Imperial Guards, 2nd infantry (Tokyo)	3	2	1	–	–
1st division 49th infantry (Kōfu)	3	2	1	1	4
2nd division 30th infantry (Takada)	2	5	–	2	5
3rd division 18th infantry (Toyohashi)	–	–	–	–	–
4th division 61st infantry (Wakayama)	2	–	–	4	4
5th division 11th infantry (Hiroshima)	4	–	–	2	2
6th division 45th infantry (Kagoshima)	–	2	–	1	6
7th division 27th infantry (Asahigawa)	1	1	1	2	1
8th division 5th infantry (Aomori)	2	2	1	–	1
9th division 9th infantry (Kanazawa)	2	–	–	1	7
10th division 39th infantry (Himeji)	6	4	2	3	2
Taiwan 1st	–	3	1	2	4
Kwantung 2nd (Hōten)	2	–	–	3	4

pre-modern Japan showed a considerable regional variation. By the eighteenth century the best-quality soy sauce was produced by commercial
brewers clustered in large cities, in particular Edo, while the rural population relied overwhelmingly on home-made soybean paste (*miso*) for
flavouring.[83] The use of soy sauce by most farm households, which were
largely self-sufficient in food, was restricted to special occasions such as
festivals and weddings. They purchased soy sauce from local brewers,
since only wealthy farmers could afford to brew soy sauce at home. The
situation was different in central Japan (Aichi, Mie and Gifu prefectures),
where so-called *tamari shōyu* – much less complex in manufacture and
different in taste from the conventional soy sauce consumed in cities – was
brewed in most households.[84]

Throughout the twentieth century, owing to urbanization, rising
standards of living and a shift towards industrialized mass manufacture,
not only did soy sauce become the dominant flavouring for the ever
increasing number of Japanese, but its taste was becoming increasingly
standardized. This was due to the modernization of production, which
came to rely more and more on chemical knowledge and machinery rather
than centuries-old know-how and experience among regional brewers.
Moreover, the market share of major manufacturers steadily increased and
hundreds of local varieties were gradually replaced by national brands.[85]
In 1937 the five largest firms were responsible for a quarter of Japanese soy
sauce production.[86] The soy sauce case illustrates perfectly the increasingly

homogenizing effect of industrially processed food on taste preferences of the Japanese population throughout the twentieth century.

Contrary to the navy, which after adopting a Westernized diet in 1890 gradually returned to the native pattern based on rice and soy sauce, the foundation of the army diet rested firmly on the pre-modern urban meal pattern supplemented by Western and Chinese elements. The main reason that the armed forces included non-traditional dishes in their menus was because they provided more nourishment. Serving nourishing and filling meals at the lowest possible cost was the general rule of military cookery, and the adoption of Western and Chinese recipes made this possible. In 1910 the daily energy requirement for army soldiers was set at the level of 2,500–2,700 calories, and was raised in 1929 to 4,000 calories. Moreover, the authorities suggested that on the occasion of heavy training or a battle this standard should be further increased by 500–1300 calories.[87] Approximately two-thirds of this amount was to be supplied by the staple, which left 1,200–1,300 calories (and in the case of heavy training or a battle even up to 2,600 calories) for side dishes.[88] Budgetary constraints made it virtually impossible to provide so many calories from lean traditional foodstuffs – vegetables, *tōfu*, seafood. The best solution proved to be the large-scale adoption of foreign cooking techniques, such as deep-frying, pan-frying and stewing, and foreign ingredients, such as meat, lard and potatoes. High-calorie fried dishes were a cheap source of energy, and also a method of using up ingredients of questionable quality – practically everything qualified for being breaded and deep-fried. Moreover, adding curry powder to Japanese-style dishes perked up the bland taste of ingredients of inferior quality. Curry powder also helped to mask the unpleasant smell of spoilt fish and meat. In short, the military's adoption of Chinese and Western dishes made a high-calorie diet economically possible.

There was also another reason for including foreign-inspired dishes in military menus – they helped to bridge regional differences in taste. Recruits hailed from all over the country and had been used to different kinds of food. For example, during the experiments conducted in the winter of 1936–7 by Major-General Kawashima Shirō (1895–1986) of the Army Provisions Depot 22 per cent of soldiers who participated in the experiment found the *miso* soup served too sweet, while 10 per cent found it too salty.[89] Military cooks experienced problems in making the food suited to the taste preferences of the majority of soldiers and sailors, and tried to overcome regional differences in diet by including local dishes, such as *miso* soup with pork, vegetables and sweet potatoes (*Satsumajiru*) from southern Kyushu or *Kantōni* (also known as *oden*) from the Tokyo region, in the military menus. Methods were also developed to determine the 'average taste' of each unit, like the one described below:

> In the case of military cookery, where in one kitchen meals for several hundred and even for more than a thousand people are prepared, the flavouring can by no means be adapted to the taste preference of each soldier. However, this does not mean that the aspect of taste is completely ignored. Of course, it is impossible to satisfy different likes and dislikes as to minute details, but it is possible to prepare food with a taste that is close to the majority of soldiers. In this way the aim could be reached that, just as the age and bodily exercise of all soldiers are similar, so too can they have relatively similar taste preferences. For this reason, the problem is how to cook meals suited to the taste of as many soldiers as possible. The following points should be considered:
>
> *Determining the 'standard taste' of the Military Unit*
>
> First, I shall explain with the example of *miso* soup how to determine the 'standard taste' of the unit, or in other words, which taste is favoured by the majority of privates. Prepare three sorts of *miso* soup containing different amounts of *miso* and let it be tested by as many soldiers as possible (when selecting soldiers, take into consideration their occupation before entering the military). The 'standard taste' of *miso* soup (the amount of *miso* to be used) will be the taste most favoured of the three. . . . The amount of soy sauce and sugar used for cooking fish, and the quantity of vinegar used in *sunomono* can be determined in the same way. In addition to this, according to the same method it is possible to learn about the salt taste of each military unit, and to compare it with the salt taste of the entire army.[90]

Provided that rice remained the staple, the 'de-Japanization' of side dishes turned out to be the perfect solution for making the taste of military menus agreeable to the majority of conscripts, since most men were *equally unfamiliar* with Western and Chinese food. These dishes were not only hearty, relatively inexpensive and convenient to cook in large quantities, but also unknown, and therefore relatively uncontroversial. We may presume that it must have been somehow easier for recruits to get used to a completely

Conscripts at table, 1938.

new taste than to change one they had acquired in childhood. By serving
foreign foods that were new to all recruits, army and navy cooks not only
helped to level regional and social distinctions in the military, but also
speeded up the process of nationalizing and homogenizing Japanese food
tastes. Indeed, by the time that the (second) Sino-Japanese War broke
out in 1937, curries, croquettes and Chinese stir-fries had become soldiers'
favourites and acquired a clear military connotation. Historical records
indicate that many conscripts during the 1920s and '30s considered food to
be among the most memorable experiences of their time in the military.[91]
Some even included entire menus in their diaries.

The main impact of modern warfare on human food tastes may
lie in the fact that the thousands of conscripts are not free to choose
the food they eat, and that this experience shapes their future food
preferences.[92] Military menus in Japan reinforced the nationwide spread
of the ideal of rice as the centrepiece around which a meal was constructed, and of soy sauce as a crucial flavouring agent. The inclusion
of side dishes that contained (canned) meat – motivated by the goal of
strengthening the military – set army meals apart from the daily diet of
the majority of the population. By virtue of their conscription, the sons
of farmers and other lower-class households enjoyed the new 'luxury'
of being sustained by menus that would have been considered too

Menu served in the 14th cavalry regiment, 21–30 March 1933.[93]

DATE	BREAKFAST	LUNCH	DINNER
21 March 1933	*miso* soup	simmered burdock root and carrots	rice cakes (*ohagi*)*, *udon* noodles
22 March 1933	*miso* soup	noodles in curry sauce	fish *teriyaki*
23 March 1933	*miso* soup	deep-fried, breaded fish or meat	rice with meat and vegetables flavoured with tomato sauce
24 March 1933	*miso* soup	simmered beef on rice	rice curry
25 March 1933	*miso* soup	*udo* stalks in vinegar dressing	(no record)
26 March 1933	*miso* soup	soy-stewed pork and vegetables	rice with vegetables and meat
27 March 1933	*miso* soup	*miso* soup with pork, vegetables and sweet potatoes	simmered squid with taros and lotus root
28 March 1933	*miso* soup	pork and vegetables in *miso* sauce	*udon* noodles made of ship's biscuits
29 March 1933	*miso* soup	*oden*	mackerel in *miso* sauce
30 March 1933	*miso* soup	grilled pickled cod	canned salmon and vegetable stew

* We may presume that rice cakes were served especially on 21 March to celebrate the Spring Equinox, a national holiday at the time officially labelled Imperial Ancestors' Spring Memorial Day.

extravagant for daily consumption where they came from. Furthermore, a military canteen was for thousands of drafted peasant sons the site of their first encounter with eclectic dishes that represented multicultural urban mass gastronomy. On their discharge, the soldiers returned home and shared their newly acquired taste for Western and Chinese dishes

Soldiers preparing rice balls, 1937.

with their families and neighbours. By doing so, they were instrumental in carrying the ideal of new, national cuisine to the furthest corners of the country.

Four
Reforming Home Meals

Conscription was not the only powerful factor in homogenizing taste preferences in Japan; home economics education was also influential in disseminating a national standard for home cookery. This transformation, like that of the modernization of the armed forces, was grounded in the reforms of the Meiji government. The newly launched ideal of womanhood, known by the rubric 'good wife, wise mother' (*ryōsai kenbo*), promoted housewifery as the crucial symbol and the sole aspiration for adult women. It was part and parcel of the modern ideal of the home that revolutionized family and gender relations in Japan. The legal foundation of this transition was laid in the Meiji Civil Code promulgated in 1898, and persistently, though gradually, the rhetoric of reform was put into practice.

At first, both the domestic ideology and the concept of 'good wife, wise mother' acquired a strong bourgeois connotation. Step by step, however, largely through their proliferation in the mass media, middle-class domestic ideals began to transform conceptions of family and womanhood among the working classes as well, ultimately assuming the status of a national ideal. By the 1970s the attributes of *ryōsai kenbo* became practically synonymous with womanhood, and the actual circumstances of most Japanese households matched the middle-class domestic models created at the beginning of the century.[1]

Reforming domestic space in Japan was a highly political project. Modern nation states, the ranks of which Japan aspired to join, drew their strength from the productive and reproductive capacities of their populations, since they relied heavily on industrial labour for their economic potency and universally drafted conscripts for military power.[2] Therefore, the Meiji government considered well-functioning, healthy households instrumental in manufacturing loyal and fit citizens who were to put the goal of 'rich country, strong army' (see chapter Three) into practice.

Although serving the interests of the state, however, the reform of domestic space in Japan was by no means a state-sponsored, top-down project comparable to 'civilization and enlightenment' (see chapter One). To be sure, the state provided the legal foundation and institutional framework for the reform, but it proceeded through the interaction of various initiatives.[3] The reform also opened up a myriad of business opportunities for producers of furniture and cooking equipment, publishers of magazines and cookbooks. All these players were in constant negotiation with each other, not to mention the men and women who adjusted their family life to the newly emerging concepts and expectations.

In his *House and Home in Modern Japan*, Jordan Sand meticulously explains the creation of domestic space in modern Japan, in both abstract and concrete terms. In this chapter, based on Sand's insights, I will illuminate aspects that were critical for the elevation of the family meal into a cult of family performance and the glorification of cooking as the epitome of housewifery. These two developments are central to the construction of Japanese national cuisine and contemporary attitudes towards cooking. Home economics classes, sustained by nationally circulated magazines and later by radio and television, helped to disseminate the nationally homogenous repertoire of home cooking. They were also responsible for the popularization of the culinary aesthetics hitherto restricted to gastronomy as the characteristic feature of 'Japaneseness'.

The Family Meal as the Hub of Domesticity

The launch of the domestic discourse in Japan was fertilized by the exposure to the Victorian 'cult of domesticity', manifested by the sentimentalization of home life and the romanticization of motherly duties in British and North American middle-class homes. This family morality that had developed under the influence of industrial capitalism and Protestant reform movements found no parallel in Japan. By the end of the nineteenth century, however, the Anglo-American domestic ideal received the increasing attention of Japanese social reformers and was widely featured in the Japanese media. The neologism *katei* – a term that soon entered the Japanese language as the equivalent of the English word 'home' – was especially constructed in order to express the full meaning of the new concept. *Katei* soon became a trendy word and a '*katei*' column became a standard component in popular mainstream magazines and newspapers. In conjunction with *katei*, the phrase *ikka danran* (the family circle) became ubiquitous in the language of Japanese domestic reform. The term denoted the pleasure of family members gathering together, along with the moral and educational value that these occasions entailed.[4]

Thus conceived, the ideology of domesticity centred on the conjugal unit, as opposed to the lineal extended family that had prevailed in Japan, and the middle-class household was the chief site at which the ideal was targeted. At first, model families that embraced the concept of *katei* belonged to the new class of professionals – company directors, elite bureaucrats, university professors and military officers. After World War One, this select group was extended to include civil servants, educators, office workers and others who could classify as 'white-collar' professionals, and were labelled *sarariiman* ('salary men', male salaried workers). They formed the 'new middle class' that emerged at the time in Japanese cities and clearly distinguished themselves from the bourgeois elite of the previous generation – for example shopkeepers and craftsmen, who remained a significant presence in urban and rural areas. By 1920 such households constituted merely 5–8 per cent of the entire population in Japan, but in Tokyo the share reached 21.4 per cent.[5]

The chief source of this new class were second and third sons who, according to custom, did not inherit family property. Propelled by the new opportunities for upward mobility provided by the Meiji reforms, they moved away from their extended families to the rapidly expanding urban centres, where they found employment in the newly emerging banks, schools and offices. These young men and their wives started their married life in completely new circumstances, as nuclear families without houses of belongings, and modelled themselves increasingly on the new ideology of domesticity. They assigned to themselves, as David Ambaras observes, the mission of 'ensuring the well-being and progress of the nation':

> As part of their ideological engagement, members of this group implicitly posited their difference from and superiority to other classes in terms of values, everyday practices, and technical expertise. And to implement the reforms and techniques they deemed essential to achieving the twin objectives of national progress and self-empowerment, new groups of experts worked to capture key sections of public opinion to cement alliances with state agencies.[6]

Secondary education and a white-collar profession for the household head were the two indispensable factors for a family to be recognized as belonging

'A Page from the Accounting Book', a poster from the Industrial Hygiene Exhibition of 1924.

to the new middle class. Professional housewifery was the designated role for a woman within this new class. As phrased by one of the reformers, the husband was to function as prime minister and foreign minister, while the wife was to serve as finance minister and home minister.[7] Diligence and thrift in household operations, and meticulous attention to keeping accounts, were emphasized as virtues critical to competent housekeeping. The wife's assumption of chief responsibility for all domestic matters revolutionized existing conventions and resulted in the gendering of housework for the rest of the twentieth century. It has only been recently that the aphorism *otoko wa soto, onna wa uchi* ('man outside, woman inside') began to decline in Japan.[8]

It is difficult to generalize household circumstances of the Tokugawa period, considering the differences conditioned by class, income, occupation and local custom. Nonetheless, with the exception of the wealthy warrior and merchant families, who employed servants to do most of the domestic work in their households, the household was an economic unit of production with both productive and reproductive activities taking place, and female and male members of the household fulfilling both functions. For example, Tokugawa fathers were involved in education and the physical care of children, and male householders were engaged in shopping and housework.[9] Industrialization and urbanization, propelled by the Meiji reforms, interrupted the unity between the place of work and the place of residence for an increasing number of Japanese. The ideology of domesticity, in turn, led to the emergence of the new profession of 'housewife' (*shufu*).

The word *shufu* was not commonly used in Japan before the 1880s. It literally bears the meaning 'mistress (of the house)', but gradually, embraced by the rhetoric of domesticity, *shufu* became an independent label, 'reflecting its transformation from a status designation within a household to a universal occupational category'.[10] The emergence of a professional housewife was crucial for the transition of the Japanese domestic space, since she would be the one who defined its every detail, including the character and content of the home meals. 'No part of the house' – Sand explains – 'was more heavily invested with importance in the texts of the new profession than the kitchen, for it was here that the modern *shufu* was to establish herself as an expert.'[11] Infrastructural improvements such as electricity, piped water and gas fundamentally transformed domestic labour. Equipped with technological innovations and new knowledge with which to handle them, the 'good wife, wise mother' was then dressed in a white apron to complete the transformation into a professional housewife. The apron reflected the professionalism of her future role as a scientist of the modern home, with the kitchen serving as her 'laboratory'.[12]

'Reform of the Home Begins with the Kitchen Equipment', a poster from the Industrial Hygiene Exhibition of 1924.

91

A middle-class family at dinner, a poster from the Industrial Hygiene Exhibition of 1924.

The crucial factor responsible for the particular importance that the kitchen acquired within the home was the centrality of the family meal within the ideal bourgeois lifestyle. Eating together as a family was invested with new moral meanings. Media slogans proclaimed that 'there is no greater pleasure of the family than when old and young, big and small gather in a happy circle and enjoy a meal together'.[13] It would be incorrect to assume that gatherings around food were lacking in pre-modern Japan. However, the focus shifted from strengthening the relationship within peer groups between the non-kin members of the community towards the 'closed circle' of family members. In pre-modern Japan, sharing food was not associated with the family.[14]

The suggestions that reformers made to synchronize mealtimes among family members, to share eating space, even to share the same dining table, were all revolutionary to late nineteenth-century Japanese. In the past, meals in most Japanese households were taken on individual trays (*zen*), with one tray for each member of the household. Barriers of status had commonly been maintained by segregating the time and space in which food was taken by different members of the household. Meals were usually shared among household members of the same sex or age, so that men, women, old and young did not customarily eat together; the room in which the husband dined was often off limits to his wife.[15] The domestic ideology

Two men dining on individual trays, from *Nenjū sōzai no shikata* (1893).

considered that changes in these practices would be morally significant for the integrity of the entire household. During the first decades of the twentieth century, new objects that were to facilitate the diffusion of the new practices and rules that were to guide them were enthusiastically propagated by domestic ideologues, and successively reshaped the conventions within urban families.

A home meal was, in the first place, to become a site of relaxation for the head of the family. The introduction to a cookbook of 1905, one of the first that prominently used the term *katei* in its title, described this ideal in the following manner:

> When he leaves the house in the morning, complicated public affairs are awaiting him. Regardless of the type of occupation, every wage earner comes home in the evening absentmindedly, with tired body and enfeebled spirit. His knitted eyebrows loosen

An urban working family at a shared table, 1932.

at last when the child welcomes him on the road, and the wife greets him at the door. Meanwhile, the family is seated in front of the table, the mixed smell of rice and fish cooked by the wife saturates the air. Then, when he starts eating, he relaxes, the hardships of the whole day are gone without a trace, and the room brims with a peaceful spirit of satisfaction.[16]

Three changes were necessary in order to achieve such an atmosphere: mealtimes of all family members needed to be synchronized; individual trays had to be replaced with a shared table; and the quality and variety of home meals had to be improved. After the turn of the century, an increasing number of middle-class families abandoned their trays and began to take meals sitting on the floor around a low table. They were soon followed by working-class families; by the 1920s a large proportion of them adopted shared tables, mainly due to practical considerations – one large table with folded legs took less space than several individual trays and could be used for other purposes as well.[17] The new shared table, commonly referred to as *chabudai*, was either round or rectangular, with the diameter of approximately 60–70 centimetres. Such tables had long been used in Nagasaki restaurants that served *shippoku* cuisine, a Chinese-Japanese fusion cooking.[18] By the 1920s *chabudai* had become the heart of the domestic ideology in Japan, and half a century later, when Western-style dining tables and chairs were adopted by a growing number of Japanese households, they were labelled 'traditional'.[19]

The second concern in the reform of family meals was related to the quality and variety of the food to be served on the new tables. As I noted earlier (see chapter Two), a differentiated gastronomy has operated in urban areas since the seventeenth century. Restaurants and food stalls were a regular feature of urban life, and professional caterers often delivered food for special occasions to homes. Even rural households relied on such services for big celebrations, such as wedding banquets.[20]

In contrast, home meals in pre-modern Japan were austere, even in relatively wealthy families (see chapter Three). The average urban citizen subsisted mainly on rice and pickles, supplemented by *miso* soup and a side dish for lunch and dinner. Compared to what Japanese consume on a daily basis today, the number of side dishes served with rice and soup was much smaller and their variety very limited. *Tōfu* in hot broth or fresh *tōfu*, seafood preserved in soy sauce (*tsukudani*) and ubiquitous simmered vegetables (*nimono*) were served day after day, occasionally interrupted by grilled or simmered fish.[21] Since most women relied on a narrow range of recipes, the only variation in home menus was provided by the (seasonal) availability of ingredients. Their range, however, must have been rather narrow, if we consider that the assortment provided by the food pedlars who delivered foodstuffs to most urban households was restricted by what they could carry. All these aspects combined suggest that monotony was the dominant feature of daily menus. Little variation in home-cooked meals was observed and none was expected.

Seafood pedlar, from *Shiki mainichi sanshoku ryōrihō* (1909).

An issue of the magazine *Fujin zasshi* ('Ladies' Journal') in 1916 stressed the need to change this situation and reform Japanese home cooking:

> Westerners have sophisticated 'family dishes' – specialities of the house – in their families. Japanese order dishes for special occasions from restaurants, but Westerners enjoy family meals at home. In my opinion, this tremendously helps to keep peace within the family.[22]

Like other aspects of the discourse on domesticity in Japan, the ideal of the family meal was clearly inspired by Western example. Its practical application, however, was a compromise between the ambitions of reformers and the commitment of housewives, as well as the economic condition of each household.

'Home Cooking' under Construction

The call for the reform of home meals initiated the process of the professionalization of home cookery. Professional chefs became increasingly involved in educating amateur women in cooking skills. One of the pioneers was Akabori Minekichi (1816–1904), who in 1882 set up the first amateur cooking school for women. Located in the centre of Tokyo and known at the time under the name Akabori Kappō Kyōjō (Akabori Cooking Class), the school was at first targeted at the wives and daughters of progressive upper-middle-class families. Soon, however, the scope of influence of the Akabori business expanded and began to shape Japanese cookery on a national scale. Akabori Masako (1907–1988) rounded off the family's mission during the 1960s, when her radio broadcasts and television cooking shows reached practically every household. By that time, the number of graduates of the Akabori school exceeded 800,000.[23]

At first, the Akabori Cooking Class focused on Japanese cooking, but from 1887 classes in Western cookery, which fascinated Minekichi and were much in vogue at the time, were also set up. Minekichi, his son Minekichi II (1853–1904) and grandson Minekichi III (1886–1956) also furnished cooking classes at several girls' higher schools in Tokyo. Targeted at upper-class women, the modern curricula of these schools, influenced by successes in American home economics education, included classes on nutrition and 'scientific' cookery. Young girls dressed in white aprons

Students of the Akabori Cooking School, from *Katei nenjū ryōri no shikata* (1912).

Students of a Higher Girls' School during a home economics class, c. 1930s.

became a standard sight at Western-inspired 'household management' classes at state-sponsored higher schools.

The introduction, in 1881, of the subject of 'Housework Economics' (*kaji keizai*) into primary schools marked the formal beginning of home economics education in Japan. However, needlework rather than cooking remained the central topic of this new subject well into the 1940s.[24] Girls' higher schools, with curricula tailored to educate professional housewives, became the chief site of culinary education for women in pre-war Japan. The number of girls enrolled at girls' higher schools grew rapidly after World War One; the percentage of female students at primary schools who continued education at a secondary level increased from 39.7 per cent in 1920 to 46 per cent in 1925, and reached 53 per cent by 1935.[25] These figures suggest that by the 1930s the middle-class ideal of home cooking was disseminated beyond that specific class. Sand explains that the combination of rapidly expanding secondary education and economic stability after World War One produced new white-collar households 'with pretensions to bourgeois status but without the social privilege or financial security of the generation educated earlier'.[26] These new households, managed on very tight budgets by housewives educated in higher girls' schools, set the stage for the transformation of the bourgeois lifestyle into a national standard.

Experts in the history of Japanese home economics education point out that before the Secondary School Law of 1943, which placed emphasis on practical training, cooking lessons at higher girls' schools were largely theoretical.[27] Despite this, however, they proved essential for the modernization and standardization of home meals in Japan. The pre-World War Two home economics curriculum may not have provided girls with practical culinary training, but it effectively disseminated knowledge concerning nutrition and hygiene. Moreover, most importantly, it changed the attitudes of future housewives towards home cooking. Ōe Sumi (1875–1948), a prominent reformer of women's education in Japan, argued that the aim of home economics did not lie in merely transmitting skills, but was also to raise women's interest in housekeeping.[28] Even if formal schooling did not have enough impact to change directly the way pre-World War Two housewives cooked, it certainly contributed to the spread of knowledge and attitudes that laid the foundation for the post-war changes accelerated by economic growth.

Jordan Sand argues that a characteristic feature of the modern transformation in Japan with regard to houses and the things kept and consumed in them was that 'the mass market in print and images of modern commodities came in advance of a mass market in the commodities themselves'.[29]

Front page of the
magazine *Ryōri no
tomo*, 1910s.

This experience of mass-mediated modernity was critical in shaping the
desires, tastes and consumption practices of future consumers. This holds
particularly true in reference to home cooking. Cookbooks and periodical
mass media targeted at middle-class Japanese housewives, and later at all
Japanese women, provided a steady stream of information and recipes that,
if not always used in the kitchen, engraved the new ideal of home cooking
in the minds of their readers. This was an interactive process, with women
themselves participating in it via correspondence columns, send-in recipes
contests and various events organized by the publishers.[30] Such discourse
shaped the national standard of the home meal, which would be put into
practice by future generations of housewives.

It is difficult to assess to what extent the recipes depicted in household manuals, cookbooks and cookery columns reflect reality, and how

they affected the cooking practices of the people at whom they are targeted. Anne Murcott, for example, argues that cookery books 'conveniently freeze something of the period at which they were produced', but are not a reflection of reality.[31] Stephen Mennell, however, points out that this does not hold true for cookery columns in magazines, identifying a strong connection between their content and the diet of the 'real people':

> It is easier to feel more confident about the connection between what appears in the cookery columns and what actually happened in the domestic kitchen than was the case with the cookery books . . . It appears to be broadly true that women's magazines, in cookery as in other supposedly feminine concerns . . . sought to set high standards for their readers, leading them but taking care not to run too far ahead of them – which could have demoralised the housewife and been bad for the magazines' circulation.[32]

It would be misleading to assume that the cookery columns of Japanese women's magazines published in the 1920s and '30s reflected the reality of home meals consumed by middle-class households at the time.[33] However, there is a striking continuity between the recipes and menu suggestions that appeared in the mass media at the time and the mainstream home cooking repertoire that began to prevail throughout Japan since the 1960s. This continuity clearly indicates that middle-class home cooking as projected in the periodical mass media of the pre-war period served as a model in the development of the post-war national standard.

Four themes dominated in cookery columns of Japanese women's magazines during the 1910s, '20s and '30s: hygiene/nourishment, economy, convenience and novelty.[34] They reflected the four principles of the new Japanese home cooking that these columns helped to construct. Ideal home meals were to ensure the physical well-being of the family members – and, therefore, follow the scientific principles of hygiene and nutrition – while keeping family finances restrained. They were not supposed to be difficult to prepare, but needed to attract the appetite of the family members, while suiting their taste preferences.

Such ideal home cooking came to be known under the name *katei ryōri* ('home' + 'cooking'). The new term consciously used the neologism *katei*, emphasizing a strong connection with the ideology of domesticity. Along with home economics textbooks, the new genre was disseminated through the cookery columns of women's magazines. Periodicals devoted entirely to cookery, such as *Ryōri no tomo* ('Cook's Companion'), *Katei to ryōri* ('Home and Cooking') and *Ryōyū* ('Provisions' Companion') also emerged. They were accompanied by dozens of cookery books with the term *katei ryōri* in their titles, and these mushroomed after the turn of the twentieth century. The new home recipes rested on professional cookery simplified to suit the purpose of home meals – home dishes should be neither too expensive nor too time-consuming to prepare. In view of the requirement that home meals should be nourishing and novel, the Western foodstuffs and dishes that had entered Japan since the 1860s suited the purpose of kitchen reformers. Foreign elements were carefully selected and accommodated to the taste preferences of an average middle-class family. This creative process resulted in a new genre of cooking that came to be known as *wayō setchū ryōri*, or 'Japanese-Western fusion cuisine'. This term was by no means restricted to the experiments carried out in home kitchens. *Wayō setchū ryōri* was an umbrella concept that also included the hybrid Japanese-Western creations that emerged in *yōshokuya* and military canteens. This hybrid genre was instrumental in downgrading the image of an exclusive cuisine for the elite that Western food had acquired during the first decades of the Meiji period. *Wayō setchū ryōri* served at mass urban restaurants, the military and (occasionally) in middle-class homes gradually lost its foreign connotation and entered the category of Japanese cuisine. Many hybrid recipes that emerged in the early twentieth century have by now acquired a nostalgic label of 'mother's cooking' (*ofukuro no aji*).

In view of the monotonous character of pre-modern home meals, the need to improve the variety of home cooking was emphasized already in early writings on home reform. For example, the following advice was included in a 1904 issue of the alumni magazine *Katei shūhō* ('Home Weekly'), published by students of Japan Women's College, one of the few institutions in Japan that trained home economics instructors: 'Enlarge the number of cooking techniques as much as possible. For example, when preparing Western dishes blend them with Japanese and Chinese elements into a proper combination. This way you will increase variety.'[35] Sand argues that the quest for novelty 'was inherent in the logic of the period-ical mass media, which introduced culinary features in order to attract and keep female subscribers'.[36] In my opinion, the emphasis on variety was also prompted by the general tendency in consumer cultures towards the expansion of variety, in turn propelled by a continuous increase in the range of things available routinely on a commercial basis.[37] For example, by the 1920s a wide range of novel processed foods became available, such as canned vegetables and ready-to-use sauces, which inspired housewives

Students of Japan Women's College at a Japanese cookery class, from *Tourist Library 14: Japanese Food* (1936).

to try new recipes and made homemaking more interesting and less labour consuming. Moreover, variety in diet was at the time considered beneficial for one's health; varied diet was propagated by physicians as a means to improve appetite. For example, in 1898 the British popular magazine *Home Chat* drew the attention of its readers to the monotony of school meals, stating that

> unvarying monotony with which each day brings forth its regular menu is a real hindrance to the proper nourishment that ought to be conveyed to those growing bodies ... All medical men plead for variety of food as being one of the chief things to be aimed at towards supplying the waste and building up of our bodies. ... All this variety need not necessarily mean expensive.[38]

In 1911 Sasaki Sachiko, a culinary instructor at Japan Women's College, explained that the general 'progress of life' was the reason behind the need for more variety in the Japanese home diet. She remarked as follows:

> Nowadays, the knowledge and interests of people have progressed. The advanced style of work and general rules of life have become elaborate and complicated. In such circumstances our body can no longer stand simple traditional food, nor can this type of food satisfy our souls ... Following the development of our interests, we also have come to desire novel tastes with regard to food.[39]

Novelty as such was not mentioned among the six points indicated as guidelines in the preparation of family meals by the regular textbook of home economics published by Japan Women's College two years earlier. However, novelty was a natural outcome if the six principles were followed, because they could not be achieved without thorough reform of home menus: 1) nourishment and digestibility; 2) inexpensiveness; 3) suitability to the occasion (e.g. breakfast requires a different menu from dinner) and particular needs of each individual (e.g. white-collar versus manual workers, invalids, etc.); 4) taste; 5) suitability for age (e.g. children need different food from the elderly); 6) aesthetics of presentation.[40]

Yanagita Kunio (1875–1962), a pioneering Japanese ethnographer, noted an increased variety of food as one of the significant changes that the patterns of food consumption in Japan underwent in the early twentieth century.[41] The introduction of new foodstuffs from abroad, along with the development of new dishes inspired by foreign cuisine, constituted the core of this shift. The ideology of domesticity, with its emphasis on reforming monotonous meals of the past, propelled the dissemination of the new elements, since it revolutionized the general attitude toward home meals. Increased attention towards food cooked at home, and greater efforts to improve its quality, resulted in the growing differentiation between the home menus of members of the same neighbourhood. Many middle-class housewives strove to make their cooking varied and distinctive, and they were aided in this task by cookery columns of women's magazine, which not only provided them with new recipes, but also regularly published weekly menu suggestions (see overleaf). Variety in the menu is striking; even *miso* soup – the breakfast's mainstay – uses a different type of vegetable each day. The high concentration of Western-style dishes during the weekend (chicken and peas in creamy sauce and pork balls on Saturday, and a Western-style fish dish on Sunday) indicates that these dishes were considered somehow special.

Send-in-recipe contests organized by women's magazines proved very popular among their readers. For example, in the early 1920s the magazine *Shufu no tomo* ('Housewife's Companion') conducted a contest with the theme 'Side Dishes that our Home is Proud of'. *Shufu no tomo*, first published in 1917, was the most influential women's magazine in pre-war Japan, with a nationwide circulation of 230,000–240,000 copies twice monthly.[42] The results of kitchen experiments from virtually the entire country were entered in the 'Side Dishes that our Home is Proud of' contest.[43] Many of the awarded recipes were Japanese-Western hybrid combinations, such as pork steamed in soy sauce, mashed potatoes with

A weekly menu (side dishes to be served with rice)
suggested in July 1920 by the magazine
Shufu no tomo.[44]

	BREAKFAST	LUNCH	DINNER
Monday	*miso* soup with cabbage, aubergine pickle	stewed squash	simmered red snapper, simmered *tōfu*
Tuesday	*miso* soup with wax gourd, simmered beans	simmered fish cake and lotus root	grilled aubergine, hamburger steak
Wednesday	*miso* soup with *tōfu*, dried seaweed (*nori*)	grilled horse mackerel, cucumber	chilled savoury egg custard, simmered young taros and Egyptian kidney beans, grilled squid
Thursday	*miso* soup with taros, *tsukudani*	simmered wax gourd sprinkled with minced fish, pork or beef	simmered squash, stewed rock trout with ginger
Friday	*miso* soup with leek, *miso* with vegetables	simmered thin-sliced deep-fried *tōfu* and *udo* stalks	skipjack in *wasabi* dressing, *Ryūkyū* style soup with chicken, burdock root and devil's tongue jelly
Saturday	*miso* soup with aubergine, mashed preserved skipjack	chicken and peas in creamy sauce, fish *teriyaki*	*myōga* and dried shrimps in vinegar dressing, pork balls stewed with cabbage
Sunday	*miso* soup with snap beans, grated *daikon*	grilled cherry salmon, soused spinach	aubergine, *sōmen* noodles, Western-style fish dish (with bread)

A weekly menu (side dishes to be served with rice) suggested in 1915 by the magazine *Fujin zasshi*.[45]

	BREAKFAST	LUNCH	DINNER
Monday	*miso* soup with *nattō*, scrambled egg	grilled horse mackerel, simmered lotus root Korean style	deep-fried pork cutlet, simmered wax gourd
Tuesday	*miso* soup with clams, simmered snap beans	*myōga* and mackerel in vinegar dressing, simmered taros	deep-fried aubergine, simmered horse mackerel
Wednesday	*miso* soup with *tōfu*, fried egg	simmered mackerel, soused rape seedlings	yam soup, grilled chicken
Thursday	*miso* soup with *tōfu* lees, simmered beef with ginger	Korean-style beef, seaweed (*wakame*) and *myōga* in vinegar dressing	mackerel *sashimi*, snap beans with sesame dressing
Friday	egg with *nori* seaweed, aubergine simmered in *miso*	pork stew	grilled salmon, simmered sweet potatoes
Saturday	soup with grilled wheat gluten (*yakifu*) and *myōga* ginger, simmered snap beans	simmered vegetables, grilled fish cake	*miso* soup with pork, vegetables and sweet potatoes; cucumber in sesame-vinegar dressing
Sunday	*miso* soup with *daikon* radish, *Narazuke* pickles	hamburger steak, deep-fried lobster, apple jelly	beefsteak, mashed potatoes

Chinese chives, 'convenient salad' (potatoes, carrots, tomatoes, cucumbers in a dressing made of boiled and mashed egg yolk, butter, mustard and vinegar) and vegetable stew.[46]

An array of methods was employed by early twentieth-century culinary reformers, and by middle-class housewives themselves, in order to accommodate foreign elements into the Japanese home menus. The easiest way to achieve an innovative character in a meal was to combine Western and Japanese dishes in their forms close to the original. In the example below, which derives from the alumni magazine of Japan Women's College, the eclectic character is achieved by including grilled fish as a component of a Western-style breakfast:[47]

BREAKFAST
Pear jam with cream
Grilled fish
Bread
Coffee

Meals with a Western structure were unusual in early twentieth-century Japanese homes, and therefore considered more exclusive than meals with a Japanese structure. Consequently, they were often suggested for Sunday menus.

The 'rice–soup–side dishes' pattern that had for long prevailed in the urban diet dominated the reformed home cooking of the early twentieth century as well. However, the number of side dishes was enlarged and their variety increased through the incorporation of Western and hybrid Japanese-Western dishes. Even minimal innovations, such as spicing up the simmered vegetables with curry powder or serving an omelette with ketchup, had a considerable modernizing effect.

The making of Japanese home cookery was basically a process of trial and error; hundreds of recipes that were invented in the early decades of the twentieth century vanished without a trace. Only a handful became deeply rooted in Japanese homes, acquiring the status of hallmarks of Japanese home cookery. It is impossible to determine why certain experimental dishes succeeded and others failed. Generally speaking, wide availability and low price increased the chances for acceptance of the ingredients, while the need for special equipment, such as an oven, was clearly an impediment to a recipe's popularity. As I explained in chapter Two, a spectacular growth in demand for onions, cabbage and potatoes, which had been generated by Western-style restaurants and cafeterias, resulted in a steady fall in their prices. It is, therefore, not surprising that these vegetables were most extensively used in the economy-conscious middle-class kitchens. Beef and pork were incorporated chiefly because of their nourishing properties, since they still remained relatively expensive. Even if we take these aspects into consideration, however, it is still difficult to explain why certain recipes succeed and others failed. The following selection includes experimental recipes that did not catch on:

Shiso and potatoes roll
Boiled potatoes cut small and rolled in *shiso* leaves soaked in plum vinegar.[48]

Potatoes and *nori* roll
Mashed potatoes flavoured with *dashi*, sugar, and soy sauce rolled in roasted seaweed (*nori*).[49]

Potato dumplings
Mashed potatoes mixed with cooled rice gruel and salt, shaped into oval dumplings and boiled. Served with sugar and roasted soybean flour or in sweat *azuki* bean soup (*shiruko*)[50]

Crab and *tōfu* rolled in cabbage leaves
Boiled crab meat mixed with broiled *tōfu*, wrapped in blanched cabbage leaves, simmered in *dashi* with sugar and soy sauce.[51]

Onion *furofuki*
Boiled whole onions served with a sauce made of crushed sesame seeds, sugar, *dashi* and *miso*.[52]

Stew with *sōmen* noodles
Stew made of meat and leeks, seasoned with pepper, with boiled *sōmen* noodles cut into pieces.[53]

Adding foodstuffs of Western origin to the existing Japanese dishes, often replacing Japanese foodstuffs that they resembled (for example, substituting macaroni with Japanese noodles in the above recipe), or cooking them according to Japanese techniques were the prevailing methods to make meals appear less foreign. The main objective was often to mask their unfamiliar taste. This was particularly relevant in the case of foodstuffs with a very strong, distinctive flavour, such as meat and milk. For example, the author of an article of 1906, 'Some new culinary ideas' featured in the magazine *Katei zasshi* ('Home Journal') gave readers advice on how to use Western foodstuffs in an innovative way. Among the proposed novelties were sweet *azuki* bean soup with milk, crushed *mochi* and (optional) vanilla essence. This new snack was recommended for people who 'do want to drink milk but cannot stand its smell'. Three advantages of this novel drink were advocated – it was nourishing, fashionable, had a taste similar to what the Japanese were used to and, above all, masked the milky smell.[54] The idea never really caught on, but this example clearly indicates the difficulties involved in reforming Japanese home cookery – in order to be accommodated successfully, the proposed reforms not only needed to match the aspirations of the new urban middle class, but also had to fit within established practices and tastes.

Japanese Culinary Aesthetics and Kaiseki

Within the newly created canons of Japanese home cookery Japanese-style tableware prevailed. Japanese housewives were familiarized with the rules and methods of food arrangement that had hitherto guided professional cookery in Japan, and were encouraged to devote attention to the aesthetic aspects of home meals.

The high aesthetic value of Japanese cuisine was already singled out in the late nineteenth century to weigh its merits against Western and Chinese food (see chapter One).[55] This emphasis was reinforced in early twentieth-century cookery books and the cookery columns of popular magazines and through home economics education. For example, a housekeeping textbook published in 1919 explained the difference between Japanese and Western cuisines in the following way:

> Japanese cuisine has a plain taste, its form and colouring are excellent, and it harmonizes perfectly with the tableware. Western cuisine places digestion and nourishment before presentation. It is rich in variety and often has a rich taste.[56]

As mentioned earlier, Japan Women's College propagated the aesthetic aspect of food as one of the six principles that should guide a domestic cook. We may presume that the appropriation of the cult of tea (*chanoyu*) in female education also indirectly contributed to the increased emphasis on the aesthetics in cooking. *Chanoyu* – a highly ritualized ceremony during which powdered green tea is prepared by a skilled practitioner and served to a small group of guests in a tranquil setting – had until the late nineteenth century been primarily a pastime of male literati. However,

An illustration from
the magazine *Ryōri
no tomo*, 1914.

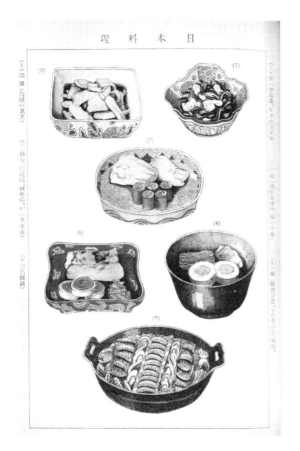

理　料　本　日

girls' schools embraced it as a useful device to inculcate among young
women rules of comportment and behaviour for the reception of guests.
Chanoyu masters wholeheartedly welcomed the role that the cult of tea was
to play in female education, realizing the financial and other advantages
that were to be gained through the popularization of their pursuit.[57]

There was, in fact, a close connection between the cult of tea and the
aesthetic principles that guided professional cookery in Japan. A particular
style of serving food, which emerged in the sixteenth century among the
practitioners of *chanoyu*, successively acquired a dominant position on
the Japanese culinary scene. By the nineteenth century, the style began to
prevail in prestigious restaurants; during the twentieth its main principles
were extended to encompass gastronomy and home cookery as well; today,
it is considered the defining feature of culinary 'Japaneseness'.

The style is known nowadays under the name *kaiseki*, but the term itself did not come into general use before the second half of the nineteenth century.[58] Kumakura Isao, a leading scholar of *chanoyu*, explains that the fundamental principles of *kaiseki* were developed by the renowned tea master Sen no Rikyū (1522–1591), the founding father of *kaiseki*, but the style kept changing after his death. For example, a meal served by Rikyū on one of his tea gatherings in 1590 consisted of rice, soup with vegetables and sea bream marinated in sake, followed by broiled salmon and fresh *tōfu*.[59] Today, a conventional *kaiseki* meal consists of the following courses:

First course: rice, soup, *mukōzuke* (vinegared dish or *sashimi*)
Second course: simmered dish in hot broth (*nimono*)
Third course: grilled dish (*yakimono*)
Fourth course: 'special dish' (*shiizakana*)
Fifth course: soup (*suimono*)
Sixth course: pickled vegetables, a jug with hot water[60]

The main distinguishing feature of *kaiseki* was its sequential character. The style established a set of courses that were served in a carefully timed sequence, each item being brought to the table at its optimum temperature. As Kumakura explains, *kaiseki* attached significance to the sentiment of hospitality conveyed by the food rather than to how luxurious it was; it was supposed to reflect a sense of the season and sensitivity to human feelings. 'To serve well-prepared foods with consummate timing, so that hot foods can be eaten hot and cold foods cold – this was its very natural (yet extremely ambitious) aim; the issue of quantity, etiquette, and style simply followed from that goal.'[61]

Kaiseki revolutionized the sixteenth-century conventions of formal dining in Japan, which were characterized by sumptuous flamboyance, with lavish quantities of food arrayed simultaneously in a dazzling ornamental display of several small tables (the so-called *honzen ryōri*). In contrast, *kaiseki* followed *wabi* aesthetics, which emphasized the beauty of restraint, penetrating to the true essence of things to discern beauty therein.[62] A typical *honzen*-style banquet included a large quantity of food that could not be eaten during the course of the meal, and a prominent place was occupied by food that served merely ornamental purpose. In contrast, the *kaiseki* style, influenced by the meal etiquette of Zen temples, demanded that only small quantities of food should be served. The menu was limited to allow for better appreciation of the taste of the food.

Although simplicity was a defining feature of the original, sixteenth-century *kaiseki*, over time the style gradually became less austere and more beautiful to the eye. This change became particularly pronounced when, in the course of the nineteenth century, *kaiseki* was embraced by prestigious restaurants. Restaurant chefs changed somewhat the succession of the courses; for example, instead of serving rice at the beginning of the meal, they served it at the very end in order to keep their customers hungry and let them enjoy a long sequence of dishes.

A Conventional Restaurant *Kaiseki* Meal:[63]

First course: an assorted dish (*kuchitori*)
Second course: *sashimi*
Third course: simmered dish (*nimono*)
Fourth course: grilled dish (*yakimono*)
Fifth course: steamed dish (*mushimono*)
Sixth course: deep-fried dish (*agemono*)
Seventh course: vinegared dish (*sunomono*)
Eighth course: rice, soup, pickled vegetables

Restaurateurs not only altered the structure of *kaiseki*, but also made it more extravagant, changing the character of the meal from that of ritualized tranquillity to that of epicurean enjoyment of excellent food. At this point two different styles of *kaiseki* began to diversify – a specialized meal served at tea gatherings and generally referred to today as *chakaiseki* (tea *kaiseki*), and an exclusive haute cuisine served at restaurants generally known as *enkaiseki* (banqueting *kaiseki*). In order to distinguish clearly the tea *kaiseki* from its restaurant copy, a new set of ideograms (but pronounced exactly the same) came into wider use. While the original set of characters had an ordinary meaning of a 'banquet', 'meal' or 'menu', the new set of characters, which began to appear in tea-ceremony literature from the middle of the seventeenth century, had a strong ideological connotation. In a literal translation it meant 'rock held to one's bosom', referring to the fact that in the same way that Zen monks, during the course of their austerities, placed warm stones in the bosoms of their robes to stave off hunger, this was a simple meal intended to help people bear hunger pangs.[64] The new set of characters stressed the spiritual value of tea *kaiseki*, and the popularization of the new term during the nineteenth century was clearly a reaction to the increasing dominance of the more flamboyant version of *kaiseki* in prestigious restaurants.

However, the principles of beauty of restraint and the harmony between the food, the tableware, the season and the surroundings, which had been a source of spiritual tranquillity of tea *kaiseki*, were not fully developed by nineteenth-century restaurateurs. It was after the turn of the twentieth century, largely under the impact of the artist and cook Kitaōji Rosanjin (1883–1959) and the chef Yuki Teiichi (1901–1997), that these principles came into their own in Japanese gastronomy. Kitaōji, himself a renowned potter, is considered chiefly responsible for reinforcing the aesthetic unity between the food and tableware. Yuki, the owner of the Kitchō restaurant – the most celebrated Japanese restaurant today – put into practice the *kaiseki* ideal of full harmony between the meal and the surroundings in which it is served. Both men elevated Japanese haute cuisine to its climax, at the same time enlarging the classic repertoire through the incorporation of local dishes and foreign foodstuffs.[65]

The circumstances of the 1960s economic growth created a perfect climate for the spread of the *kaiseki* ideal beyond the exclusive circle of tea practitioners and gourmands, turning it into a trademark of modern Japanese cuisine, the defining feature of culinary 'Japaneseness'. Today, the aesthetic harmony between the food, the vessel, the setting and the season is projected as if it had *always* guided food preparation on the Japanese archipelago, as if *every* Japanese has an innate tendency to follow and appreciate these rules.[66] The *kaiseki* aesthetics functioned as a vital homog-

An appetizer from a *kaiseki* menu, from *Yamazato: Kaiseki Cuisine. Hotel Okura, Amsterdam* (2003).

A simmered course (*nimono*) from a *kaiseki* menu, from *Yamazato: Kaiseki Cuisine*. *Hotel Okura, Amsterdam* (2003).

enizing component in the process of the making of Japanese national cuisine, and televised media played, and still continues to play, a critical role in its dissemination among the Japanese population.

Since the 1960s the proliferation of electric appliances, such as washing machines and rice cookers, along with the rapid growth of the food processing industry, greatly diminished the load of housework, allowing women to devote more time to cooking (see chapter Seven). On the other hand, through the medium of television, members of the general public who rarely had the opportunity to sample exclusive cuisine were familiarized with *kaiseki* and its aesthetics. Professional chefs eagerly appeared on television cooking shows, encouraging Japanese women to mimic their skills. Before the late 1980s, when simple dishes that could be prepared quickly with little effort began to gain ground, complicated and labour-intensive recipes prevailed on most cooking shows. Two major messages were conveyed by television and the other media in relation to cooking. First, cooking was projected as a way of showing every woman's affection for her family. In other words, since electric appliances and products of the food industry made meal preparation easier, women were prompted to raise the level of their cooking, including the aesthetic aspects. The second message pleaded with Japanese housewives to protect the 'tradition' of

Japanese home cookery for future generations by continuing their efforts in the kitchen and not being tempted to be negligent (*tenuki*).[67]

Under such persistent media influence, and the economic affluence in the backdrop, by the 1970s and '80s the cooking skills and repertoire of Japanese housewives reached the highest level in the history of Japanese home cookery. The ideal of a home meal designed by the early twentieth-century reformers was finally put into practice. The same holds true for the atmosphere surrounding the meals. Memoirs and oral testimonies of children who grew up before the 1960s indicate that even in middle-class households (which took the lead in embracing the ideology of domesticity) family meals had not been an occasion for relaxation, but rather a stage to exercise home discipline by the head of the family.[68] Since the 1960s, however, when fathers became increasingly absent during home meals, working long hours to stimulate economic growth, the ideal of domestic cosiness was finally achieved.[69]

Recent accounts indicate that with the closure of the twentieth century the ideal of the Japanese home meal has begun to crumble. Cosy family meals are nowadays taken more often at Skylark, Royal Host, Denny's and other 'family restaurants' (*famiresu*) rather than at home; between 1965 and 1996 an average percentage of the household budget assigned to food that was spent on eating out increased by more than 10 per cent (from 7.2 to 17.6 per cent).[70] According to a survey conducted in 2003 among citizens of large cities, Japanese in their forties and older mention 'family cosiness' (*ikka danran no tame*) as one of the three most important reasons for dining out, as well as 'to enjoy good food that cannot be made at home' and 'for a change of atmosphere' (*fun'iki o kaeru tame*). For the younger generation (in their twenties and thirties), enjoying food that cannot be made at home also ranked among the three top answers, along with reasons such as 'because I like eating out in general' and 'because I want to leave the house'.[71] Other surveys suggest that young women who were born after the 1960s find everyday cooking boring and rely heavily on fast-food and ready-to-eat groceries to feed their families.[72] Still, the twentieth-century ideal of Japanese home cooking is unlikely to disappear. It will certainly be kept alive on Japanese television, which continues to educate the public about Japanese culinary traditions and their history, perpetuating the myth of a common culinary heritage and the instinctive quest for harmony between the food, the tableware and the season.[73]

Five

Wartime Mobilization and Food Rationing

The fifteen-year period between the outbreak of the Sino-Japanese War in 1937, which marked the beginning of World War Two in the Far East, and the end of the occupation of Japan by the Allied Forces in 1952 constituted a very important stage in the construction of Japanese national cuisine. The wartime mobilization of people and resources, which was successively tightened as the war progressed, had an unprecedented homogenizing impact on Japanese cuisine. World War Two was perhaps the most powerful democratizing force in the history of Japanese diet. The divide that had for centuries separated the rural and urban diet rapidly declined – urban citizens were forced to rely increasingly on staples other than rice, which had thus far dominated peasants' fare. As I explained earlier, although rice was a preferred staple, there had not been enough of it to feed the entire population. Therefore, the most underprivileged sections of the Japanese society, such as the majority of peasants and the urban poor, were sustained by other staples, or at best on a mixture of rice with vegetables and other grains (see also chapter Three). Since the fixed components of the urban landscape, such as public transport, cinemas, department stores and restaurants one by one disappeared under the pressure of mobilization for total war, urban life increasingly came to resemble rural existence.

Preparing for Total War

'Total war' means total mobilization. It requires the commitment of massive armed forces to battle and strong industrial economies to sustain them.[1] In waging total war, supporting the war machine is as essential in the pursuit of victory as sheer military might. In these circumstances, the management of food resources assumes unique strategic significance, since

City dwellers planting vegetables before the Parliament Building in Tokyo, 1945.

it ensures the working efficiency and morale of the population. The Japanese authorities were aware of the fact that the days of 'national wars' had arrived, demanding total mobilization of soldiers as well as civilians. Already in 1915, the statesman and general Tanaka Giichi (1863–1929), in his speech to reservist officials, called for national mobilization:

The outcome of future wars will not be determined by the strongest army, but by the strongest populace. A strong populace is one which has physical strength and spiritual health, one which is richly imbued with loyalty and patriotism, and one which respects cooperation, rules, and discipline. The populace which has this kind of education will not merely have a strong army, but will also be successful in conducting agricultural, manufacturing, commercial, and other industrial efforts. The reservists must achieve the reality of becoming good soldiers and good citizens and exert their influence (for these goals) in their home community.[2]

The preparations for total war began in the late 1920s. It was only in 1938, however, with the ratification of the National General Mobilization Law, that the state was provided with an unprecedented controlling power over people and resources.[3] These totalitarian circumstances facilitated successful implementation of far-reaching reforms that aimed at cost-effective production of food and efficient distribution. For example, industrial food processing received strong backing from the government and small retail foodstuff dealers were replaced with dealers' co-operatives and ultimately by state-controlled distribution stations.[4] Such measures went hand in hand with wide-ranging efforts to disseminate scientifically grounded principles of efficient nourishment among the population. In line with the doctrine of 'total war', nutritional knowledge was rapidly transformed from a scientific domain of specialists into a practical advice for the people. A variety of state institutions singled out diet as an important home-front weapon essential for preserving order and productivity.

These actions stand in contrast with the image of wartime Japanese society sketched by the American anthropologist Ruth Benedict. In her bestseller *The Chrysanthemum and the Sword*, published in 1946 and commissioned by the US Office of War Information, Benedict portrayed Japanese as irrational people who 'do not recognize the one-to-one correspondence which Americans postulate between body nourishment and body strength'.[5]

Equally misleading is the patriotic symbolism of the 'Rising Sun Lunch Box' (*Hinomaru bentō*), consisting of plain boiled rice and plum pickle (*umeboshi*) placed in the centre of a rectangular lunch box, which together resembled the Japanese flag. This meal of questionable nourishing quality is totally unrepresentative of the general approach to nutrition in wartime Japan. The origin of the *Hinomaru bentō* is attributed to an initiative of 1937 in a girls' school in the Hiroshima prefecture, where this

The 'Rising Sun Lunch Box' (*Hinomaru bentō*).

patriotic lunch box was consumed by pupils each Monday as a token of solidarity with the troops fighting in China. By 1939 the idea was adopted by schools all over the country, and during subsequent years the 'flag lunch' rose to the symbol of wartime mobilization and national unity.[6] However, the daily reality of the majority of the population stood in sharp contrast to this image, if only because after 1941 plain boiled rice became a luxurious item on the menu. Since the summer of 1940 the authorities had prohibited Tokyo restaurants from serving rice dishes.[7]

The knowledge of how to make maximum use of the limited resources – scientifically grounded practical advice on nutrition – was propagated on a large scale by a variety of state institutions. State propaganda had elevated the knowledge of eating healthily at a low cost to a level of a patriotic virtue. The confidence in a scientific solution for wartime food shortages remained strong until the very end – the inaugural meeting of the Dietician's Association of Great Japan was held on 21 May 1945.[8] The military provided the example of an efficiency-driven approach towards food preparation and consumption. The totalitarian character of the Japanese state bolstered the effectiveness of the reforms. The political innocence of food, on the other hand, ensured their longevity. Unlike ideological aspects of wartime life, which were persistently erased by the occupying forces after 1945, the knowledge and skills of healthy diet disseminated in wartime were perpetuated undisturbed despite the fall of the regime.

The extensive involvement of the wartime Japanese state in the consumption practices of its population exposes the intricate connections between power, welfare and knowledge that developed in Japan during the first decades of the twentieth century.[9] As Turner has pointedly observed, scientific advances did not liberate the body from external control, but, on the contrary, intensified the means of social regulation.[10] The application and dissemination of nutritional science through a range of state institutions constituted a technique for making Japanese civilians objects of knowledge and power. It was not an oppressing and dominating power, but rather a kind of a government 'at a distance'. While the autonomy of individuals was preserved, they were controlled through the establishment of rules and by shared expert knowledge and conceptual frameworks.[11] Such 'government at a distance' played a critical role in homogenizing Japanese cuisine.

The foundations for the modern science of nutrition were laid in the first half of the nineteenth century: in 1803 gastric digestion was shown to be a chemical process; in 1814 fats were demonstrated as being composed of fatty acids and glycerol; and in 1827 food constituents were classified into three categories – sugars, fats and proteins.[12] The new science developed at first as part of organic chemistry and medicine, and was later subsumed under the field of 'hygiene', which was defined as anything pertaining to the maintenance and strengthening of health as opposed to the cure of diseases. Gradually, however, nutritional science developed as an independent discipline and featured increasingly highly on political agendas. The development of capitalist production and the introduction of general conscription made modern nation states dependent on the bodies of their populations as never before. The interest of capitalist governments in dietary matters steadily increased when a direct link between the health of these bodies – and thus the productivity of workers and the strength of the soldiers – and daily nutrition became apparent. In other words, dissemination of nutritional knowledge among the populations was proved essential for the progress of modern capitalist states.

Two factors inspired the governments of European countries to take concrete actions in order to develop sound policies related to public nutrition. First, the rise of Newer Knowledge of Nutrition during the early twentieth century underscored the fact that an adequate diet comprised substances other than proteins, carbohydrates and fats – substances that later came to be referred to as 'vitamins' – and emphasized the potential of proper nutrition as the *preventive* measure for the health improvement.[13] Second, World War One, and particularly the German case, disclosed the far-reaching consequences of the inadequate handling of food shortages by the authorities.[14] Both factors heavily influenced state polices in Japan.

Nutritional knowledge began to be transmitted in Japan from the late 1850s by the Dutch physicians in the employ of the Tokugawa government, such as J.L.C. Pompe van Meerdervoort (1829–1908), A. F. Bauduin (1822–1885) and K. W. Gratama (1831–1888). In the 1870s, when the Germans began to take over the leadership in disseminating Western medicine in Japan, the emphasis on nutritional science was further strengthened, since German scientists headed the new field.[15] The Hygiene Experiment Stations, set up in the 1870s by the Home Ministry, marked the first steps in creating an institutional basis for the dissemination of nutritional knowledge in Japan.[16] Their establishment was in line with the policy of 'civilization and enlightenment' that aimed at furthering the country's progress through the appropriation of Western science and technology. In 1887 Tawara Yoshizumi (1855–1935), who was an employee of the Hygiene Experiment Station in Tokyo, compiled the very first nutritional table of Japanese foods.[17] Before the 1920s, however, military rather than civilian institutions played a leading role in matters related to nutritional science in Japan. As we have observed in chapter Three, the Imperial Japanese Army and Navy were deeply concerned with dietary issues, because they were directly confronted with the consequences of malnutrition. The army was the locus of the first nutritional survey, which was carried out in 1881 and coordinated by the chief of the Medical Headquarters of the Army, Koike Masanao (1854–1913).[18] Along with Takagi Kanehiro and Mori Rintarō mentioned earlier, Koike was one of many military surgeons who played a pioneering role in Japanese nutritional research. From the 1920s the army also became increasingly involved in disseminating nutritional knowledge among the general public.

A direct participation of the Japanese civilian government in the matter of public nutrition was stimulated not only by the developments in Europe, but was also propelled by the consequences of World War One experienced in Japan itself. The economic recession and restricted rice imports from South-East Asia confronted the government with the so-called Rice Riots. Because urban dwellers relied heavily on rice for their daily sustenance, in 1918 hundreds of thousands of them went out to the streets protesting against the soaring price of rice. In an immediate response to the riots, in 1919 the Home Ministry Sanitary Bureau issued two pamphlets, one entitled 'Recipes for Rice Surrogates' and the other 'Nutrition and Economizing on Food'.[19] The long-term response included the Campaign to Increase Rice Production in the colony of Korea (see chapter Six) and the establishment of the Imperial Government Institute for Nutrition (also known under the name State Institute for the Study of Nutrition). These steps set the stage for the increasing involvement of the Japanese state in the diet of its citizens.

The institute was set up by an Imperial Ordinance on 16 September 1920, and the formal opening took place in December the following year. It was one of the first institutions in the world devoted entirely to the issue of human nutrition.[20] Its activities ranged from fundamental research and its practical application (for example in industrial food processing) to the propagation of knowledge about a healthy and economical diet among the general public.[21] A generative power behind its establishment was Saiki Tadasu (1876–1959), a true 'founding father' of Japanese dietetics, a holder of a PhD from Yale University. In 1914 Saiki established his private Nutritional Laboratory – the first research institute in Japan to deal exclusively with human nutrition. In 1917 he organized the very first lecture programme on nutrition, and two years later successfully lobbied for state financial backing for grounding nutritional science in Japan.[22] It is beyond doubt that Saiki's personal commitment was largely responsible for the establishment of the Imperial Government Institute for Nutrition. However, it cannot be denied that the spirit of the times was very propitious for the realization of his ambitions.

Saiki's aim was twofold: to ground dietetics as an independent scientific discipline in Japan and to disseminate practical advice on nutrition among the public. Both goals could be achieved only with state support, which Saiki was granted after 1920. Exemplary menus were prepared and made public on a daily basis by the Imperial Government Institute for Nutrition. Easy-to-follow instructions and recipes were propagated via cooking demonstrations, exhibitions and lectures. In 1924 Saiki himself held the very first radio lecture on the issue of nutrition, and in the year 1933 alone the institute carried out nearly 300 lecturing tours throughout the country.[23] The popularization of the ideal of professional housewife, who was to ensure the health of her family while watching over the household finances, provided a fertile ground for the activities coordinated by Saiki and other professionals involved in the propagation of nutritional knowledge. From the 1920s nutritional advice came to be featured regularly in home economics textbooks, cookery books and women's magazines. A decade later, the emphasis on nourishment became increasingly dominant in the printed media, including publications targeted at rural households. The commitment of the Japanese state towards improving dietary conditions was largely responsible for this trend. In 1929, in an official notification to the local administrative organs throughout the country, the Home Ministry underscored the importance of nutritional reforms in bolstering the physical condition of the population.[24] Three years later a directive of the Ministry of Education provided primary schools with financial support for their canteens. By 1940 more than 12,000 schools throughout the country were serving food to their pupils.[25]

The Militarization of Nutrition

The establishment of the Public Welfare Ministry, a year after the outbreak of the Sino-Japanese War, accelerated the growing involvement of the state in public nutrition. For example, between 1939 and 1944 ten new institutions training dieticians were established, while only one such institution – set up privately by Saiki in 1925 – had been in operation thus far.[26] A major difference between dieticians educated by Saiki and those who graduated from the new schools was the fact that the latter were inculcated with knowledge and skills much more attuned to the practical application on a daily basis in the wartime circumstances of growing food shortages. Moreover, the new schools operated on a far larger scale. For example, the School of Provisions managed by Ryōyūkai, a foundation with strong military ties, had a potential of educating up to 500 students per year. In 1941 the school offered two one-year daytime courses, one in dietetics and one in canning, a six-months daytime course in bread-making and a six-months evening training in nutrition for professional cooks.[27]

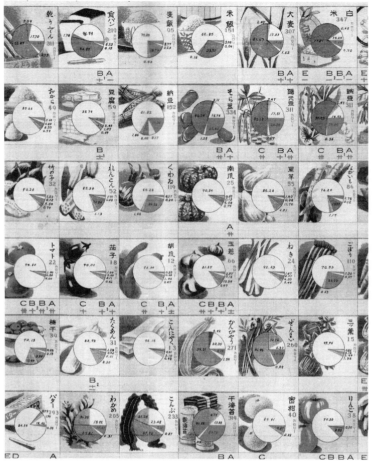

A fragment of an educational poster indicating nutritional value of different food-stuffs, issued by the Tokyo Institute for Nutrition and Provisions, 1938.

Graduates of the school were offered employment in a variety of institutions related to mass catering, food processing, food rationing and public nutrition, as well as Ryōyūkai's own infrastructure throughout the Japanese empire.

As an umbrella organization through which the influence of the military on civilian consumption practices was channelled, Ryōyūkai played an important role in the construction of the uniform model of mass catering in Japan. By the late 1920s, army kitchens – with modern equipment, motivated and well-educated personnel, and economical yet nourishing menus – were propagated as an example to follow by civilian canteens at schools, factories and hospitals. Although officially Ryōyūkai was not part of the military structure, its ties with the armed forces remained very strong. It was established in 1925 by the staff members of the Central Provisions Depot in Tokyo under the leadership of the First Army Accountant Marumoto Shōzō (1886–1961), who was later promoted to Major-General. Various projects carried out by Ryōyūkai over the years were coordinated by the staff of the depot and financed largely by the food industry. As I explained in chapter Three, orders for the army and navy had been essential for the growth of the Japanese food industry. Before Japanese canned products were able to enter the global market in the 1910s, the industry was entirely dependent on the orders for the (first) Sino-Japanese War (1894–5) and the Russo-Japanese War (1904–5). During the 1920s and '30s the use of canned food among the civilian population in Japan gradually increased, sustained by the 'militarization of nutrition'. This is perhaps the most appropriate label to describe an array of measures that resulted in the proliferation of the military model of efficient nourishment among the civilian population, under Ryōyūkai's leadership.

A variety of activities coordinated by Ryōyūkai aimed chiefly at persuading the general public to mimic the military mass catering. For example, most schools that set up canteens after 1932, propelled by the financial support of the Ministry of Education, followed the example of the military – tried and tested menus, aluminium tableware and industrially processed provisions were widely used throughout the country.[28] Along with educational courses for civilian caterers, Ryōyūkai provided practical advice on a regular basis through its monthly magazine *Ryōyū* ('Provisions' Companion'). From nutritional information and model menus to newly available equipment and means of economizing on fuel, for nearly twenty years *Ryōyū* disseminated the military experiences in efficient mass nourishment among civilian caterers. The wartime mobilization for total war greatly accelerated the militarization of nutrition, since the efficiency-driven military models were extended to encompass the entire society.

It was in the industry's vital interest to finance Ryōyūkai's activities. By popularizing military catering among civilians, food processing enterprises were able to enlarge the civilian market for their products. The advertising campaign for ship's biscuits (*kanpan*), launched in 1937, is a case in point. It illustrates the increasingly intricate connections between the military, the food industry and public nutrition in wartime Japan. The preparation for the campaign of 1937 began ten years earlier, when 33 Japanese producers of ship's biscuits formed a cartel. The Industrial Guild

Biscuits advertisement, 1940.

of Ship's Biscuits Manufacturers was formed in 1932, propelled by the Manchurian Incident (1931) that marked the starting point of Japan's direct military confrontation with China.

Kanpan had been the staple in the Japanese armed forces for decades, but before 1937 remained largely unknown to civilian consumers. Approximately 90 per cent of total biscuit production in Japan at the time was constituted by products other than *kanpan*. By 1944 the ratio was reversed: *kanpan* constituted 96 per cent (36,000 out of the total of 37,000 tonnes) of all biscuits manufactured in Japan that year.[29] The new product was widely advertised, often carrying patriotic texts that called for solidarity with the soldiers at the front:

> In order to let one soldier fight at the battlefield hands of eight people are required at the home front. The amount of food they need is enormous. Saving and storing rice – our staple – has become the necessity. Using foods made of flour as a substitute for rice can make a difference. Once we learned that *kanpan* next to being a staple of the front is also a defence food guaranteeing

Ship's biscuits factory, c. 1940s.

perfect preservation, we feel our duty to store it not only for the calamities of peacetime, but also as an air defence at wartime.[30]

Ship's biscuits are rationalized portable food. They have always been an important military provision for the brave warriors of the Imperial Army in every location. Let's all together experience the real value of soldier's food.[31]

Using the image of the armed forces for advertising purposes was not limited to *kanpan*. Military elements were also featured in advertisements of foodstuffs associated with a hearty military diet, such as vegetable oil and curry powder. Obviously, this trend was prompted by the fact that the developments at the China front constituted the focus of public attention in late 1930s Japan. However, one more factor contributed to the selling power of the military images – the armed forces enjoyed extreme popularity among the population. In the eyes of commoners only the military seemed aware of the kind of problems that people faced in their daily lives. Local reservist organizations were increasingly successful in building a social basis for militarism, especially in the rural areas. From the early 1930s 'it was increasingly to the military that the people looked for the solutions they hoped would bring them a better future'.[32]

Military imagery aside, the multi-facet efficiency of *kanpan* was considered its major advantage. *Kanpan* provided three times more calories

Salad oil advertisement, 1938.

Curry powder advertisement, 1938.

than rice (which became increasingly scarce after 1937); it was easy to store and transport; and it was ready-to-eat. The last point was particularly important, since fuel for cooking was rationed. Moreover, confiscation of scrap metal, needed for the production of aeroplanes, tanks and other front-line necessities, deprived many households of cooking equipment. Due to the shortage of cans, after 1942 canned provisions were destined exclusively for the battlefield. The home front had to make do with the ceramic substitutes patented by the Great Japan Air Defence Provisions Co. (see p. 129). They used the same principle of food conservation as metal cans – sterilization by heat in a hermetically sealed container – and could be safely stored in case of emergency.[33]

Early wartime initiatives, such as the 'Rising Sun Lunch Box' and the 'Meatless Day', which prohibited the consumption of meat in Tokyo on the 8th and 28th day of each month, were merely the beginning of dietary deprivation that would continue throughout the 1940s.[34] Rationing of sugar and matches was introduced in June 1940, followed by firewood in October and milk in December. The following year marked a dramatic shift towards the rationing of a wide range of foodstuffs, from luxuries such as sake, beer and confectionery, to daily necessities like rice, wheat

Distributing rationed firewood, 1943.

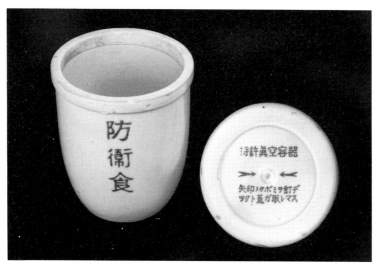
'Defence food' container, c. 1942–7.

flour, eggs, fish and vegetable oil.[35] The Food Management Law of February 1942 introduced a uniform, nationwide system of staple food rationing, replacing a variety of measures instituted thus far by the authorities of each prefecture. The daily ration of 2.3 *gō* (approximately 322 grams) of partly polished rice was determined as the national standard; Rice Polishing Restriction Regulation of December 1939 had already prohibited the sale of white rice. Since provisioning of the rapidly increasing man-power of troops was considered a priority, however, less and less rice was left for the home front. Between 1940 and 1945 the amount of rice supplied to the armed forces rose from 161,000 to 744,000 tonnes, making it impossible to retain the rationing standards for civilians.[36] Consequently, the government was compelled to adulterate rationed rice with wheat, barley and soybeans, and from 1943 substitute 10–30 per cent of the rice ration by other grains or sweet and white potatoes. Moreover, the actually distributed quota was usually much lower than the quantity that people were entitled to buy according to their purchase permits.[37] All this meant a steady reduction of available food, so that tubers and vegetables grown in school yards, river banks and parks became critical sources of food in urban areas. In the countryside, supplementing the official food supply was easier, since mudfish and eels could be fished for in irrigation channels, birds caught in especially erected nets, crickets collected in the rice-fields and mushrooms and tubers in the woods.[38]

In the long run, the wartime rationing of rice had a two-sided effect on consumption practices in Japan. On the one hand, it forced urban consumers to rely on staples other than rice, in particular wheat flour (in the form of noodles and bread) and potatoes. For example, between 1934 and 1955 the total consumption of wheat in Japan rose threefold, from 1,180,000 to 3,620,000 tonnes.[39] The incorporation of noodle dishes of Chinese origin, such as *rāmen* and *yakisoba*, in the canon of national cuisine was sustained by the wartime food shortage. Even culinary purists, such as the Society for Research into Japanese Cuisine – an association of professional chefs founded in 1930 for the sake of protecting Japanese cuisine from Western influences – had no other choice but to embrace substitute staples. Among the winning dishes in the 'Substitute Food Contest' held by the association in September 1940 were buttered toast sprinkled with shrimp powder, deep-fried noodles in curry sauce, and potato pancake sandwiches.[40]

It is generally claimed that the American occupation (1945–52) was chiefly responsible for the spread of wheat-based dishes in Japan. The fact that the food aid consisted mainly of flour undoubtedly contributed to the popularization of bread in Japan. It must be stressed, however, that American initiatives sustained a tendency that had become increasingly pronounced since the late 1930s. Although a handful of cookery books with American recipes were published already in the late 1940s, the real impact of American food culture on Japan began in the 1970s with the expansion of fast-food and other restaurant chains and convenience stores (see chapter Seven). Most food-related publications issued during the 1950s show a clear continuity with the 1940s and, after the food supply situation stabilized, with the 1930s.

Along with propelling the consumption of staples other than rice among urban consumers, the nationwide rationing of rice had the opposite effect on social groups that hitherto could not afford rice as a daily staple, such as peasants and urban poor. In order to ensure the smooth functioning of essential war industries such as mining, shipbuilding and the iron and steel industry, supplementary rations (on the top of the standard 2.3 *gō*) were allotted to workers employed in these industries.[41] Between 1937 and 1944 about two million peasants switched to lucrative employment in the war industries. Many also became part-time farmers, since these industries began to relocate their factories to rural areas, which were less threatened by air raids. Farm families whose members had supplementary jobs in the industry increased from 31.4 per cent in 1940 to 62.7 per cent in 1944.[42] Moreover, the introduction in 1941 of the system of dual-pricing

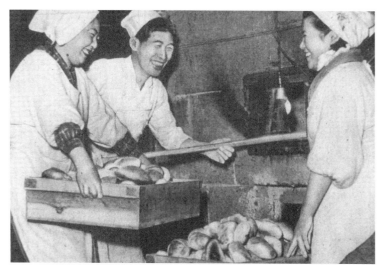
Baking bread from American flour, 1946.

for rice – a higher price was paid by the government to actual cultivators of land and a lower price to the big landowners – led to the improvement of the real income of farmers. All in all, as the war historian Bernd Martin phrased it, 'in the final years of the war the farmer actually had a better income than ever before' and 'for the first time since the enforced industrialisation of the Meiji era the Japanese peasant could make a decent living'.[43] It seems obvious that in such circumstances the consumption of rice, the preferred staple, increased in the countryside. Accounts of the harsh reality of rural existence in wartime are by no means false.[44] However, when placed in the national perspective, the relative improvement is obvious, and the levelling of living conditions in urban and rural areas during the 1940s beyond dispute. The mass return of urbanites to their native villages provides evidence that, as the Pacific War approached its end, city dwellers became much worse off than the Japanese living in the countryside.

The wartime food rationing system had an enduring effect of singling out rice as the national staple. The Food Management Law of 1942 granted *all* Japanese the right, even if only in theory, to a rice-centred diet. For more than half a century, the production and distribution of rice in Japan remained under state control, and it was only after 1995 that rice re-entered the free commodity market. The wartime rationing of rice provided a firm foundation for the regional and social homogenization of Japanese cuisine during the 1950s and '60s.[45]

Wartime communal cooking provided another incentive for dietary homogenization. With the introduction of food rationing, the position of the family as the basic unit of consumption was shifted to the 'neighbourhood associations' (*tonarigumi*). From 1940 towns and villages were divided into 'neighbourhood associations', comprising approximately 10–20 households, and 'block associations' (*chōnaikai*), consisting of approximately twenty 'neighbourhood associations'. Food rations were allocated not to individuals or families, but to 'neighbourhood associations'. This necessitated the joint purchase of food and joint cooking by the members of each association. The land for vegetable gardens and the seeds were also allotted to the 'neighbourhood association' as a unit. Dieticians employed at the government-controlled food distribution centres provided the associations with recipes and other advice on how to cook the relatively unknown foodstuffs in an efficient manner.[46] Since this knowledge was manufactured at the centralized organs of the state, it greatly contributed to dietary homogenization. We may presume that in the circumstances of communal dining, the distributed advice was followed more closely than would have been the case in individual family kitchens.

It is difficult, if not impossible, to assess whether the dissemination of practical advice on nutrition by the wartime authorities made a difference in the daily struggle for survival. Half of the troops that the Japanese Imperial Army lost between 1937 and 1945 died not on the battlefield but from starvation and malnutrition-related diseases.[47] These figures do not necessarily discredit the military catering system and military nutritional policies. They simply imply that the logistical capacities of the Japanese armed forces were unable to catch up with the expansionist ambitions of their leaders. The food supply at the home front deteriorated hand in hand with the losses at the front line. By 1944 the content of public campaigns had shifted from rice substitutes and instructions on maintaining vegetable gardens to emergency advice on edible weeds and how to use eggshells and brew soy sauce out of fish bones. Advertisements of various nutritional supplements frequently appeared in the printed media. For example, the Yeast Plant Institute in Uji developed a remedy for indigestion in the form of yeast-based pills, and Hoshi Pharmaceutics invented heroin-based pills, which were supposed to stimulate digestion, relieve constipation and generally improve the physical constitution. The product marketed under the name *Shokueiso* was advertised as a cooking activator that improved the taste of food, removed the bad smell of stale ingredients, softened fibrous vegetables and generally halved the cooking time.[48] These desperate attempts to nourish the nation through the use of

chemical supplements explicitly illustrate the persistent trust of the wartime government, and perhaps the public as well, in scientific solutions to
remedy food shortages.

The Legacy of War

The suffering of the home front became most severe in the immediate
post-war years. On the top of millions of hungry Japanese in the homeland, more than six million military men and civilians who by 1948 had
been repatriated from the colonies and occupied territories had to be fed.
The late spring and summer of 1946 are recorded as the time of the most
serious food crisis in Japan's modern history. In his bestseller, *Embracing*

Defeat: Japan in the Wake of World War II, John Dower described the conditions in urban Japan during the immediate post-war years:

> Defeat did not merely sever Japan from the food supplies of Asia. It also occurred in midsummer, when the previous year's rice harvest was running out. With the empire now cut off and millions of exhausted civilians and demobilized soldiers about to return, it was imperative that there be a bumper crop. Instead, due to adverse weather, manpower shortages, insufficient tools, and a fall-off in fertilizer production, 1945 saw the most disastrous harvest since 1910, a shortfall of almost 40 percent from the normal yield. . . . For a quarter of the families, gruel constituted the major part of all meals. Soups with leafy vegetables were another mainstay of the daily diet, as were homemade bread and dumplings along with steamed sweet potatoes. Typical diets of desperation also included acorns, orange peels, roots of the arrowroot plant, rice-bran dumplings, and a kind of steamed bread made from a wheat bran that in normal times was fed to horses and cattle. . . . Many farmers engaged in a gratifying barter trade with once-condescending city folk who flocked to rural areas in search of food. Kimonos as well as watches, jewelry, and other treasured possessions were traded for food, giving rise to one of the most famous phrases of the time: *takenoko seikatsu*, the 'bamboo-shoot existence.' The edible bamboo shoot can be peeled off in layers, and the *takenoko seikatsu* phenomenon referred to city people stripping off their clothing, as well as other possessions, for food.[49]

There can be no doubt that the 1940s constituted the most tragic episode in modern Japanese history. However, despite, or rather because of wartime mobilization and food shortages, this decade bore witness to the incredible progress in the implementation of nutritional knowledge in Japan, a development that set the stage for considerable improvement in public nutrition in the post-war era. For example, the Secondary School Law of 1943 revolutionized the system of home economics education. It divided the subject into four categories: home management, child-rearing, health preservation and clothing. Cooking was included in the health preservation category and, in contrast to the situation before the reform, much time and effort were devoted to the transmission of practical skills.

The authorities clearly outlined the goal of this reformed education to be the dissemination of nourishing and economical methods of food preparation. The high level of science implementation was distinctive in the new curriculum; following the model of military cooking manuals, new textbooks indicated the nutritional value of each dish that was to be prepared in class. This reform provided the foundation for home economics education in post-war Japan and was responsible for the widespread awareness and sincere concern of contemporary Japanese homemakers about the nutritional value of their meals.[50]

In his analysis of the relationship between total war and social change, Arthur Marwick distinguished the 'test-dimension' of war. He argued that the supreme challenge that total war poses to political structures and social and economic systems that have outlived their vitality may provoke change in the direction of greater efficiency in order to mobilize the full potential of a society and its resources.[51] This is exactly what happened in wartime Japan. In the long run, wartime mobilization created the basis for sound nutritional policies in post-war Japan that encompassed the entire population. For example, the nutritional survey initiated by the Dietician's Association of Great Japan in June 1945 was interrupted in August by Japan's surrender, but the collected material served as the basis for the National Nutrition Survey initiated in occupied Japan six months later.[52]

Nutritional research continued in the same institutes with slightly changed names, and the dissemination of nutritional knowledge continued under the leadership of the same experts. For example, in November 1946 Arimoto Kunitarō (1898–1984), a recognized expert in the world of Japanese dietetics, was appointed director of the newly established Nutrition Division in the Welfare Ministry's Bureau for the Preservation of Public Health. Arimoto's publishing record alone convincingly demonstrates the trans-war continuity in the popularization of nutritional knowledge in Japan. Similar lists by other experts can easily be compiled.

Selected publications by Arimoto Kunitarō (single or multi-authored):

1937 *Jissen eiyō to chōri* [Practical Nutrition and Cooking]
1941 *Tabemono no kagaku* [The Science of Food]
1941 *Eiyō kagaku* [Nutritional Science], last edition 1977
1943 *Eiyō kikakusho* [Nutritional Programme]
1950 *Eiyō, shokuhin jiten* [Dictionary of Food and Nutrition]
1952 *Ryōri kondate kādo* [Menu Cards]
1952 *Eiyō shidō no jissai* [The Reality of Nutritional Guidance]

1955 *Eiyō no seirigaku* [Physiology of Nutrition]
1956 *Eiyōgaku gairon* [An Introduction to Nutritional Science],
   last edition 1976
1961 *Eiyō no chishiki to ryōri no jissai* [Nutritional Knowledge and
   the Reality of Cooking]
1963 *Tabemono I* [Food I]
1965 *Tabemono II* [Food II]
1966 *Eiyōgaku sōron* [General Remarks on Nutritional Science],
   last edition 1980
1966 *Eiyōgaku no gaisetsu* [The General Theory of Nutritional
   Science]
1973 *Chōri to kakō no tame no shokuhin kagaku* [Food Science for
   Preparation and Processing], last edition 1981.

The wartime experience wrapped up the construction of Japanese national cuisine. First of all, the austere diet that had continued for more than a decade bridged the gap between the urban and rural areas so characteristic of the pre-war period. While city dwellers experienced the hand-to-mouth existence of farmers, a great number of peasants' sons enjoyed the luxury of having rice three times a day and became acquainted with multicultural military menus drawn from pre-war urban gastronomy. The food industry continued to profit from the same products, which were now focused primarily on the civilian market.

The dietary influence of the military continued long after the disappearance of the Imperial Japanese Army and Navy from the political arena. The same people who under the auspices of the military were involved in activities geared towards the improvement of public nutrition continued their efforts after 1945. For example, in February 1946 the magazine *Shufu no tomo* ('Housewife's Companion') began to publish a series of articles dealing with the scientific aspects of cookery written by ex-Major-General Kawashima Shirō (1895–1986). Kawashima began his military career in 1930 at the Army Provisions Depot in Tokyo, where he carried out research into field rations and provisions for air squadrons. He was also involved in various activities of Ryōyūkai, publishing extensively in professional and popular journals. In 1942 he was awarded a doctorate from Tokyo University for his research on portable rations for Japanese soldiers fighting in Siberia. In August 1950, shortly after the Korean War (1950–53) broke out, the Americans commissioned him to design portable rations for Korean troops; apparently, American rations did not agree with them, having a negative impact on their combat strength.[53]

Military menus reproduced in civilian canteens: rice, *miso* soup and pork cutlet with shredded cabbage, 1980s.

The militarization of nutrition, and the chronic shortage of rice, set the stage for the post-war transformation of Japanese diet represented by the diminishing quantitative importance of rice and increased consumption of bread, noodles and industrially processed food. The work initiated by the Army Provisions Depot and supported by the wartime government continued. Military menus were reproduced in restaurants and civilian canteens, where military cooks and dieticians, and those educated during the 1940s under the strong influence of the military model, found employment after the war ended. Gradually, the militaristic connotation of the food and the innovations implemented by the armed forces disappeared, amalgamated into the mainstream civilian culture of the post-war era.

Six

The Culinary Consequences of Japanese Imperialism

The powerful role of the West in the construction of modern Japan has been widely recognized and rarely questioned. There is a general consensus among the general public and scholars alike that the building bricks of Japanese modernity were material goods, practices and ideas of Western origin that were gradually integrated into the Japanese context and ultimately acquired a Japanese identity.[1] In contrast, the contribution of non-Western ethnic minorities in the making of modern Japan remains largely unacknowledged, despite the growing body of scholarship on the topic.[2] As John Lie argued in 2001 in the introduction to his book *Multiethnic Japan*, 'the assumption that Japan is a monoethnic society is widely shared not just by scholars of Japan and the Japanese themselves, but also by virtually everyone else'.[3] Although the dominant paradigm of Japanese ethnic homogeneity has since the 1990s become significantly lower in voice, it remains unchallenged, partly due to a relatively small proportion of ethnic minorities in Japan. The estimated total of non-Japanese living in Japan in the 1990s was 4–6 million in a country of 125 million people.[4] However, Lie claims that it is not so much the demographic estimate, but the constitutive role of ethnic minorities in modern Japan that makes the monoethnic myth problematic. Cuisine provides a vivid testimony for Lie's argument that multi-ethnicity occupies a central role in modern Japanese society and culture.

The Japanese-Western-Chinese Culinary Tripod

I argued in chapter One that the formation of the dual Japanese and Western styles of dining among the Meiji elite initiated the construction of a Japanese-Western-Chinese tripod, which by the mid-twentieth century had become the fundamental structure within modern Japanese cuisine. One of the first signals indicating that Japanese cuisine would assume such a structure came into view in 1880, in the form of a treatise on food and drink by Noguchi Hokugen. The treatise dealt generally with the differences between Japanese, Western and Chinese cuisines.[5] It is by no means surprising that Noguchi chose these three cuisines for his gastronomic theorizing. China had since ancient times been the cultural force in terms of which Japan defined itself; it had been a source of inspiration for many Japanese practices and ideas. The West, in turn, was a dominant influence in modern Japan; during the late nineteenth and twentieth centuries it replaced China as the matrix against which Japan measured its strengths and weaknesses. At the time of the publication of Noguchi's treatises, a uniform cuisine that the majority of the Japanese population could identify as 'theirs' had yet to emerge. Moreover, both Chinese and Western cuisines were unknown in Japan except to the members of the elite and a handful of Japanese who interacted with the foreign communities in the treaty ports. Most inhabitants of the Japanese isles in the late nineteenth century subsisted on food produced and processed in the immediate vicinity of their place of residence. The developments described in the previous chapters were yet to begin.

During the following decades, as the concept of 'Japanese' cuisine crystallized and familiarity with Western and Chinese dishes, ingredients and cooking techniques increased, the Japanese-Western-Chinese tripod gradually acquired validity and practical meaning for the ever growing number of Japanese. By the 1960s the tripod had become deeply rooted in the consciousness of the majority of the population, reinforced by the media and endorsed by the education system. Today, it no longer denotes the totality of the culinary scene in Japan, which since the 1980s has become far more complex, including new genres, such as fast-food and the so-called *esunikku* ('ethnic') category that is composed largely of South-East Asian and South Asian cuisines. Rather, the Japanese-Western-Chinese tripod epitomizes the structure of modern Japanese cuisine as it began to take shape during the 1920s and '30s. *Washoku* ('Japanese food') manifested the Japanese tradition; *yōshoku* ('Western food') functioned as edible national icon of universal Japanese modernity; and Chinese cuisine (*Shina ryōri*) stood for Japanese imperialist expansion into Asia.

As was mentioned earlier, the reliance on Chinese borrowings had been long-standing in Japan. For example, such essential components of Japanese cuisine as soy sauce and soybean paste (*miso*) are of Chinese origin. The prototype of soy sauce and *miso*, the semi-liquid flavouring called *hishio*, is recorded to have been used in Japan as early as the eighth century AD. *Miso* became the staple in the Japanese diet since the thirteenth century. Soy sauce similar to the contemporary product was based on a Chinese recipe that was transmitted to Japan in the seventeenth century.[6] The use of chopsticks and the structure of the Japanese meal were also largely influenced by the civilization of ancient China. However, by the mid-nineteenth century, centuries after their introduction, Chinese elements had become fully integrated in local consumption patterns and entirely stripped of their foreign connotations. With a few exceptions, such as the exclusive Japanese-Chinese style of cooking (*shippoku ryōri*) that was developed during the eighteenth century in the merchant enclave of Nagasaki, pre-modern Japanese never really tasted Chinese food.[7] It was during the 1920s and '30s, when the rhetoric of imperialist expansionism began to dominate public discourse, that Chinese cuisine came to be widely consumed in Japan.

The formation of the Japanese Empire began in 1876 with Japan forcing neighbouring Korea to open ports to trade, in a fashion resembling the tactics of Commodore Perry two decades earlier (see chapter One). The victory in the Sino-Japanese War in 1895 provided Japan with its first major colony – the island of Formosa (Taiwan). Korea became Japan's protectorate ten years later and was officially colonized in 1910. Taiwan and Korea constituted Japan's two major colonies before the establishment in 1932 of the Japanese-run puppet state of Manchukuo. In 1945 Japan lost all its colonies, except for the neighbouring islands of Hokkaido and Ryūkyū (Okinawa), which were seized shortly after the Meiji Restoration.[8] However, the colonial legacy continued to influence Japanese food habits even after the collapse of the empire. More than a million Japanese who resided in Korea, Taiwan, Manchuria and other Chinese territories under Japan's domination, not to mention hundreds of thousands of soldiers who fought on the continent, acquired a taste for foreign food and played a critical role in its popularization in post-war Japan. For example, returnees from Manchukuo were responsible for the dissemination of northern Chinese dishes, such as *gyōza* dumplings. They found themselves jobless in the midst of devastation and food shortages, and many embarked on the making and selling of *gyōza* to their hungry customers.[9] *Gyōza* were particularly suited to the circumstances of wartime Japan, since they were made of wheat flour which was easier to acquire than rice and practically anything qualified as stuffing. In a survey conducted in 2002 among 15,000 respondents, *gyōza* ended up third among the dishes most frequently served at dinner tables in contemporary Japan.[10]

Fried *gyōza* and *rāmen* noodles rank among the most popular dishes in contemporary Japan.

The popularization of other Chinese dishes in Japan dates further back than that of *gyōza*, however. The influx of Westerners into Yokohama, Nagasaki and Kobe during the 1860s set the stage for the diffusion of Chinese cuisine in modern Japan. Although the Chinese had no legal right to remain in Japan before the first Sino-Japanese treaty was concluded in 1871, they were brought in under the legal protection of Western powers. Western merchants relied heavily on their Chinese staff – servants, clerks and middle-men – to run the households and enterprises that they relocated from the China coast. During the 1870s and '80s independent Chinese merchants began to settle in Japan as well, so that Chinese soon constituted the majority of the foreign population residing in the ports. By 1890, for example, 200 Chinese firms operated in Yokohama, compared to slightly more than 100 firms from all other nationalities combined. Most

A Chinese servant waiting on Westerners, from *Seiyō ryōri tsū* (1872).

A Chinese servant accompanying his master to a market in Yokohama, from *Seiyō ryōri tsū* (1872).

of the Chinese migrants hailed from southern China: Guangdong and Fujian – the 'traditional' areas of Chinese emigration – and the treaty ports of Shanghai and Ningbo.[11] Western travellers in Japan did not fail to notice the dominant Chinese presence in Japanese treaty ports. Miss Isabella Bird noted that

> one cannot be a day in Yokohama without seeing quite a different class of orientals from the small, thinly dressed, and usually poor-looking Japanese. Of the 2,500 Chinamen who reside in Japan, over 1,100 are in Yokohama, and if they were suddenly removed, business would come to an abrupt halt. Here, as everywhere, the Chinese immigrant is making himself indispensable.[12]

Major Henry Knollys was of similar opinion and remarked:

> The ubiquitous Chinamen crop up here again in the shape of domestic servants, in which capacity they are far superior to, and more reliable than, the natives. . . . The plodding, business-like unlovable Chinese on the other hand will at any sacrifice adhere to their contracts, and great as is their unpopularity, monopolise most of the important posts in English firms. They keep themselves very much apart as a class community, and, as a matter of course, are abhorred by the Japanese.[13]

Japanese generally resented Chinese because of their advantageous associations with Westerners. Chinese warehouse keepers and skilled negotiators of Western firms easily manipulated relatively inexperienced Japanese businessmen and shared in the prosperity deriving from the Western monopoly of Japan's foreign trade.[14] On the other hand, the negative image that the Chinese community acquired at the time was caused by poor hygiene in the residential areas that accommodated Chinese labourers, with cheap hotels, grog-shops and the drunken sailors they attracted. Despite many practical skills such as Western-style tailoring and hairdressing that Chinese passed on to the Japanese, the latter held the former in very low esteem, an attitude that was further inflamed by the Japanese victory over China in the Sino-Japanese War (1895). As elsewhere, a prejudice against Chinese was strong and Chinatowns were perceived as ethnic ghettos infested with crime and disease.[15]

It is by no means surprising that in such circumstances Chinese food did not appeal to the Japanese and they hardly ever ventured into a

Chinatown restaurant. Only a handful of Chinese restaurants operated outside the Chinatown areas in late nineteenth-century Japan. For example, in the 1880s Tokyo counted three Chinese restaurants: Eiwasai (opened in 1879), Kairakuen (established in 1883) and Shūhōen (set up in 1884). They were all very exclusive and recreated the nostalgic atmosphere of the pre-modern merchant enclave of Nagasaki. Although frequented by the Japanese political elite, they were far less fashionable than Western-style establishments.[16] As Gennifer Weisenfeld observed, 'defining and differentiating "Japaneseness" vis-à-vis the West and within Asia was an ongoing project requiring constant renegotiation in relation to changing geopolitical conditions'.[17] In the late nineteenth century there was as yet no place for Asia in the construction of new forms of consumption in Japan; borrowings from the West constituted at the time the marrow of modernizing processes.

The situation changed after the turn of the century. With the 'unequal treaties' revised and victory over Russia in the Russo-Japanese War (1905) under its belt, Japan's confidence in the international arena increased and the infatuation with the West cooled off. The time was ripe for the Chinese food boom to begin.

Popular restaurants serving Chinese food, either Chinese-owned or run by a Japanese proprietor but employing Chinese cooks, mushroomed in Tokyo during the second and third decade of the twentieth century. Their number is reported to have increased from two establishments in 1906 to fifteen hundred in 1923.[18] Similar restaurants also emerged in other cities. In Sapporo, for example, which would later become famous for its Chinese-style noodles, seven Chinese-style eateries opened during the first half of the 1920s. The first one, Takeya Shokudō, catered primarily to the Chinese students of Hokkaido Imperial University, but they were soon outnumbered by Japanese customers.[19]

The restaurant Rairaiken, set up in Tokyo in 1910, went into history as the first establishment to serve *Shina soba* ('China' + 'noodles') in Japan.[20] It was owned and run by Ozaki Kan'ichi, a former official at the Yokohama Customs Office, and employed thirteen Chinese cooks hailing from the Yokohama Chinatown. On busy days up to 2,500 Japanese customers gobbled down the Guangdong-style food served there.[21]

Shina soba was one of the signature dishes of Rairaiken. The name was easy to remember, since most Tokyo dwellers were familiar with *soba* noodles sold in the streets of the capital since Tokugawa times. However, *Shina soba* acquired the status of a 'national' dish in Japan under a different name – *rāmen*. The change of name from *Shina soba* to *rāmen* took place during the 1950s and '60s. The word *Shina*, used historically in reference to

China, acquired a pejorative connotation through its association with Japanese imperialist aggression in Asia and was replaced with the word *Chūka*, which derives from the Chinese name for the People's Republic. For a while, the term *Chūka soba* was used, but ultimately the name *rāmen* caught on, inspired by the chicken-flavoured instant version of the dish that went on sale in 1958 and spread nationwide in no time.[22] In 2004, 5.53 billion meals of instant *rāmen* were sold in Japan. This translates into 42.8 meals per capita, not counting fresh *rāmen* sold at ubiquitous restaurants and stalls. Although the average per capita consumption in Japan remains the highest in the world, compared with 15 for entire Asia, 7.9 in North America, 5.3 in Latin America and 1.3 in Europe, the worldwide popularity of *rāmen* is tremendous and still growing.[23] Within less than a century, not only did the status of *rāmen* shift in Japan from a novelty to an everyday food, but it has also been turned into a Japanese symbol.

The transformation of the Chinese original into the Japanese-style *rāmen* that we know today took place gradually. We may presume that *Shina soba* prepared in the early 1910s by the Chinese cooks at Rairaiken resembled one of many noodle dishes served at the Yokohama Chinatown. The process of Japanization intensified as more and more establishments serving *Shina soba* emerged and the recipe was adjusted to the specific

A selection of instant *rāmen* in an average supermarket, 2006.

A typical *rāmen* restaurant in rural Japan, 2006.

circumstances of each location and the taste preferences of the customers. The culinary historian Kosuge Keiko suggests that the inclusion of *Shina soba* in the menus of noodle shops that had originally specialized in indigenous *soba* greatly contributed to its Japanization. The Japanese invasion of Manchuria in 1931 also played a role in this respect, since many Chinese cooks were propelled to leave Japan and the kitchens of Chinese restaurants were instead populated by Japanese cooks.[24] However, two major factors continued to differentiate the newcomer in the Japanese noodle arena: the noodles and the broth.

> The Chinese-style *rāmen* noodles of Japan are more elastic and hence chewier than the traditional Japanese wheat noodles (*udon, sōmen*, and *kishimen*). The difference results from the Chinese technique of adding alkali to the salty water that is used to knead the wheat dough. This also gives the noodles a pale yellow hue and a particular aroma. . . . The dish consists basically of noodles in a pork or chicken broth seasoned with black pepper and topped with slices of pork and various other items.[25]

The meat-based stock gave the dish a distinctive flavour, since Japanese cooks relied exclusively on seafood and seaweed while preparing broth for their noodles. Yet the spirit of the times seems to have been equally critical for the growing popularity of *Shina soba* as its attractive taste. Japanese imperialist expansion into China fostered a China boom in Japan. Chinese-style decorations, Chinese costumes and Chinese products were eagerly consumed by the Japanese public, as they translated colonialism into a concrete experience. By physically interacting with China through the ingestion of Chinese food and drink, the Japanese masses were brought closer to the idea of empire. In 1932 Chinese dishes began to be served in the Hankyū department store in Osaka, and soon every respectable department store operated a Chinese restaurant alongside the already furnished Japanese and Western ones.[26] In 1936 the Takashimaya department store in Osaka organized a promotion campaign for Chinese wines with sales personnel dressed in Chinese dress. The prestigious grocer Meidi-ya, with stores throughout the country, regularly advertised Chinese wines and liquors, offering a detailed description of their production processes and taste differences.[27]

Following the early Meiji tactics, it was reported that Chinese cuisine appeared on the emperor's table, which undoubtedly enhanced the fashion for Chinese food.[28] The rise of a pan-Asian imperialist vision, and growing public interest in the colonies, opened up new opportunities for cultural representations of Japanese empire to shape Japanese modernity. For example, the number of cookery books devoted to Chinese cuisine dramatically increased during the 1920s and '30s, as did the frequency of Chinese recipes in the cookery columns of women's magazines. In 1929 the magazine *Shufu no tomo* introduced four Chinese recipes suggested by the wife of Yamamoto Teijirō (1870–1937), agriculture minister in the cabinet of Tanaka Giichi. The magazine explained that Mr and Mrs Yamamoto had spent some time in Taiwan, and brought their Taiwanese cook with them on their return to Japan.[29] Thousands of bureaucrats, professionals and businessmen had departed for Taiwan since 1895, and later Korea and Manchuria, to manage the colonial establishment and economy. Many of them acquired a taste for local food and disseminated their eccentric liking after returning to Japan. However, it was not until the late 1920s, a time of growing imperialist sentiment, that their exotic preferences received public attention.

From the 1920s onward Chinese-style dishes began to play an important role in military menus as well. The first military cooking manual to incorporate Chinese recipes was the *Kaigun shukeihei chōri jutsu kyōkasho* ('Catering Textbook for Navy Accountants') published in 1918. In the same year, the Army Provisions Depot arranged for a regular transfer of cooks from China, and dispatched them throughout the army units to provide the catering sections with necessary supervision and advice.[30] Reformers of military catering began to view Chinese dishes as an alternative to *yōshoku*, since Chinese dishes contained meat and fat, while being close to Japanese cuisine in, for example, the use of soy sauce. Historical records imply that in the 1930s conscripts singled out Chinese dishes, along with *yōshoku*, as the favourites on military menus (see chapter Three). The wartime militarization of nutrition and the shortage of rice sustained further popularization of Chinese-style dishes, in particular wheat-based dumplings, buns and noodles (see chapter Five).

Chinese and Western cuisines played a very important role in the process of Japan's culinary self-definition. Representations of the West and Asia provided the space to negotiate new practices and meanings, fulfilling a unifying and democratizing function in the construction of modern Japanese cuisine. Ambiguities and contradictions of this process are clearly reflected in the Japanese-Western-Chinese tripod. On the one hand, the Japanese-Western and Japanese-Chinese hybrids have become fully integrated within Japanese consumption patterns, and have acquired a solid position as components of Japanese national cuisine. On the other hand, they retained their distinctive identity as the *yōshoku* and *Chūka* categories.

The passionate embrace of Chinese cuisine by the Japanese masses cannot be explained by its gustatory qualities alone. The imperialist expansion into China was equally important for the popularization of Chinese food in Japan as the policies of 'civilization and enlightenment' (see chapter One) were for the popularization of Western food. Imperialism constituted a critical force in the making of a Japanese national cuisine.

Embracing Korean Food

The incorporation of Chinese food into Japanese cuisine is the most visible, but not the only, channel through which Japanese imperialism shaped the culinary culture of twentieth-century Japan. Another important process was the gradual embrace of Korean cuisine, which has been completed only in recent years.

Contrary to the case of Chinese food, Korean cuisine was practically unknown in Japan prior to the 1940s. Publications that introduced Korean cuisine to the Japanese public were limited to guidebooks for settlers and tourists heading for the colony. Korean restaurants in Japan were rare and rather exclusive. For example, Meigetsukan – the most famous Korean restaurant in Tokyo – charged 3–7 yen for a set menu at a time when a bowl of *Shina soba* could be had for 0.10 yen and a meal of sushi for 0.25 yen. The very first Korean restaurant that opened in Japan was Kansanrō, set up in Tokyo in 1905 by a Korean named Yi In-sik. Establishments such as these were targeted chiefly at Korean diplomats and intellectuals residing in Japan, as well as the Japanese elite composed either of gourmands hungry for exotic experience or former members of the Korean colonial establishment. A much greater number of cheap eateries operated within Korean residential areas in Japan – 160 such establishments were counted in 1930.[31]

The migration of Koreans to Japan remained very limited during the first decade following the annexation of Korea in 1910. The situation, however, began to change during the 1920s, stimulated by the recruitment of colonial labour in Japanese heavy industry. Between 1920 and 1930 the number of Korean migrants in Japan increased almost tenfold (from approximately 30,000 to 298,091). By 1939 nearly a million Koreans resided in Japan, and another million arrived during the following five years under labour mobilization programmes and forced 'labour conscription' to supplement shortages of manpower in the war industries.[32] After Japan's defeat in 1945, approximately 600,000 Koreans remained in Japan, while most were repatriated, either under the official repatriation programme or through illegal channels.[33]

Despite the presence of such a large Korean community, Korean food was practically unknown beyond Korean residential areas. The Japanese public encountered Korean food in the midst of the period of severe food shortage, which lasted from 1945 to 1949. Koreans operated food stalls at black markets, where thousands of undernourished civilians flocked in pursuit of something to assuage their hunger.[34] Black markets functioned as the centres of business and trade in Japan between 1945 and 1951. The black market in Tokyo emerged within a few days after capitulation. By October 1945 an estimated 17,000 open-air markets had blossomed nationwide, mostly in large cities. They were run by gangster gangs headed by godfather-type individuals. For example, in Tokyo the market in the Shinbashi district was controlled by the Matsuda gang, Asakusa by the Shibayama gang, the Ginza area by the Ueda gang, Ikebukuro by the Sekiguchi gang, and Shinjuku by the Ozu and Wada gangs. Well-organized Formosan and Korean gangs were also involved. The black market

A Korean restaurant Meigetsukan in Tokyo, c. 1950s. Under the name of the restaurant, the phrase 'Keijō ryōri' (Keijō cuisine) appears on the signboard, Keijō being the colonial name of Seoul.

was supplied, largely illegally, by tapping into food supplied in the countryside and former military stockpiles. American goods also made their way onto the market, via prostitutes who received them from American clients or through vendors who struck private deals with occupational personnel.[35]

The chief ingredients of the dishes served at Korean stalls were tripe and offal – foodstuffs that did not fall under the food rationing system. Koreans had a long tradition of cooking and eating the internal organs of animals, and eateries serving them operated within the Korean community in Japan during the 1920s and '30s. The hunger and deprivation of the mid-1940s for the first time compelled Japanese to break the prejudice against what in their view was unclean food. During the immediate post-1945 years, marked by malnutrition and even starvation, grilled tripe and offal – commonly known as *horumonyaki* – were a real treat. After 1949, when the rationing of meat was lifted, grilled meat gradually replaced offal on the menus of eateries run by Koreans. The two most famous Korean eateries of the 1950s were Shokudōen in Osaka and Meigetsukan in Tokyo. They were labelled *Chōsen ryōriten* or *Chōsen ryōriya* (meaning 'Korean restaurant'), *Chōsen* being the Japanese name for Korea throughout the colonial period and before. In time, however, these restaurants began instead to be called *yakinikuya* ('grilled meat restaurant'). The reason behind this shift was because the word *Chōsen* acquired a strong association with North Korea, since the conventional names of North Korea and South Korea were respectively *Kita Chōsen* and *Kankoku*.[36]

Contemporary *yakiniku* restaurants are direct descendants of the Korean eateries of the 1950s, and the major change in their menus over the years consisted in the quality and quantity of the served meat.[37] Per capita yearly consumption of meat in Japan increased from 3 kilograms in 1955 to 9.2 kilograms in 1965, 22.5 kilograms in 1980 and 28.5 kilograms in 1990. This dramatic growth went hand in hand with the popularization of *yakiniku* restaurants. For example, between 1963 and 1979 their number in Tokyo increased from 17 to 1,118; in 1992, Tokyo counted 1,600 and Osaka 1,500 *yakiniku* restaurants.[38] These figures imply that a large proportion of meat consumed in Japan since the 1970s took the form of *yakiniku*, which was more affordable than beef stew (*sukiyaki*) and steak. The consumption of grilled meat at home also increased at this time, demonstrated by the skyrocketing sales of ready-to-use *yakiniku* dipping sauces.[39] Today *yakiniku* ranks among most popular 'classic' meat dishes in Japan. Its Korean roots are still recognized, similarly to the Chinese and Western origins of the *Chūka* and *yōshoku* categories in the culinary tripod discussed earlier. However, *yakiniku* has become utterly domesticated and has spread as a favourite food in urban as well as rural areas.[40]

The *yakiniku* case clearly demonstrates the role of Koreans in the popularization of meat eating in Japan. In fact, this role was far more

A typical *yakiniku* restaurant in rural Japan, 2006.

historically embedded than is generally known. While the West provided the ideological incentive for the rise of meat eating in Japan (see chapter One), since the nineteenth century Korean beef has provided the means toward its realization.

The import of Korean cattle was conducted on a private scale from the 1880s, but the trade intensified drastically during the Russo-Japanese War (1904–5). Following Korea's annexation in 1910, the stimulation of the Korean beef industry became a priority for the colonial authorities. In the following years, the stock increased by approximately 200,000 head per annum; by the 1920s the number of cattle in the colony more than doubled.[41] A steady supply of cheap Korean beef enabled the Japanese urban masses to embrace culinary modernity represented by dishes served at *yōshokuya* and other mass eateries that emerged in the Japanese cities in the early twentieth century (see chapter Two). During the late 1930s, with the rapid build-up of the Japanese armed forces, Korean beef acquired importance in military strategies as well, since it became increasingly critical in provisioning Japanese troops. The export of beef cattle to Manchuria increased from 100 to 400 head during the first half of the decade to more than 2,000 in 1937. Japanese policy makers, however, envisioned a dramatic increase of up to 10,000–30,000 head as necessary to support Japanese expansion into China.[42]

The Japanese consumers of Korean beef had no knowledge of its Korean origin. The situation was different in the case of *yakiniku*, which had clearly been associated with Korean eateries from the outset. Still, it was not embraced by the Japanese as part of Korean culture. Contrary to the popularization of Western cuisine, which was sustained by the ideology of 'civilization and enlightenment', and that of Chinese cuisine by the rhetoric of militarist expansion into China, the spread of *yakiniku* relied strictly on its gustatory merits. In view of a generally negative attitude towards Koreans, the Korean origins of *yakiniku* were a predicament, rather than a stimulant, in its popularization in Japan. The circumstances were very different in the case of *kimch'i* (in Japan known as *kimuchi*) – the Korean pickle made of salted vegetables fermented with red chilli pepper, garlic, green onions, ginger, seafood and other ingredients. No Korean meal is complete without the pickle and it is considered a potent symbol of Korean identity. A wide range of vegetables is fermented throughout Korea, but the most popular version is made of Chinese cabbage.[43]

While *kimch'i* was served as a side dish at *yakiniku* restaurants, its popularity fell far behind that of grilled meat. Its pungent taste did not agree with most Japanese customers and the strong, garlicky odour of the pickle itself, and even more so the breath of the eaters, was not socially

acceptable. However, during the 1990s a drastic increase in the sales of *kimch'i* took place in Japan. Between 1990 and 2000 the production of Korean pickle in Japan increased nearly fourfold, while its import from Korea increased from 3,432 to 30,000 tonnes. The growth during the final two years was particularly spectacular – from 15,000 to 30,000 tonnes. In the year 2000 *kimch'i* ranked as number one among all the pickled vegetables produced (and consumed) in Japan, far ahead of such traditional products as *asazuke* (22,500 tonnes), *takuan* (90,600 tonnes), *fukujinzuke* (60,500 tonnes) and *umeboshi* (40,300 tonnes). *Kimch'i* is not only the most popular pickle at the moment, but it is also an ingredient of dishes such as *buta kimuchi* (pork pan-fried with *kimch'i*) and *kimuchi nabe* (*kimch'i* stew), which have become mainstays of contemporary Japanese diet.[44]

Kimch'i production in Japan, 1980–2001.[45]

YEAR	AMOUNT (IN TONNES)
1980	34,059
1985	46,636
1990	83,474
1995	93,304
1997	120,560
1998	180,147
1999	250,000
2000	300,000
2001	360,000

A combination of factors stimulated the swift popularization of *kimch'i* in Japan. Manufacturers' efforts to revive the stagnating market for pickled vegetables, and the tough competition between them, is considered to have played an important role.[46] The ethnic food boom and health food fashion that swept Japan during the 1990s were also significant, because they led to shifts in attitude, particularly among women, towards spices and garlic. *Kimch'i* was embraced as a delicious food with healthy properties, such as the ability to increase stamina, prevent cancer and even generate weight loss.[47] The third factor behind the rapidly growing popularity of *kimch'i* in Japan was the changing attitude toward Korea. This change was inspired by two international sporting events that took place in Seoul – the 10th Asian Games in 1986 and the 24th Olympic Games in 1988. The publicity surrounding both events engaged the interest of the Japanese public, leading to the growth of Japanese tourism in South Korea. A general shift, in the midst of the economic recession of the 1990s, from (expensive) Europe to (cheap) Asia as the most popular tourist destination provided additional stimulus to travel to South Korea, in particular among young women. After 1994, when a visa was no longer required for Japanese nationals to enter the country, the stream of tourists increased rapidly (from 1.5 million to nearly 2.5 million in 2000). The decline caused by the terrorist attacks of 11 September 2001 and the SARS epidemic of 2003 was only temporary. In 2004 the number of Japanese tourists in South Korea recovered, again reaching nearly 2.5 million.[48]

The co-hosting of the World Cup of 2002 by Japan and Korea, and the years of preparations preceding the event, undoubtedly generated further interest in Korea and contributed to the gradual decline of its negative image in Japan.[49] However, the Korea boom, which gained momentum in 2004, was only loosely connected to football. It was largely carried on the shoulders of Japanese women of 40 and older – all fans of the Korean television drama *Winter Sonata* and its leading character Bae Yong-joon. The series began to be aired on the NHK terrestrial channel in April 2004 and soon become a phenomenal hit, with viewer ratings of more than 20 per cent. Armies of middle-aged Japanese women travelled to Korea en masse to visit filming locations and sample the culture they had witnessed on screen. The popularity of the drama has definitely changed Japanese perception of Korea, and with it the attitude towards its cuisine.[50]

There is no doubt that the 'Korean Wave' – as the spread of South Korean pop culture throughout Asia during the last decade is commonly referred to – was critical for the final embrace of Korean food by the Japanese public. It would be misleading, however, to characterize the popularization of Korean food in Japan as a late twentieth-century phenomenon. Like many other aspects of multiethnic Japan, it has its roots in the colonial ambitions of the Japanese Empire.

Seven

Multiple Circuits of Affluence

From LARA to Starbucks

After 1945 the United States emerged as the most influential outside force in the political, economic and social development of Japan. Officially, from August 1945 to April 1952 the country was subject to occupation by the Allied Powers. In practice, however, their influence was negligible; the United States determined the policy and exercised decisive command over all aspects of the occupation.[1] Initially, the Americans imposed the agenda of 'demilitarization and democratization', but they soon reversed course and began to rearm Japan as a subordinate Cold War partner. The operative document for the reverse course was drafted in September 1947 and envisioned a Japan that would be '"friendly to the United States," amenable to American leadership in foreign affairs, "industrially revived as a producer primarily of consumer's goods and secondarily of capital goods," and active in foreign trade; militarily it would be "reliant upon the US for its security from external attack"'.[2] In the American international objectives of counter-revolution and support of a capitalist mode of development, Japan was to play the role both of a buffer zone against communism in Asia and an alleged Asian model of the advantages of gradual, non-revolutionary development along capitalist lines.[3]

The outbreak of the Korean War (1950–53) sealed the Japanese-American alliance, embedding Japan firmly in the structure of US global strategy. It also proved an 'elixir' that revitalized Japan's economy. War orders for the US and South Korean armies benefited the Japanese textile, construction, automotive, metal, communication and chemical industries. As Michael Schaller explains,

> during the three years of fighting in Korea, Japan earned nearly $2.5 billion from procurements, more than the value of

American aid from 1945–1950. During the two years following the Korean armistice, Japan earned an additional $2 billion from military procurements. These orders initiated a twenty year period of nearly uninterrupted 10 percent annual growth in the Gross National Product (GNP).[4]

Before this miraculous economic growth began, however, the Japanese population experienced long years of deprivation (see chapter Five). The food crises experienced during the first two years of the occupation were more severe than any during wartime shortages. A sudden and unprecedented population increase was largely responsible for this situation. Between 1945 and 1950 the Japanese population increased by 11.2 million, more than half of this increase resulting from the repatriation of Japanese civilians and military personnel from the colonies and other overseas areas.[5] Moreover, in 1945 the country encountered the poorest rice crop in years, while food imports from the colonies came to a halt. The first shipments of grain from the United States did not arrive until March 1946. The food collection and rationing machinery that had been developed by the Japanese government during the war period was retained intact by the American occupying forces. The administrative confusion surrounding the surrender, however, along with increased resistance among farmers to comply with food collection quotas, resulted in a deficit in the food supplies available to meet the rationing requirements.[6]

In 1947, with the aim of easing malnutrition among Japanese children, the occupation authorities initiated a programme of school lunches. At first, this was carried out in large cities, whose populations suffered most from food shortages. The meals were prepared using canned meat and fish from the remaining stockpiles of the Japanese Imperial Army and food donations of the Licensed Agencies for Relief in Asia (LARA). LARA was a group of private American charitable and religious organizations formed in 1946 with the aim of contributing food, clothing, medical supplies and other relief items to Japan and other Asian nations after World War Two.[7]

In 1951 the school lunch initiative was expanded to encompass children all over Japan. The directive issued the previous year prescribed that a school lunch was to provide 600 kilocalories and 25 grams of protein, and should be centred on bread and milk. Skimmed powdered milk was considered the most cost-effective remedy for strengthening malnourished children and was donated by various aid organizations, such as LARA, the United Nations International Children's Emergency Fund (now known under the name UNICEF) and the US Government Appropriation for Relief

School lunch centred on bread and milk, 1951.

in Occupied Areas (GARIOA). The reliance on bread was determined less by its nutritional qualities and more by the fact that the US government was eager to dispose of the wheat flour surplus from the American market.[8]

Ironically, it was a similar reason – the overproduction of rice – that prompted the Japanese government in 1976 to direct schools to start using rice in their lunches. While by the 1970s rice production had flourished under the government's protectionist policy (both farmland and rice production being subsidized), the demand for it steadily decreased. Daily consumption of rice dropped from 360 grams per person in 1960 to 170 grams in 1996, compelling the government to continue to store huge quantities of surplus rice.[9]

This decline in rice consumption in Japan was not the result of a shift from rice-centred to bread-centred diet. Rather, it was a marker of the rising standard of living. Along with the rapid increase in the consumption of meat (see chapter Six), the consumption of fats and oils nearly tripled between the early 1950s and '60s.[10] In other words, the position of side dishes was shifting from that of complementing the rice-based meal to that of the centre of the meal, accompanied by rice. For example, the proportion of household expenditure for staple foods declined from 22.2 to 13.1 per cent over the decade 1965–75, whereas those of non-staple foods increased from 49.6 to 52.3 per cent.[11] The Japanese ate less rice, because they could now afford to include former 'luxury' foods, such as meat, fish and fruit, in their daily diet. Rapid urbanization and the transition of the patterns of income distribution (as a result of the movement of people from rural areas to improve their income positions) are considered chiefly responsible for the changing consumption patterns in post-war Japan.[12] Those who moved to cities embraced the urban lifestyle more rapidly than their counterparts who remained in the countryside. In time, however, under the steady influence of the media and profit from the land and rice subsidies, farm households began to emulate urban consumption patterns persistently and to follow new trends. One of the most notable shifts that took place during the 1960s and '70s was the proliferation of industrially processed food and electrical household appliances in the growing number of Japanese kitchens.

Japan's infatuation with the American lifestyle had begun already during the first years of the occupation. As Simon Partner reports, American movies, jazz music and well-fed American servicemen handing out chewing gum and money to clamouring Japanese children provided Japanese with a first-hand evidence of American affluence. With the devastated Japan of the 1940s as a backdrop, the United States 'seemed to be a paragon of efficiency, productivity, good living, and happiness, a place where even the unemployed had flush toilets; where used cars still gleamed like new'.[13] Although the occupation policies were not specifically designed to reproduce American economic successes and lifestyles in Japan, the focus on economic recovery that gained ground after the 'reverse course' of 1947 led to technology transfer and managerial assistance on the part of the Americans and helped to transform wartime producers of munitions and military equipment into producers of consumer goods. During the 1950s Japan's new leaders and farsighted entrepreneurs who envisioned Japan as a mirrored image of the United States embarked on the mission of creating a consumer market for electrical goods.[14] In 1955, with strong government support, the 'bright Japan' (*akarui Nihon*) campaign and the New Life Movement Association propagated the idea of rational, 'bright life' (*akarui seikatsu*) as the symbol of Japan's future.[15] Electric goods companies began to invest heavily in advertising their new products. Next to smaller appliances, such as toasters, electric rice cookers and 'hot plates' that could be used to fry foods directly at the table, the three major status symbols of the 1950s were a television set, a washing machine and a refrigerator. By 1965, more than 50 per cent of all Japanese households owned an electric refrigerator, and five years later the share of refrigerator-owners reached nearly 90 per cent. This percentage was higher than the average in European countries.[16]

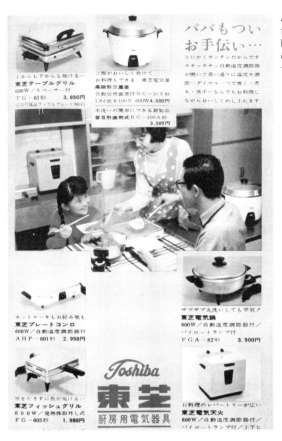

An advertisement for various electric kitchen appliances of the Toshiba brand, 1962.

The emergence of a consumer market for electrical household appliances in 1950s Japan was spectacular because most Japanese were entirely unfamiliar with such luxurious items. As Partner explains, Japan was at the time by any objective measure an underdeveloped nation, with average earnings only a fraction of American incomes and much lower than those in Western Europe, including the defeated Germany.[17] The economic recovery and the rhetoric of 'bright life', which followed a decade of extreme deprivation, turned electrical appliances into symbols of affluence, providing irresistible stimulus for their purchase.

The proliferation of refrigerators in Japanese households went hand in hand with the rapid popularization of frozen foods. Their production increased from 5,000 tonnes in 1960 to 141,000 tonnes in 1970, 562,000 tonnes in 1980, and in 1990 surpassed a million tonnes. The spread of industrially prepared foods (excluding canned food that had already been popularized earlier) at first proceeded less rapidly (from 3,000 tonnes in 1960 to 64,000 tonnes in 1970), but their production surpassed a million tonnes only four years after frozen foods.[18] In 1996, only 31.8 per cent of food consumed by an average Japanese was in the form of fresh foodstuffs cooked at home, as opposed to 41.6 per cent of foods purchased in a prepared form, 9 per cent in the form of ready-to-eat meals delivered to homes, and 17.6 per cent consumed while dining out. Between 1965 and 1996 the share of unprocessed foodstuffs in the Japanese diet declined by nearly 17 per cent.[19] This rapid change was generated by the persistent influence of the media and the advertising power of the food industry. However, the impact of the school lunch system initiated in 1951 should not be underestimated. Since school lunches differed remarkably from the meals most children ate on a regular basis at home, they not only influenced the children, but also, by extension, the attitudes of their families toward hitherto unknown foods.

Like military diet, school lunches were composed with the goal of efficient nourishment in mind. The aim of 600 kilocalories and 25 grams of protein specified in the directive of 1950 were to be provided by a roll, a glass of milk and a warm dish. Further details were left to the discretion of

A selection of instant curry in a rural supermarket, 2006.

the catering departments of each school, and it does not seem surprising that military mainstays were well represented in school lunch menus. We may presume that military cooks and other individuals educated during the 1940s system of militarized nutritional education (see chapter Five) found employment as school lunch caterers. During the 1950s and early 1960s curries, deep-fried whale meat, deep-fried bread (*agepan*), *tenpura* and macaroni with vegetables ranked among the most popular dishes among children.[20] The creativity of caterers increased hand in hand with economic affluence .

Dishes served in 1965 along with bread and milk at schools in different parts of Japan.[21]

DISHES	LOCATION
Whale meat simmered with ketchup	Ōita prefecture
Borsch, apple	Tottori prefecture
Sweet and sour whale meat	Tokushima prefecture
Beef curry	Mie prefecture
Deep-fried breaded cod with Tartar sauce, boiled potatoes, strawberries	Saitama prefecture
Whale meat and liver in tomato sauce with cheese, *tōfu* with peanut dressing, *karintō*	Okayama prefecture
Pieces of deep-fried chicken dusted with seasoned flour and boiled cabbage	Hyōgo prefecture
Deep-fried breaded horse mackerel, French salad	Ehime prefecture
Croquette, vegetables in vinegar dressing	Ōita prefecture
Egg salad, cheese	Akita prefecture
Stew, green tea confection	Gunma prefecture
Fruit salad, cheese	Fukushima prefecture
Spaghetti with meat sauce, breaded deep-fried pork cutlet	Kanagawa prefecture
Spaghetti with meat sauce, boiled egg, tangerine	Wakayama prefecture
Spaghetti mixed with dry curry, French salad	Ibaraki prefecture

DISHES	LOCATION
Sweet potato in tomato sauce, egg-drop soup	Kanagawa prefecture
Tōfu stir-fried with curry, margarine	Wakayama prefecture
Miso-flavoured stew, jam	Miyagi prefecture
Minced beef and *tōfu* dumplings, shredded cabbage, Japanese summer orange	Yamaguchi prefecture
Western-style *oden*, jam	Miyagi prefecture
Deep-fried whale meat, soused Chinese cabbage	Ōita prefecture
Stewed soybeans and pork	Kyoto prefecture

The popularization of bread and familiarizing the post-war generation with the custom of milk drinking, hitherto practically non-existent in Japan, are clearly the chief legacies of the school lunch programme.[22] As Ehara Ayako explains, however, school lunches are also responsible for the indiscriminate mixing of foods in one meal; the school lunch system provides an explanation for the bizarre combinations that adult Japanese today tend to assemble at buffet-style restaurants and even serve to their children at home.[23]

One of the distinctive characteristics of menu planning in the schools is the prevalence of meals of indeterminate nationality – a combination of Japanese and Western elements. For example, a meal might consist of *udon* noodles, curry stew, *age-pan*, and milk. *Udon* is a traditional Japanese food and carbohydrate that stands on its own as a complete meal when served in a broth with additional ingredients. To combine it with bread seems odd, therefore, whether from a Japanese or a Western perspective. Another meal might consist of a breaded and deep-fried boiled egg, *zōni* (a seasoned broth with simmered vegetables and rice cakes, traditionally served at New Year's), fruit, bread and yogurt.

This sort of East–West hodgepodge provided sufficient energy and protein, but it was hardly a model of balance in either content or taste. It complicated the job of teaching children mealtime etiquette and interfered with the transmission of Japan's traditional dietary culture. In short, the initial imperative of providing maximum nourishment at low cost, without regard to the balance or harmony of the menu, set the tone for

Japan's school lunch program, which continued in the same vein for many years. The impact of this program on the eating habits of Japanese children and their families was profound.[24]

Despite the evident impact of the school lunch programme on the food preferences of the post-war generations of Japanese, it was by no means responsible for the popularization of American cuisine. Hamburgers, French fries, milk shakes and doughnuts began to permeate the daily diet of the Japanese population during the 1970s via a different route.

McDonald's was introduced in Japan in 1971 by Fujita Den (1926–2004), then a University of Tokyo student. He started with five restaurants and the early years were tough, the year 1973 ending with a net loss. By 1984, however, McDonald's ranked first in the total sales of Japan's restaurant industry. Twenty years after the opening of the first outlet, the number of McDonald's reached 860 and more than quadrupled in the following decade. The ambitious plan of '10,000 outlets by 2010' announced around the turn of the new millennium is not likely to materialize, but the company remains the largest fast-food chain in Japan today, with nearly 4,000 restaurants operating throughout the country.[25] As Emiko Ohnuki-Tierney explains, the American identity of McDonald's contributed to its popularity in Japan:

A McDonald's outlet in Japan, 2006.

Despite founder Den Fujita's claim that McDonald's was not promoted as an import ('from America'), the company has clearly capitalized on the fact that it is associated with American culture. Fujita did, however, depart from the 'suburban approach' that characterizes McDonald's in the United States by locating his first restaurant on Ginza, the most fashionable street in Japan. He placed another outlet in the Mitsukoshi department store, which is not only the oldest but also the most prestigious of all Japanese department stores. The location of these two restaurants helped create an image of McDonald's as a prime example of Americana, as imagined by Japanese people whose understanding of United States culture is limited. Furthermore, the fact that McDonald's opened in fashionable locations helped convince young people that eating while standing – an act that violates Japanese table manners – is chic. During the summer of 1986, in an extra effort to dramatize McDonald's American identity, Fujita sponsored a visit by the full troupe of the Broadway musical '42nd Street,' which played a one-month run in Tokyo.[26]

Although undoubtedly fuelled by their American image, this factor was not chiefly responsible for the popularity of McDonald's, Kentucky Fried Chicken and other American fast-food chains in Japan. Rather, they benefited from a general trend towards dining out. Dining at restaurants – a genuine luxury for most Japanese before the 1970s – was transformed into a routine component of daily life, especially in urban areas. The number of eating and drinking establishments operating throughout the country more than doubled between the 1960s and 1990s. The growth of sales, however, was much more impressive – from 410 billion yen in 1960 to 13,135 billion yen in 1992.[27] In 2004 an average household spent 19.6 per cent of its food budget on dining out (as opposed to 7.9 per cent in 1970).[28] Dining out ranks as the most popular leisure activity in Japan, prevailing over domestic travel, driving, karaoke and watching videos.[29]

The Japanese dining-out market is extremely dynamic, with new trends not infrequently fading as abruptly as they emerge. As John Clammer explains in his sociological study of consumption in Japan, the concept of trends (*būmu*) is very important to the understanding of Japanese consumer culture, because consumption activities have a strong group preference. 'Trends are followed', Clammer argues, 'partly because it is difficult not to follow them – shops simply cease to carry stock reflecting the previous trend – but equally because to be trend-conscious is to adapt to one of the most powerful mechanisms of social integration in a culture which does not value so much those who stand out.'[30]

The first case of 'mad cow' disease, or BSE (bovine spongiform encephalopathy), in Japan, reported in September 2001, proved devastating for the hamburger business, leading to reduced sales, falling profits and eventually a drop in the number of McDonald's outlets.[31] While recognizing the harmful effect of the BSE scare, economic analysts argue that McDonald's 'cannibalized' its own success by saturating the market with too many stores. By the end of the 1990s McDonald's trendy appeal was over and it has joined the ranks of mundane eating places, like curry houses and noodles shops. A victim of a similar phenomenon, although proceeding in a much more rapid tempo, is the more recent symbol of Americana in Japan – the Starbucks chain of coffee shops.[32]

Starbucks opened its first coffee shop outside North America in the centre of Tokyo, and Japan remains the company's most important overseas market. During the first five years since the opening of the first store in August 1996, the expansion rate of Starbucks in Japan was phenomenal. By the end of 2001 Starbucks Coffee Japan operated 300 outlets and its sales growth more than doubled between 1998 and 2002. In March 2006 there were 602 Starbucks coffee shops in operation throughout Japan, but their trendy appeal has certainly passed its peak.[33] Nevertheless, Starbucks' business in Japan is far from fading. In September 2005 the company launched

A Starbucks outlet in Japan, 2006.

the sales of ready-to-drink chilled coffee in two flavours, Starbucks Discoveries Milano (espresso) and Starbucks Discoveries Seattle (latte). They are produced by Suntory Ltd, a market leader on the Japanese beverage market, and sold at the ubiquitous 'convenience stores' (*konbini*) that are open 24-hours a day. Immediately after their launch, the drinks were so popular that sales far exceeded initial projections. A decision was made to focus on the production of the Starbucks Discoveries Seattle and temporarily discontinue the other flavour. Starbucks and Suntory have doubled the production capacity for the coffee drinks and in April 2006 reintroduced Starbucks Discoveries Milano in convenience stores in and around Tokyo.[34]

Organic Farming and Nostalgia for Local Produce

Affluence is clearly a defining feature of the culinary scene in contemporary Japan. A wide range of fresh and processed provisions, snack foods and ready-to-eat meals are available at supermarkets, convenience stores and through home-delivery services. Dining establishments serve a wide variety of native and foreign dishes and omnipresent vending machines dispense not only soft drinks, beer, sweets and ice cream, but also steaming noodles and grilled rice balls. Food is big business and every opportunity to sell more of it is exploited. Long-distance train travellers can dine in buffet cars or purchase food from catering carts to eat in their seats. Catering carts and rail station kiosks also stock a large variety of food souvenirs, usually specialities of the region, such as locally grown fruit and vegetables, pickles and confections. They are distributed among colleagues, friends and family to mark the end of a journey and offer a vicarious sharing of the experience. Food has for centuries been a typical and welcome gift in Japan; it is relatively inexpensive, easy to choose, can be shared and is easily disposed of.[35] However, the recent celebration of local produce in Japan has acquired connotations that go beyond the simple notion of a souvenir (*omiyage*).

Economic affluence and a growing familiarity with foreign culinary trends since the 1970s have occasioned an emerging pride in domestic produce and local specialities. Imported foods, which had long been regarded somehow superior, have lost their attractive appeal. Instead, domestically harvested or produced foods have generally become equated with high quality, safety and perfection of form.[36] Along with urbanization and the rapidly changing lifestyles of an ever growing part of the Japanese population, the nostalgia for the vanishing, allegedly more 'authentic'

A kiosk with food souvenirs is indispensable at every large train station, 2005.

rural life – the so-called *furusato* ('native place') – has become increasingly pronounced, effectively perpetuated by the media and the domestic tourist industry.[37] This nostalgic reverence for *furusato*, in turn, generated the celebration of local produce all over Japan. The revival of traditional vegetables from Kyoto provides a model example of similar processes taking place elsewhere. Marketed under the label *Kyō yasai* (Kyoto vegetables), the 'restored' vegetables include the varieties of vegetables produced by Kyoto farmers before World War Two, but which after the war were replaced by new varieties with their promise of higher yields and a greater resistance to disease.

During the 1960s and '70s the authorities of the city and prefecture of Kyoto took the first steps towards preserving local vegetables threatened with extinction, successfully reintroducing them to the marketplace. They were aided in this endeavour by Kyoto-based restaurant owner-chefs who were dissatisfied with the taste of commonly available vegetables, and by Kyoto farmers eager to reclaim a market advantage. By the 1980s, greengrocers and restaurants specializing in 'heirloom' vegetables opened, and 'the taste of historical Kyoto' was shared throughout Japan via gift packs and souvenirs of aubergines (eggplants), turnips and yams. Most vegetables are produced without or with very few chemical fertilizers and pesticides, and are usually available only seasonally, unlike conventional vegetables available at supermarkets throughout the year. By revitalizing the cultivation of seasonal vegetables, the image of Kyoto as the capital of Japanese culture and culinary heritage was greatly enhanced. However, as Eric Rath's investigation revealed, the claim that a specific geographic location is a cultural and historical origin point, in this case for certain vegetables, is fraught with problems and contradictions. Cases like that of the 'Kyoto vegetables' raise questions about both the historical authenticity of local culinary revivals and their role in the recent reinvention of Japanese culinary history (see Conclusion).[38]

Such instances notwithstanding, it is obvious that organic farming is successively gaining ground in Japan, constituting a major counter-current to the mainstream consumption behaviour described above. As in other parts of the world, economic affluence of the 1960s and '70s fostered a growing concern among Japanese consumers about food safety. An important factor that contributed to this concern were some widely publicized food poisoning cases. The most famous example was the Morinaga milk poisoning incident of 1955; arsenic contamination of milk additives led to 12,000 cases of poisoning and 138 deaths, among them many babies and infants. Another well-known poisoning scare was the Kanemi rice-oil case of 1968, which resulted in 1,900 officially recognized cases of poisoning. These and other incidents had a negative impact on public perceptions of the food industry and prompted Japanese consumers to take action by organizing themselves into co-operatives and other grass-roots-based movements. Increasing awareness over environmental degradation, also widely publicized by the media, further contributed to the rapid growth of these organizations.[39]

Concurrent with the trends described earlier in this chapter, the organic farming movement in Japan has experienced a phenomenal growth since the 1970s. Integral to its success were the very diverse networks of grass-roots organic food distributors, retailers and, above all, consumer co-operatives that worked together, jointly attracting a wide section of Japanese society. Darrell Moen argues that Japan has one of the best-developed consumer co-operative movements in the world. In 1990 the largest consumer co-operative alone – the Japan Consumers' Co-operative Union (JCCU), commonly known under the name Seikyō — had a national household membership of 14.14 million. If the family members of each co-op member are counted, this translates into more than 40 per cent of the Japanese population.[40]

Seikyō was established in 1951, with a strong backing from the leftist movement, but it experienced steady growth only from the late 1960s. The fact that it began to offer to their members organically grown produce directly from the farm, at prices lower than those at conventional supermarkets, contributed greatly to its expansion. As mentioned earlier, public concern about food safety and environmental damage steadily increased from the 1970s and Seikyō capitalized on this trend. Its affiliation with the trade union movement and the Japanese Communist Party and the Social Democratic Party (formerly Japan Socialist Party) is also responsible for the fact that many low-income and working-class families do their shopping at Seikyō. The co-op operates through retail outlets and through a group ordering system, the core of which is the *han* (delivery post) composed of several households. Deliveries are made weekly, and consist of a variety of organically grown fresh produce, as well as non-brand-name processed foods that are obtained through direct marketing structures and face-to-face negotiations with organic farmers' groups.[41]

With more than 14 million member households throughout Japan, Seikyō is a major player in the Japanese organic farming movement, greatly influencing the direction in which the movement progresses. However, although the largest, it is merely one out of many similar organizations that operate all over Japan. During the 1990s, for example, more than 900 groups of consumers have established co-partnerships with local organic farmer groups.[42] Such initiatives give farmers an opportunity to become less dependent on the conventional distribution systems of wholesalers, while providing consumers with a reliable source for their food supply. As Moen observes, 'direct-marketing relations give both farmers and consumers the opportunity to establish long-term relations based on trust. Contracting with the same farmers year after year, consumers are able to identify who grew their produce and consumer visits to farms are learning experiences for both consumer and farm families.'[43]

Considering the enormous commercial potential of the organic food market in Japan, it does not seem surprising that the mainstream industry has recently expressed a growing interest in organic farming. One of the pioneers in this respect was the hamburger chain Mos Burger. Since the establishment of its first outlet in 1972, and despite the fierce competition of McDonald's, the enterprise managed to increase its market share steadily: from 50 stores in 1976, to 100 in 1979, 200 in 1983, 500 in 1986, 1000 in 1991 and 1500 in 1998.[44] The story goes that Mos Burger developed its marketing strategy by studying that of McDonald's and then doing the opposite in order to exploit a different market niche – thick French fries instead of thin, stores on side streets and alleys instead of McDonald's main street locations, emphasis on quality instead of McDonald's speed and low price.[45]

Seikyō delivers
groceries in rural
Japan, 2006.

Cutlet-Curry-Rice-Burger – one of the latest additions to Mos Burger's menu, 2006.

モスライスバーガー　カツカレー
（価格：350 円 / 税込）
株式会社モスフードサービス

　　One of the characteristic features of Mos Burger has always been a highly innovative, frequently altered menu. In 1973 the first hit product – soy-sauce-flavoured Teriyaki Burger – was launched, soon turning into a standard item on the menu of all hamburger chains in Japan. Fourteen years later Mos Burger became the talk of the town with the introduction of its Rice Burger, which substituted conventional buns with bun-shaped wedges of pressed rice, an invention inspired by grilled rice balls. Other unusual items on Mos Burger's menu over the years included a hotdog served on *nan* bread with curry sauce and the so-called Japanese Burger Takumi Judan – at first sight a conventional de-luxe hamburger, which combined a meat patty with bacon and fried egg, lettuce, onions and tomatoes, all flavoured with mayonnaise and *miso*-based sauce.[46]

　　Since the late 1990s, partly aiming to distinguish itself from other fast-food chains, Mos Burger has put an increasing emphasis on the quality and safety of its ingredients. Today, all Mos Burger outlets use organically grown vegetables, each outlet displaying detailed information (farmer A in B prefecture) about the origin of lettuce, tomatoes, onions, cabbage, and other vegetables used on a specific day. Moreover, in 2003 Mos Food Services, Inc. entered into the home delivery business with organically grown vegetables that can be ordered online at www.mosbatake.jp.[47] Such examples demonstrate that, along with the mundane activities of Seikyō, organic food is becoming a major trend on the Japanese culinary scene.

　　A rough overview of the transformation of Japanese cuisine during the last half-century indicates that Japanese affluence has developed in many different directions. The 1960s was the period when the mass urban culture of the pre-war era, amalgamated with the experiences of military catering, wartime food shortages and school lunches, turned into a national standard. This was also the time when the pre-war ideal of home cooking was being put into practice in a growing number of Japanese households. The circumstances of economic growth extended pre-war trends to encompass the entire society, whereas before they had been characteristic of a middle-class urban lifestyle. The 1970s and '80s brought new trends, such as electrical household appliances, industrially prepared foods and the phenomenal growth of the dining-out market. In tandem with these developments, growing public concern about food safety and environmental damage generated the rise of organic farming. Concurrent with the embrace of foreign culinary trends, a nostalgic longing for an allegedly more 'authentic' rural life and local produce emerged. Different circuits of Japanese affluence coexist, providing evidence of the extreme complexity and dynamism of the Japanese culinary scene today.

It seems that despite all the changes, food managed to retain its spiritual and religious connotations in Japan, largely due to the prominent role it plays in Shinto and Buddhist rituals.[48] As in other societies, the connection between food and religion remains particularly pronounced on festive occasions, such as the New Year's celebration when a pyramid of pounded rice cakes (*kagamimochi*) is displayed in almost every household, or during the *obon* (autumn equinox) festival when ancestors are worshipped with offers of fruit, vegetables and sake, in addition to the food they favoured when they were alive. Gravestones covered with tangerines and small sake containers are familiar scenes in cemeteries throughout Japan. Food and drink remains, meaningful in daily ritual as well; many householders still

A Shinto 'groundbreaking' ceremony held before a new house is built. Food offerings include fruit, vegetables, sake and *mochi*, 2003.

Home Buddhist altar with offerings of flowers, fruit and two cans of beer, 2003.

offer the day's first bowl of cooked rice to the Buddhist altar (*butsudan*) housing the memorial tablets (*ihai*) of deceased family members.[49] As the illustration above implies, however, even the dead are incapable of escaping the forceful encroachment of the food industry.

Conclusion

The Making of a National Cuisine

During the course of the twentieth century, the daily meals of people of different social and economic status who resided in different parts of Japan grew both more varied and increasingly similar. The patchwork of localized and diverse consumption practices of previous centuries was gradually replaced by a set of foods, practices and tastes with which the majority of Japanese willingly identified. The main objective of this book has been to explain this phenomenal transformation. Each chapter identified the chief processes that were involved in the making of modern Japanese cuisine. Since the shifting of the culinary scene in Japan continues, some attention was also devoted to signalling, although not fully analysing, the most recent phenomena.

Japanese cuisine as it is projected and valued today is a modern construct conceived in the midst of the twentieth-century historical dynamics. Even the term *washoku* ('Japanese cuisine'), nowadays saturated with a sense of timeless continuity and authenticity, is a modern invention. It emerged in the late nineteenth century in response to the growing prominence of foreign cuisines in the Japanese culinary discourse.[1] This by no means implies, however, that Japanese cuisine is a twentieth-century fabrication; that it does not rest upon time-honoured foundations. As this book has demonstrated, the construction of Japanese national cuisine was deeply embedded in the existing environment and relied on knowledge, skills and values that the Japanese people had accumulated over time. Many of the constitutive elements that today stand for culinary 'Japaneseness' are indeed deeply rooted in Japan. They often date back several centuries and are intricately tied to the past of a particular community, class or region. Some of these elements were embraced as national icons relatively unchanged, others were transformed by new technologies, needs and tastes. As with any other cultural constructs, a cuisine is a mixture of old and new, with clear continuity with the past. It is both tenacious and volatile – neither virtually immutable, 'like some slow-moving glacier which only shifts a few metres every year, preserving continuity while changing', nor 'ever reinvented, ever spurious' in its pretence of continuity.[2]

Like the concept of the Japanese nation itself, Japanese cuisine was built on two pillars – 1) a variety of local consumption practices, customs and attitudes; and 2) elements imported from abroad. The following four facets were critical in the demarcation of Japanese national cuisine:

1. the spread of the urban meal pattern based on the 'rice–soup–side dishes' structure, with rice as the staple and soy sauce as the dominant flavouring agent;
2. the construction of a 'traditional' culinary repertoire through the nationwide diffusion of regional dishes, and the proliferation of Edo and Kyoto gastronomy;
3. the gentrification of taste and the extension of aesthetic qualities of *kaiseki* cuisine to all genres of cookery, and its propagation as the epitome of culinary 'Japaneseness';
4. the delineation of the Japanese-Western-Chinese tripod as the normative structure of professional and home cookery in Japan.

Not all the relevant issues could be addressed in this volume. Instead of being comprehensive, I have aimed at demonstrating the most critical processes, paying careful attention to the changing political circumstances that provided a persistent stimulation for dietary change. First, the policies of 'civilization and enlightenment' set the stage for the entire transformation; they inspired adoptions from the West that became building blocks in the creation of modern Japan. Second, the rhetoric of 'rich country, strong army' and 'good wife, wise mother' generated the development of an advanced military catering and prompted the modernization of home cooking. Third, the militarization and economic mobilization of the wartime period facilitated the nationwide proliferation of a standardized cuisine that had developed under the influence of military dieticians and home economics experts. Fourth, imperialist ambitions were critical in outlining Chinese and Korean food as the integral components of modern Japanese cuisine. Finally, post-war economic affluence brought about the gentrification of taste and democratization of diet, which sealed off the construction of a Japanese national cuisine.

Culinary nation-making was by no means peculiar to Japan. The proliferation of the concept of 'national cuisine' is a characteristic feature of the nineteenth and twentieth centuries, clearly a result of the expanding horizon within which people framed their existence. The sense of identity and other cultural values that in the past had developed merely around local life have been during the last two centuries extended to include national and global perspectives.[3] This change obviously finds articulation not only in what we eat, but also in the way we perceive and label food. Today, we tend to describe different types of food by referring to their 'nationality'. However, when talking of French, Italian, Mexican, Brazilian, Chinese, Vietnamese, Lebanese, Eritrean and Ethiopian cuisines, we often take these labels for granted. Unaware of the short-lived origins and borrowed, reinterpreted or simply invented attributes of the food behind them, we tend to project national cuisines as far more time-honoured than they really are.

Individuals came to identify themselves as belonging to a nation relatively recently. Despite an ongoing debate among historians whether the nation is a peculiarly modern social formation or is embedded in history, there is a general consensus that the rise of the nation as the global political norm did not occurr before the nineteenth century. Another point of contention among scholars is the extent to which nations are to be seen as inventions or reconstructions shaped by earlier ethnic sentiments. Members of the 'modernist' school claim that the rise of national consciousness is rooted in modernity; that it can emerge only in a modern, politically and culturally centralized society with a pervasive social mobility and ever increasing equalization of conditions.[4] They argue that even if one might occasionally trace a national consciousness among the elites in agrarian societies, it was always secondary to religious, regional and class loyalties. Quite the opposite is true for modern nationalism, which 'effectively commands men's loyalty, overriding the claims of both lesser communities within it and those which cut across it or potentially enfold it within a still greater society'.[5]

One of the ground-breaking ideas in the scholarship of nationalism was the concept of a nation as an 'imagined community', which proposes that any community larger than a group of people who all know each other is imagined.[6] Once imagined, however, national consciousness is continuously reinforced through the unified 'national culture' manufactured by the state and distributed through its educational and bureaucratic networks. This culture does not function to reinforce and underwrite the hierarchical status system, as was the crucial role of culture in agrarian society, but rather works as the basic social bond: it makes the nation visible for its own members and for those from other nations and societies. It seems as if the members of the nation 'forget' their diverse cultural origins and instead identify themselves with one, all-embracing national culture.[7]

Food constitutes a critical component of national culture and proves particularly powerful in keeping nationhood near the surface of mundane life.[8] This is clearly reflected in the frequency of instances when eating habits have been employed to belittle other nations.[9] According to Anne Murcott, expressing nationality in terms of food is widespread due to 'the malleable, modular nature of national identity and the flexibility and ubiquity of food as a medium of communication'.[10] Because it is a biological necessity, food is impossible to avoid, along with whatever messages it carries. Moreover, a strong attachment between food and memory gives the satisfaction of visceral cravings deep emotional significance.[11] The most salient feature of a national cuisine is bridging regional, ethnic, class and gender differences, creating a cuisine with which entire populations willingly and often ardently identify. Tied to the conceptions of the national history, national cuisine acquires a sense of permanence and authenticity.[12]

Most national cuisines are grounded on the array of foods and practices characteristic of social groups and communities that occupy the nation-state territory. These foods and practices are merged with foreign elements carried by traders, immigrants and aggressors. The national cuisine emerges as a result of negotiation between the local and the foreign, through the 'interaction between practice and performance, domestic and public, high and low'.[13] The timing, pace and the main players involved are determined by the particular circumstances of each locale. In the case of the currently emerging cuisines of independent African states, for example, national governments and the members of African diasporas are playing a leading role. In contrast, the culinary nation-building in post-colonial India was carried on the shoulders of middle-class urban women, and struggles of ethnicity propelled the rise of Mexican national cuisine.[14]

Despite differences between each of these cases, they all substantiate evidence that the making of a national cuisine, although often sustained by the nation-building machine of the state, is not undertaken by a single force, but involves an array of players pursuing their particular goals. Their projects are often linked with one another, but are seldom coordinated. Still, restaurateurs and cooks, entrepreneurs and publishers of cookbooks, educators and dieticians, military caterers and all the others involved in the making of a national cuisine continuously adjust to the changing political scene and the fluctuations of the economy.

Although nation building is intricately connected with the construction of national cuisines, it is not the only factor responsible for the proliferation of the idea commonplace today that every nation has its own cuisine and that every cuisine has a 'nationality'. Culinary globalization has contributed to grounding this perception. It has become less and less obvious today for people in many parts of the world to subsist on foods produced in the immediate vicinity of their residence, as was the case for most human beings until recently. Instead, professional and home cooks all over the world rely increasingly on foodstuffs that have been produced thousands of miles away. Moreover, during the last three decades the diets of the populations of the First World have been transformed through the proliferation of hitherto unknown ingredients, flavours and dishes.[15] By the late twentieth century the appreciation of the exotic and culturally unfamiliar became an equivalent to a claim of social rank and distinction, and 'ethnic cuisines' that derive from outside the European culinary tradition were turned into hallmarks of global metropolises.[16] At first, the food was served at cheap eateries run by immigrants and refugees, and routinely labelled by referring to their homelands.[17] Today, as Sidney Mintz has cunningly phrased, a national cuisine is on its way to becoming a 'tourist artifact'.[18] Driven by commercial interests, restaurant, food and tourist industries time and again reinvent 'national cuisines', largely aided in this task by the media. Not infrequently, they fabricate historical roots and concoct myths that make 'ethnic cuisines' appear more exotic and time-honoured than they are.

This is certainly the case with Japanese cuisine. Cooks, publicists and even scholars inside as well as outside Japan tend to drape Japanese cuisine in an aura of exoticism, uniqueness and traditionalism. They are inclined to attribute the consumption practices of the past with the characteristics of the present. The most persistent tendency seems to be that of cultivating the myth of Japanese cuisine as a refined, time-honoured philosophy and practice, and extending the aesthetic qualities of *kaiseki* into a kind of eternal attribute of every Japanese meal, regardless of class and degree of affluence. Such fetishized, sentimental notions of the past do not merely falsify history but also distort our understanding of the present.

As Susan Terrio observed, 'claims of cultural authenticity in advanced capitalism are often linked to an ideal, aestheticized premodern past as well as the groups, labor forms, and products associated with it'.[19] Perhaps the most obvious motive behind the creation and perpetuation of such nostalgic interpretations of the past is the fact that their appeal to the public generates distinction and profit for those involved in these processes. Examining the strategies and agencies through which the remaking of Japan's culinary past has been deployed so far is a topic that deserves a narrative of its own, but remains outside the scope of this one. The principal aim of this book was to unveil the real story – a fascinating trajectory of the making of a Japanese national cuisine.

Japanese Cuisine Goes Global

Today, Japanese cuisine ranks among the major global culinary genres. During the last two decades, Japanese food has succeeded in penetrating a wide spectrum of the First World's gastronomy – from posh dining to healthy meal to a quick bite, Japanese cuisine is present in practically every niche of the constantly diversifying restaurant market.[1] While classic establishments proudly dish up craftsmanship and tradition for the connoisseurs of exclusive dining, *teppanyaki* steak-houses provide culinary entertainment to those with less privileged taste buds, and sushi and noodle bars – with their informal atmosphere and innovative menus – appeal to young audiences.

As the position of Japanese cuisine shifted from the periphery to the centre of North American and European dining, the dependence on Japanese know-how and ingredients imported from Japan steadily declined. Nowadays, Japanese restaurants that operate in Europe and the United States, except perhaps for the most exclusive establishments, rely largely on local recourses. They are influenced less by Tokyo and more directly by trends in Los Angeles, New York and London, which are the centres for new connections in Japanese cuisine as part of global culture. As this chapter will clarify, Japanese cuisine kept changing in the course of its global journey. Like Japanese cuisine in Japan, Japanese cuisine outside Japan was shaped by a variety of players, from macro-economic and political forces to the individual initiatives of chefs and entrepreneurs, and finally the tastes of the local public. The overseas dispersal of the Japanese – both immigrants and expatriate businessmen – constituted the foundation of the global spread of Japanese cuisine.

The first official dispatch of Japanese overseas contract labourers took place in 1885 – at the time when the construction of a Japanese national cuisine described in this book began. They were hired to work on the sugar plantations of Hawai'i, and were soon followed by thousands of countrymen heading for various destinations in East Asia, North and South America, and Australia.[2] After the turn of the twentieth century, with the rise of the Japanese colonial empire, Japanese communities in Korea, Taiwan, China and Manchuria grew rapidly and hosted the largest concentration of the Japanese overseas population. In 1930 more than a million Japanese resided in Asia, of which half were in Korea. Beyond Asia, however, the United States (including the island of Hawai'i) ranked first in terms of a Japanese resident population. Between 1910 and 1940 the number of Japanese residents in Hawai'i doubled, growing from 70,000 to more than 150,000. The Japanese population in the continental United States reached nearly 130,000, the overwhelming majority being clustered in California.[3]

Grocers and restaurants that provide native food are among the first establishments to emerge within every immigrant community, and Japanese were no exception to this rule. By the end of the nineteenth century, the Japanese quarter named 'Little Tokyo' developed in the Chinatown of Los Angeles, with several restaurants that served native fare. Their number remained stable over the years, except for the 1940s, when, prompted by the outbreak of the Pacific War, the us government ordered Japanese Americans to be evacuated from their place of residence and incarcerated in so-called War Relocation Authority (WRA) camps.[4] By the 1950s, Little Tokyo recovered as the centre of the Japanese-American community in California, still the periphery of American gastronomy. The situation began to change a decade later, when the number of Japanese restaurants in the Los Angeles area rocketed – from 15 in 1965 to 43 in 1970, 88 in 1975, and 173 in 1980.[5]

The sushi boom was born in the hub of the Californian counter-culture, the neo-bohemian youth movement of the Johnson–Nixon years that embraced organic foods and ethnic cuisines.[6] Japan's emergence as a global economic power during the 1970s, however, divorced Japanese cuisine from its association with the counter-culture and differentiated it from other types of ethnic food. The birth of sushi as a sign of class and educational standing was signified by the opening of a sushi bar in the elite sanctum of New York's Harvard Club in 1972.[7]

Within the following two decades, sushi swept the United States in two waves. First, during the 1970s and '80s, it became popular among sophisticated consumers as a sign of class and cosmopolitanism. Gradually, it gained an image of 'yuppie food'; easy familiarity with sushi held con-siderable cachet. The second wave of sushi came during the 1990s, when it ended up in supermarkets and take-away corners next to pizza, burrito, bagel and other hallmarks of contemporary American food culture. What happened? Theodore Bestor explains:

> Three things happened.
>
> One is that the economics of sushi changed. With decreasing demand from connoisseurs for authentic sushi made by skilled Japanese chefs, restaurants found they could lower their costs by hiring non-Japanese chefs. Throughout the 1990s, restaurants serving sushi have relied increasingly on Chinese, Korean, Vietnamese, Burmese, or Mexican staff – in fast-food sushi, consumers still place confidence on chefs with black hair, but seemingly do not care much beyond that. And for the really simple stuff, there are always sushi robots.
>
> At the same time, supermarket chains began to experiment with sales of simple types of sushi, hoping to lure customers with a bit of exotic food that could be easily tasted and tested without any special knowledge, and heavily promoted for its healthiness.
>
> National franchise chains supply supermarkets with raw materials, training, and costumes for employees, many of whom are part-time workers, often Asian students from local universities.
>
> And sushi became an item on the internet. Japan-Grocery.com is only one of half a dozen dot-com businesses that sell basic sushi supplies over the internet, providing people with simple kits for making sushi at home. . . .
>
> An additional factor propelling the second wave was that the innovative potential of sushi was unleashed. Following the path created by the popularity of such things as 'California Roll,' inexpensive sushi bars catering to young people began to experiment wildly with new combinations, reflecting a general popularity of fusion cuisine.[8]

The presence of a Japanese community in California was an important factor in the birth of the Japanese food trend. The Japanese community was indispensable in the initial transfer of skills and knowledge of sushi making, before the army of chef-entrepreneurs, such as Matsuhisa Nobuyuki – the most well-known and internationally celebrated Japanese chef today – began to arrive from Japan during the late 1970s and '80s.

MIYAKE Specials

●1. **Dynamite Hand Roll** 1pc 2.95
   (fish roe, green leaf)
2. **Delicleux Roll** 6pc 3.90
   (eel, tuna, green onion, cucumber)
3. **Jay's Roll** (eel, avocado, cheese, cucumber) 6pc 3.90
4. **Rock'n Roll** (eel, cucumber, avocado) 6pc..... 2.50
5. **Mamamiya Roll** (eel, yellow tail) 6pc ...3.90
6. **Kamikaze Roll** 6pc 2.50
   (yellow tail, tobiko, green onion)
7. **Tazana Roll** 6pc 3.90
   (yellow tail, fish roe, spice sprouts, wild carrot)
8. **Golden Triangle** 2pc 2.15
   (yellow tail, tobiko, mint)
9. **Palm Tree Roll** 4pc (yellow tail, ... 3.90
   fish roe, green onion, spice sprout, wild carrot)
10. **Rainbow Roll** (eel, tuna, white tuna,   6.50
    shrimp, tamago, crab stick, avocado, cucumber) 6pc
●11. **Cat's Roll** 3pc 1.70
    (black mushroom, avocado, cucumber)
12. **Kodomo Roll** (boiled egg, shrimp) 6pc..3.90
13. **Miyake Roll** 2pc 1.20
    (fried yellow tail, prawn carrot)

25. **Chicken Teriyaki Roll** 6pc ....
26. **Beef Teriyaki Roll** 6pc ....
●27. **Spicy Tuna Salad Roll** ....
28. **Tuna Salad Hand Roll** 1pc ....
●29. **Spicy Chicken Hand Roll** 1pc ...
30. **Wakame Hand Roll** (sea weed) 1pc
●31. **Tuna Appetizer** (spicy special sauce) ..
32. **Mussel** 2pc ....
33. **Apple Roll** 6pc ....
    (tuna, crab stick, avocado, cucumber)
34. **IBM Roll** 6pc ....
    (eel, crab stick, avocado, cucumber)
35. **HP Roll** 6pc ....
    (white tuna, crab stick, avocado, cucumber)
36. **Sun Roll** 6pc (salmon, Unagi, Kyuri, Tobiko)
37. **Canadian Roll** 4pc ....
    (salmon skin, salmon roe, green onion)
38. **New York Roll** 6pc ....
    (salmon, avocado, cream cheese)
39. **Hawaiian Roll** 6pc ....
    (avocado, tuna, cucumber, pineapple)
40. **Miami Roll** 6pc ....
    (barbecued tuna salad, avocado, cheese)

'Local' sushi varieties of the restaurant Miyake in Palo Alto, California, 1998.

Nobu, the name by which he is commonly known, opened his first restaurant in Beverly Hills in 1987 and in 2006 operated a total of sixteen establishments located across the United States and in London, Tokyo and Hong Kong.[9]

A strong Japanese community was not the only factor that in the long run conditioned the popularization of Japanese cuisine in the United States. The outbreak of the Pacific War and its aftermath has brought 'Japan' into the lives of every American; millions of American soldiers acquired a first-hand experience of the country and its people. In fact, the first non-Japanese customers of Japanese restaurants managed by Japanese immigrants in the US were former military men who had resided in Japan at the time of its occupation between 1945 and 1952. These individuals, and their family and friends, comprised the hub of the clientele of restaurants such as Tokyo Sukiyaki, which served up to 500 customers daily. The establishment opened in 1954 at Fishermen's Wharf in San Francisco and was set up by Yasuda Shōtarō, who had formerly run a florist shop in Oakland.[10]

Strong economic ties also paved the way for the popularization of Japanese cuisine in the United States. During the 1950s and '60s, in order

Miyako, the oldest Japanese restaurant in New York City, c. 1950s.

to strengthen the Japanese capitalist economy, which provided a bulwark against communism in Asia, the US kept its own market open to Japanese goods and made technology and capital available to Japanese enterprises. Until the 1990s the US remained a chief market for Japanese products. For example, in 1960 the value of Japanese exports to the US was six times larger than that to the countries of the European Union; a decade later it was still nearly five times larger, and by 1990 only double.[11] One of the consequences of the strong economic ties between Japan and the US was a relatively large Japanese expatriate community (on top of the already existing Japanese-American community). The number of Japanese employed overseas tripled during the period 1968–75 (from 130,000 to approximately 450,000), largely due to Japanese enterprises setting up subsidiaries in the US in order to avoid trade frictions.[12] In 2004 more than 35 per cent of nearly a million Japanese who resided abroad for longer than three months lived in the United States.[13] As the Japanese expatriate communities grew in size, Japanese from Japan began to establish travel agencies, beauty parlours, food stores, restaurants and other businesses to cater to their needs.[14] At a later stage, this 'service community' became involved in the popularization of sushi among the local population.

An important factor that familiarized the American public with the idea of dining 'Japanese-style' – in a way preparing Americans for the sushi boom – was the restaurant chain Benihana. In fact, today most

A *teppanyaki* chef
and his audience,
Leiden, 2006.

Benihana restaurants operate a sushi counter. The enterprise was set up in 1964 by Aoki Hiroaki, better known under his Americanized name Rocky Aoki. Rocky came to the United States in order to pursue a wrestling career, but ended up as a successful businessman. In 2006, 98 Benihana restaurants, franchised or company-owned, operate worldwide (78 in the United States) and many more are run by its imitators all over the world.[15]

Benihana was the first *teppanyaki*-style restaurant that opened outside Japan. *Teppanyaki* literally means 'fried on a steel griddle'. It implies a style of dining that allows the customers, who are seated around a large steel griddle plate, to watch meat, shellfish and vegetables being fried in front of their eyes. This style of dining became fashionable in Japan during the 1950s and '60s and its invention is credited to Fujioka Shigetsugu, the founder of the restaurant Misono in Kobe.[16] Shortly after Japan's capitulation in 1945, Fujioka began to run an eatery that specialized in *okonomiyaki* – wheat pancakes fried on a steel griddle with shredded cabbage and other ingredients. *Okonomiyaki* was a meagre fare that did not agree with the taste of the American soldiers who occasionally accompanied their Japanese female escorts to the restaurant. Fujioka came up with the idea of frying beef on the griddle instead of pancakes, which proved an immense success among American customers. The lore goes that Fujioka first fried thin slices of beef, similar to those used in the *sukiyaki* beef stew, and switched to steak-like chunks upon customers' requests.[17]

At first, Misono's clientele was overwhelmingly American. However, when economic growth took off under the stimulation of the Korean War (1950–53), the number of Japanese customers increased. In 1960 Fujioka opened a new location in the centre of Tokyo, which became big hype with the Japanese celebrities. Three years later, Peter Robinson, a Tokyo correspondent for the *Sydney Morning Herald* and the *Financial Times*, observed in *Fodor's Guide to Japan and East Asia* that a new genre of steakhouses had sprung out in the capital of Japan. 'The steak is grilled on a large steel

An old-fashioned *okonomiyaki* establishment in Hiroshima, 2001.

plate in front of you, chopped up into small pieces and then eaten with chopsticks. An interesting experience.'[18]

The Misono steakhouse was soon imitated by other prestigious restaurants, such as Mon Cher Ton Ton in Tokyo, Silk in Yokohama, Kitchen Tonio on the outskirts of Nagoya, Rokuban in Osaka and Candle in Kobe.[19] Newly emerging high-class Tokyo hotels, such as New Otani Hotel and Okura Hotel, also began to furnish *teppanyaki* corners in their restaurants especially to accommodate Westerners. *Teppanyaki* remained exclusive and retained a foreign image. For example, *The New Official Guide: Japan*, published in 1966, placed the original Benihana – the restaurant managed by Rocky Aoki's father – in the rubric 'Western Cuisine, Barbecue'.[20]

An important modification that Rocky implemented when introducing *teppanyaki* in the United States was to wrap this new, essentially un-Japanese restaurant style cleverly in the aura of Japanese tradition. Benihana was basically a steakhouse with a difference – familiar food served in exotic surroundings. The 'exoticism' was provided by the Asian-looking staff in Japanese dress and the interior that replicated a Japanese country inn, constructed out of building materials gathered from old Japanese houses, shipped in pieces to the United States and reassembled.[21] Benihana obviously relied on (somehow refurbished) Japanese ethnicity as far as the restaurant's ambiance was concerned, but the food itself was not much of a stretch from the American meal: steak, *filet mignon*, chicken and shrimp could either be had as entrée items or in combinations, accompanied by bean sprouts, courgettes (zucchini), mushrooms, onions and rice. The marketing strategy of Benihana clearly aimed to dissociate itself from the image of an aesthetically refined cuisine, as Japanese food was projected in the handful of cookbooks that had hitherto been published in the United States and as it was cultivated by restaurants such as Tokyo Sukiyaki. 'No exquisitely carved carrot slices. No wispy vegetables arranged in perfect flower patterns. Instead, solid food in abundance' declared a Benihana's advertisement.[22] An important selling point of the restaurant was the show-like entertainment provided by the flashy knife-swinging and pepper-mill-juggling chefs, cleverly linked in Benihana's advertisements to a 'samurai warrior':

It's a little scary at first.
    There you are sitting around this enormous table (which turns out to also be a grill) when suddenly he appears. A man dressed like a chef but with the unmistakable air of a samurai warrior.

He bows. Just to be on the safe side, you bow back. Smiling inscrutably he takes out a knife. You make a grab for your chopsticks.

He reaches into the cart he's wheeled in. From it he brings out rows of these really beautiful fresh whole shrimps.

Suddenly, the man turns into a kind of whirling dervish. *Zip, zip, zip* . . . his knife flashes through the rows like lightning. The shrimps (now cut into bite-size morsels) seem to dance to the center of the grill. He presses on. With magnificent, sweeping gesture he adds freshly ground pepper to the shrimp. Then butter. Then soy sauce. The action never stops. He even spins around and throws sesame seeds out from over his shoulder.

At last comes the moment of truth. He flips a sizzling shrimp directly on your plate. You taste it. You have a small fit of ecstasy.

Naturally, that's just the first scene. The show goes on this way . . . course after course after course. He performs. You eat. He performs again. You eat again. Steak. Chicken. Mouthwatering vegetables of every variety. You've never had such a feast. You've never seen such choreography.

Finally, it's over. He bows. You sigh. He thanks you. You thank *him*. He walks off. If you weren't so full you'd get up and give him a standing ovation.[23]

The key to the success of the *teppanyaki* formula developed by Rocky Aoki was the culinary entertainment it provided, without really challenging the customers' taste buds. The fact that *teppanyaki* was fashionable in the United States provided an additional spur for its popularity in Europe.

The first *teppanyaki* restaurants began to operate in Europe during the 1970s, before Benihana began to gain international fame. They were set up in Germany by Kikkoman-Daitokai-Europe Ltd – a daughter company of Kikkoman Corporation, a leading Japanese producer of soy sauce. The first venue was opened in Düsseldorf in 1973, soon followed by Munich, Cologne and Berlin.[24] By the 1980s, imitators of Benihana and Daitokai mushroomed, since frying beef on a steel griddle required neither specialist skills nor high investment. In the Netherlands, Chinese restaurateurs eagerly embraced *teppanyaki* in order to deal with the crisis that the Chinese restaurant business was experiencing in the country during the 1980s – the market was saturated, competition tough and profit low.[25] By switching to *teppanyaki*, Chinese entrepreneurs in the Netherlands were able to give their enterprises a financial boost, since the prestige factor of Japanese cuisine meant the possibility of a higher premium.[26] A decade later, with the rise of the sushi boom, many Chinese-owned restaurants throughout Europe were yet again being converted, this time into sushi bars.

In comparison to the United States, the popularization of Japanese cuisine in Europe proceeded quite slowly. The lack of affinity with Japan (which was provided for the Americans by the Pacific War) and a practically non-existent Japanese community were largely responsible for this situation. Since mass migration comparable to that to Hawai'i and the United States has never taken place, before World War Two Europe hosted a very modest Japanese community. In 1930, for example, there was a total of 3,696 Japanese in all of Europe, a double of their number in 1911. In Britain, which ranked first in terms of concentration of Japanese in Europe, the Japanese community never exceeded 2,000.[27] In 1960 merely 800 Japanese were registered with the Japanese Embassy in London.[28]

We may speak of a Japanese community emerging in post-war Europe only since the 1970s, rapidly expanding during the following two decades, when Japanese manufacturing strategies shifted from export orientation to a focus on local production and Japanese direct investment in Europe intensified. The UK remained to host the largest Japanese community in Europe, more than 50,000 by 2004, followed by France (nearly 35,000) Germany (30,000) and much smaller communities in other European countries. Despite this phenomenal growth, the number of Japanese residents in Europe still constitutes less than a half of Japanese residents in the United States.[29]

Similarly to the US, however, restaurants and grocers that catered to Japanese expatriates emerged in the proximity of Japanese residential areas in Europe. The fact that some Japanese housewives residing in Frankfurt and Düsseldorf (nicknamed 'Little Tokyo on the Rhine') are reported to have complained about the lack of experience of living abroad illustrates how successful certain Japanese residential areas in Europe were in recreating the infrastructure of services available in the homeland.[30] The knowledge and experience of people comprising the Japanese 'service community' were critical for the birth of the Japanese food boom in Europe, which achieved its climax around the turn of the millennium. By the mid-1990s, when economic recession compelled several Japanese firms to close their European business and recall their Japanese employees home, Japanese restaurants that had hitherto catered for them gradually turned to the local clientele.

Ōshima Akira is one of the pioneer chefs who headed for Europe in order to provide a 'home away from home' for the resident Japanese and to familiarize Europeans with Japanese cuisine. He left Japan in 1971 as a member of staff of Yamazato, the restaurant situated and run by Hotel Okura Amsterdam. Six years later, Ōshima became executive chef, and has been in charge of Japanese cuisine at the Amsterdam Okura ever since. His loyalty to the Japanese tradition finds a full expression in the culinary creations that are served at Yamazato, in particular the *kaiseki* menu that is altered seasonally.[31]

During the first fifteen years of its operation, Yamazato relied predominantly on Japanese expatriate clientele. Today, the ethnic ratio of the customers has reversed, Japanese tourists and expatriates constituting a minority. In 2002 Ōshima's efforts and creative genius were recognized by the inspectors of the Michelin Red Guide as well – 'his' Yamazato was awarded the renowned Michelin star. The Michelin Red Guide lists the leading selection of hotels and restaurants in Europe. It is particularly well known for its prestigious star-award system for evaluating the quality of the cooking of listed establishments. The guide awards restaurants between one and three stars, and they are coveted. Getting one, or one more, can create a legend; losing one can result in significant heartbreak. In 2002, at the time Yamazato was awarded, the Netherlands counted 54 restaurants with one star, seven with two and one with three. Yamazato is so far the only classic Japanese restaurant in Europe with a Michelin star. Nobu, the hip London restaurant of the chef Matsuhisa Nobuyuki, acquired the star in January 1998. This restaurant, however, serves a contemporary fusion of Japanese and South and North American cooking, and is a world apart from Ōshima's quintessential 'Japaneseness'.

A characteristic feature of the pioneering establishments serving Japanese cuisine in Europe and the United States was the endeavour of the management to recreate a 'Japanese' ambiance in their restaurants. A variety of means were used for this purpose, from Japanese background music and waiters dressed in kimonos, to interiors that evoked associations with Japan, such as red lanterns and bonsai plants.

Quite the opposite attitude emerged in European *kaitenzushi* bars, which began to gain popularity in the mid-1990s. The name *kaitenzushi*, usually translated as 'rotary sushi', refers to a restaurant that serves sushi on a conveyor belt. The system was invented by Shiraishi Yoshiaki (1914–2001), a former sushi chef and the founder of the nationwide *kaitenzushi* chain Genroku Sushi. In 1958 Shiraishi turned his small restaurant in Osaka, catering mainly to workers from nearby factories, into a *kaitenzushi* bar.

The late Hara Yōichi, the owner of the restaurant Yōichi in Amsterdam, 2000.

Advertising poster of the posh sushi bar Zushi in Amsterdam, 2000.

Customers did not order their sushi from the chef, as was the general practice, but chose from a variety of already prepared plates that rotated in front of them on a conveyor belt. The lore goes that Shiraishi got the inspiration for developing this system of serving sushi while watching a beer assembly line at a brewery.[32]

Nigirizushi ('squeezed' or 'hand-moulded' sushi), also referred to as *Edomaezushi* ('sushi from Edo'), is along with sushi rolls (*makizushi*) the most popular type of sushi. In Japan, it became well known and widely consumed beyond the Tokyo area where it originated only during the 1950s. It was a relatively expensive meal; in 1953 one had to pay 100 yen for a portion of sushi, while *soba* noodles could be had for 25–30 yen.[33] Although also available in department store restaurants, sushi was usually consumed at specialist shops (*sushiya*), which were quite costly and required familiarity with the sushi-ordering etiquette, since it had to be ordered directly from the chef. By providing a much cheaper alternative and eliminating the necessity of interaction with the chef, conveyor-belt sushi bars put *nigirizushi* within the reach of anybody. They became nationally known after the Osaka Expo in 1970, but were generally held in low esteem. The customers of Shiraishi's first bar ate standing (*tachigui*), which has negative connotations in Japanese culture.[34] Later, rather uncomfortable bar stools were provided, but generally *kaitenzushi* emanated the aura of a factory canteen. The fact that *kaitenzushi* restaurants made use of

Kaitenzushi restaurant in Osaka, 1989.

robots in sushi making, and that in general the quality of the fish did not match the high standards of the specialist *sushiya*, were also mentioned as arguments to avoid them.

Despite these shortcomings, the number of 'rotary sushi bars' in Japan grew steadily. New establishments mushroomed, while veteran giants such as Genroku Sushi, Genki Sushi and Kura Sushi, with numerous chain stores, ceaselessly expanded. It is estimated that in 2001 between 4,000 and 5,000 such restaurants operated throughout the country.[35] The biggest advantage of *kaitenzushi* was their clear pricing system. The most economical enterprises usually had a fixed price per pair of sushi, regardless of the sort. Others used plates of different colours to indicate the price of different types of sushi. Depending on taste and budget, the customers were able to choose freely from the plates passing by. By the end of the meal, the empty plates were counted and the customer paid at the cashier.

Throughout the 1990s conveyor-belt sushi bars in Japan began to acquire an increasingly positive image; they become much cleaner, more family-oriented and female-friendly than they used to be.[36] Economic recession has significantly contributed to their growing popularity. However, by the end of the decade entirely new types of *kaitenzushi* began to emerge in the fashionable districts of Tokyo.[37] They modelled themselves on European sushi bars. As opposed to the cheap-and-cheerful, get-it-down-you-and-move-on dining experience of the pre-1990s establishments, and the value-for-money character of the new Japanese enterprises, the European bars are stylish and even high class.

The first *kaitenzushi* bar in Europe opened in Paris in 1984, but the rotating bars fad was born a decade later in London. Today, a rotating sushi bar can be found in every European capital and many are operating in large cities.[38] Moreover, most sushi bars throughout Europe imitate the interiors of *kaitenzushi* bars even if they do not have a conveyor belt running. There are two reasons why London became the birthplace of the new trend. First of all, by the 1990s London had become the culinary capital of Europe in terms of dynamics and innovation; it was the place where American trends arrived first and new food fashions emerged. In the case of the European sushi boom, the fact that London hosted the largest Japanese community in Europe was crucial, since it stimulated the growth of an infrastructure and the (human) resources necessary for making and selling sushi. The pioneer of the new trend was Moshi Moshi, which opened in summer 1994 at the Liverpool Street railway station on the eastern edge of central London.[39] It was established by Caroline Bennett, a former bank employee and a graduate of the Japanese Studies Department at the School of Oriental and

The fashionable sushi bar Zushi in Amsterdam, 2000.

African Studies, University of London. During her stay in Japan, she noticed the popularity of *kaitenzushi* and decided to open a similar restaurant at home. She originally aimed at Japanese expatriates as her main business target. However, instead of businessmen in suits, crowds of London yuppies turned up at the Moshi Moshi counter.

Like *teppanyaki*, the London sushi boom was fuelled by its popularity in the United States, by the 1990s already reaching the second wave of its popularization. This popularity in the US boosted the value of sushi for Europeans. In the mid-1990s, however, sushi was still an exclusive food served, for example, at a sushi counter in the Food Halls of Harrods Department Store.[40] Within the next few years, it began to be transformed into a popular snack.

The big change came in 1997 with the arrival of the two hip *kaitenzushi* bars Itsu and Yo!Sushi, with the latter clearly taking the lead. In 2006 twenty-five Yo!Sushi restaurants operated in the UK and seven abroad (two in France, one in Greece, four in the Middle East).[41] The genius of Simon Woodroffe, the founder of Yo!Sushi, was fully recognized by the British business community, which in 1999 voted him the London Entrepreneur of the Year and a year later Group Restaurateur of the Year. Other awards, such as the Retail Interiors' Most Outstanding Retail Experience and Best

Yo!Sushi outlet on the concourse of Paddington Station in London, 2006.

Food and Supermarket Design award, followed. In his earlier career, Woodroffe had been involved in designing and staging rock concerts in London and Los Angeles. In the early 1990s he spearheaded the development of television deals to show huge international rock concerts worldwide, including Elton John and Billy Joel.[42] This background is clearly reflected in the concept of Yo!Sushi – a 'noisy hangout for the trendy Pop generation'. Glass, pine and brushed-steel interior, drinks-totting robots responding to voice commands and the techno-pop background music create an ambiance entirely free from conventional Japanese associations. As Woodroffe accurately observed: 'I don't think we're a Japanese restaurant; we're a Western restaurant that just *happens* to serve Japanese food.'[43] Yo!Sushi and its many imitators throughout Europe do not serve 'classic' Japanese food either. The menu focuses on American standards like California Roll and new British inventions like Asparagus Nigiri and Kamikaze Roll. Most plates that are transported by the conveyor belts in European sushi bars carry food items other than sushi, for example spring rolls, *tenpura*, grilled chicken skewers (*yakitori*), and even sandwiches and local deserts.

Departure from the constraints of Japanese culinary tradition has been, like in the case of Benihana, a conscious choice. Authenticity of cuisine and ethnic appropriateness seem to be the last things that mattered for

Yo!Sushi. Most customers understand so little about Japan that they are unable to recognize the false experience anyway. 'Yo! is meant to feel new and vibrant, to feel the way the British *expect* Japan to feel – young, modern and an itsy bit wacky, but with a hint of a historical connection.'[44] The case of rotating sushi bars implies that the authenticity of the food served is of little significance in Europe for the commercial success of the restaurants marketed as 'Japanese'.

This is also the case with the newest player in the genre of 'Japanese cuisine' in Europe – the noodle bar Wagamama – which has gone beyond the sushi boom and elevated the globalization of Japanese cuisine to a next level. The official Wagamama cookbook published in 1994 declared that

> Wagamama is not supposed to be an authentic Japanese noodle bar. We are not concerned with tradition for its own sake, nor with cultural purity! We believe that to be a good student is not to reproduce the same recipe as one's teacher, but to adapt it, reflecting the essence of our time and making it better by making it for ourselves and in our own way.[45]

Regular Japanese–English dictionaries translate *wagamama* as selfishness, self-indulgence, waywardness. However, many non-Japanese associate the word with the phrase 'positive eating + positive living' coined by the restaurant to stress the health-oriented philosophy of this new dining establishment.[46] The company puts particular stress on the healthy appeal of the food it serves – from freshly squeezed fruit juices and a wide choice of vegetarian alternatives to the ability to cater for customers with food allergies.

Wagamama calls itself a 'noodle canteen' and it certainly looks like one – an open space filled with communal wooden tables and benches (not chairs), with the capacity to sit up to 100–150 customers. It is an original creation of Alan Yau, the son of Cantonese immigrants who had run a Chinese take-away in Norfolk on the eastern coast of England. He has since left the company and gained fame as the creator and manager of the exclusive London restaurant Hakkasan, which is the first Chinese restaurant in Britain to be awarded a Michelin star, and currently counted as one of the most profitable restaurants in London.[47]

The first Wagamama venue opened for business in April 1992 and in April 2006 the enterprise operated 63 restaurants. Most of them are located in the UK (42), followed by Australia (11), the Netherlands (3), Ireland (2), and one each in New Zealand, Belgium, United Arab Emirates, Denmark and Turkey. The greatest challenge for the enterprise is going

ramen : big bowls of noodles in soup

all ramen excluding 28, are served with seasoned chicken and pork stock. they can be served with a vegetarian stock as an option. please ask your server

chicken ramen	€ 9.95
soup and noodles topped with slices of grilled chicken breast, seasonal greens, menma and spring onions	
wagamama ramen	€ 10.95
soup and noodles with half a boiled egg surrounded by seasonal greens, naruto, wakame, prawn, crabstick, chicken slices, fried tofu, menma and spring onions	
seafood ramen	€ 12.25
soup and noodles topped with fresh seafood including prawns, crabstick and squid, garnished with wakame, naruto, menma, seasonal greens and spring onions	
salmon ramen	€ 12.55
spiced miso soup and noodles with a teriyaki-style marinated chargrilled filet of salmon, seasonal greens, menma and spring onions	
chilli beef ramen	€ 13.55
spicy soup and noodles with sliced, chargrilled sirloin steak, fresh chillies, red onion slices, beansprouts, coriander, spring onions and a wedge of lime. the soup base includes vinegar and chilli sauce	
chilli chicken ramen	€ 10.95
same as chilli beef ramen served with grilled chicken instead of sirloin steak	
miso ramen	€ 10.55
spiced miso soup with noodles and stir-fried chicken. carrots, leeks, garlic and beansprouts. garnished with wakame, menma and sesame seeds	
moyashi soba ★	€ 8.25
vegetable soup and noodles with courgettes, snow peas, mushrooms, bean-sprouts, garlic, leeks and tofu. all quickly stir-fried and seasoned before placing on top of wholemeal ramen. garnished with spring onions. historically this ramen dish was mistakenly named soba	

chilli men : noodles in a spicy sauce

chicken chilli men	€ 10.95
stir-fried chicken, green pepper and carrot with a sauce made from fresh chillies, ginger, garlic, onion, lemon grass and red pepper. served with ramen noodles	
ebi chilli men	€ 12.95
stir-fried prawns, green pepper and carrot with a sauce made from fresh chillies, ginger, garlic, onion, lemon grass and red pepper. served with ramen noodles	
yasai chilli men ★	€ 9.95
a vegetarian version with stir-fried courgette, ginger, mushroom, carrot, snow peas, tomato and tofu in the chilli sauce. served with wholemeal noodles	

wagamama statement : genetically modified organisms (GMO)
we have worked with our food suppliers to ensure that genetically modified food stuffs are not used in our restaurants. all food served in wagamama noodle bars is GMO free. we would be happy to outline our due diligence process if you need further reassurance

side dishes : these are not starters but the perfect complement to your meal

duck gyoza	€ 6.50
five deep-fried duck and leek dumplings served with a sweet hoisin sauce	
gyoza ‡	€ 6.30
five chicken dumplings filled with cabbage, chinese leaf, chinese chives and water chestnut served with a chilli, garlic and soy sauce	
yasai gyoza ★ ‡	€ 5.95
five grilled vegetable dumplings filled with cabbage, carrot, water chestnut, onion, celery and chinese leaf. served with a chilli, garlic and soy sauce	
ebi gyoza	€ 6.95
five deep fried dumplings filled with finely chopped, king prawns, water chestnut and spinach. served with a chilli, garlic and soy sauce	
ebi katsu	€ 7.30
five deep-fried king prawns in crispy breadcrumbs, served with lime and a spicy red chilli and garlic sauce	
edamame ★	€ 4.65
freshly steamed green soya beans - lightly salted. the perfect compliment to drinks. hold up to your mouth and squeeze succulent beans from the pod	
negima yakitori	€ 6.85
three skewers of chargrilled chicken and spring onion marinated in a yakitori sauce	
yasai yakitori ★	€ 5.95
three skewers of chargrilled seasonal vegetables dipped in yakitori sauce	
tori kara age	€ 5.95
deep-fried chicken pieces prepared with soy sauce, sake, mirin, dried oregano and fresh ginger marinade. best eaten with soy sauce and seven spice pepper	
raw salad ★	€ 3.90
a combination of seasonal lettuce, red pepper, tomato and cucumber served with the wagamama house dressing	
miso soup and pickles ★	€ 2.00
a light dashi soup flavoured with white miso paste, wakame and spring onion. served with traditional pickles	

kare noodle : noodles in an coconut based soup

kare lomen	€ 10.95
same as chicken kare lomen, garnished with chargrilled king prawns instead of chicken	
chicken kare lomen	€ 10.95
a spicy sauce based dish made from lemon grass, coconut milk, shrimp paste, fresh ginger and galangal, served with ramen noodles. garnished with chargrilled chicken, beansprouts, cucumber and fresh coriander	

teppan : noodles cooked on a hot, flat griddle

yaki soba	€ 9.75
teppan-fried ramen noodles with egg, chicken, shrimps, onions, green and red peppers, beansprouts and spring onions. garnished with sesame seeds, fried shallots and red ginger	
yasai yaki soba ★	€ 8.55
teppan-fried wholemeal noodles with egg, onions, garlic, mushrooms, green and red peppers, beansprouts and spring onion. garnished with sesame seeds, fried shallots, red ginger and served on a vinegar sauce	
yaki udon	€ 10.45
teppan-fried udon noodles with shiitake mushrooms, egg, leeks, prawns, chicken, red pepper, beansprouts and japanese fishcake in curry oil. garnished with spicy ground fish powder. fried shallots on red ginger	
amai udon	€ 10.45
the flavour of this dish is both sweet and sour. udon noodles teppan-fried with egg, fried tofu, prawns, leeks, bean-sprouts, served with crushed peanuts and lime. squeeze the lime juice onto the noodles for extra flavour	

korroke : japanese potato cakes

salmon korroke	€ 9.95
three salmon and potato cakes in a sweet tamarind sauce. served with salad leaves and garnished with wakame and shredded crabstick	
yasai korroke ★	€ 8.95
three potato, green pea, carrot, onion and sweetcorn cakes in a sweet tamarind sauce. served with salad leaves and garnished with wakame and red pepper	

wok : sauce based dishes

zasai beef gohan	€ 11.95
stir-fried beef julienne with garlic, red pepper, shiitake mushrooms, spring onion, babycorn and snow peas, served on japanese-style rice and topped with a chilli shrimp paste	
zasai gohan	€ 9.55
stir-fried chicken, shiitake mushrooms, preserved and pickled vegetables, served on japanese-style rice and topped with a chilli shrimp paste	
chicken tama rice	€ 9.75
chargrilled chicken with an egg, ginger and wine sauce, stir-fried courgettes and shiitake mushrooms. served with japanese-style rice	

rice dishes

chicken katsu curry	€ 10.45
chicken fillet deep-fried in crispy breadcrumbs, served with a curry sauce and japanese-style rice. garnished with a combination of lettuce and red pickles	
yasai katsu curry ★	€ 9.55
slices of sweet potato, aubergine and pumpkin deep-fried in crispy breadcrumbs. served with a curry sauce and japanese-style rice. garnished with a combination of lettuce and red pickles	
cha han	€ 9.95
fried rice with egg, chicken, prawns, snow peas, sweetcorn, mushrooms and spring onion. accompanied by a bowl of vegetable based miso soup and pickles	
yasai cha han ★	€ 8.75
fried rice with egg, snow peas, mushrooms, sweet corn, fried tofu and spring onion. accompanied by a bowl of vegetable based miso soup and pickles	

positive eating

positive meal suggestions for positive value. unfortunately these items cannot be altered. the gyoza will be served grilled unless requested fried

absolute wagamama	€ 14.95
chicken ramen, three chicken gyoza and one kirin beer, asahi or a choice of juice	
pure wagamama ★	€ 13.55
moyashi soba, three yasai gyoza and one kirin beer, asahi or a choice of juice	
complete wagamama	€ 15.95
seafood ramen, three chicken gyoza and one kirin beer, asahi or a choice of juice	

extras

organic rice	€ 2.00
soba noodles	€ 2.55
chillies	€ 1.00
bean-sprouts	€ 2.00
pickles	€ 1.00
wholemeal noodles	€ 2.55
udon noodles	€ 2.55
4 prawns	€ 2.00
zasai chilli shrimp paste	€ 1.00
yakitori sauce	€ 1.00
curry sauce	€ 1.50
4 pieces of fried tofu	€ 1.50

www.wagamama.nl

visit our website www.wagamama.nl for information, locations, news and games. we value your opinion and are receptive to comments and suggestions. either tell the manager or fill out the opinion form online

wagamama

© januari 2005 / wagamama and positive eating + positive living are registered trademarks of wagamama limited

A Wagamama menu, 2005.

to be the recently announced launch of Wagamama's first outlets in the Boston area.[48]

Sleek and minimalist design and an emphasis on brand are the features of Wagamama that were fairly innovative in the early 1990s, and widely used in the strategies of the posh *kaitenzushi* bars that emerged in London a few years after the opening of the first noodle canteen. The concept has been one of the most successful and fashionable restaurant chains in Britain during the last decade, and the chain has been prized as the role model for the fast-food sector. In 2002, for instance, Wagamama won the British Retailers Retailer of the Year Award for Best Concept – a prestigious award voted for by senior executives within the catering and leisure industry. The following year it was awarded the Hamburg Foodservice Award for Achievements in the Industry, an award that honours pioneering concepts or outstanding personalities in professional catering. Zagat Survey announced Wagamama the most popular London restaurant of 2006.[49]

The secret of Wagamama's successes lays in a combination of factors. Trendy and exotic appeal and quick service certainly play a role, but above all the healthy image of the food served and affordable prices are crucial. As the food critic Nick Lander remarked, 'Wagamama has converted thousands of teenagers to the pleasures of eating out and to eating healthily. No other restaurateur has created restaurants where so many will queue for so long, have fun and leave wanting to return.'[50] As well as a wide range of noodle dishes, it serves other hallmarks of Japanese national cuisine (all of them actually recent hybrids), such as *gyōza* dumplings, *chāhan* (fried rice) and breaded cutlet in curry sauce on rice (*katsu karē*). Once Japanese icons of modernity and empire, these dishes are now heavily adjusted to the taste preferences of British consumers by, for example, spicing-up the curry sauce.

Wagamama does not claim to serve Japanese food, but the Japanese names of the dishes are retained. There is a fair chance that an average teenager in Glasgow, Manchester, Birmingham or Brighton is familiar with terms such as *rāmen*, *yakisoba* and *udon*. Easy-on-the-pocket Wagamama is already a phenomenon in Britain. It remains to be seen whether it will conquer the us, where the global journey of Japanese cuisine began.

References

Introduction

1 Michael Ashkenazi and Jeanne Jacob, *The Essence of Japanese Cuisine: An Essay on Food and Culture* (Richmond, Surrey, 2000), pp. 119–34.

2 Okonogi Kaori, ed., *Bessatsu NHK Kyō no ryōri: Dokusha ga eranda 21 seiki ni tsutaetai okazu besuto 100* (Tokyo, 1998).

3 Hiroko Urakami, *Japanese Family-Style Recipes* (Tokyo, New York and London, 1992).

4 Naomichi Ishige, *The History and Culture of Japanese Food* (London, 2001), pp. 115–16.

5 Nobuo Takagi , 'Japanese Abroad: Armed with Slippers and Soy Sauce', *Japan Quarterly*, 35 (1988), pp. 432–36.

6 See, for example, Ashkenazi and Jacob, *The Essence of Japanese Cuisine*, pp. 42–6.

7 See, for example, Tsuda Sōkichi, *Bungaku ni arawaretaru waga kokumin shisō no kenkyū* (Tokyo, 1977); Ishige Naomichi, 'Civilization without Models', in *Japanese Civilization in the Modern World: Life and Society*, ed. T. Umesao, H. Befu and J. Kreiner (Osaka, 1984), pp. 77–86; Kawai Hayao, *Chūkū kōzō Nihon no shinsō* (Tokyo, 1982); Sasaki Kōmei, *Nihon bunka no tajū kōzō* (Tokyo, 1997).

8 Peter N. Dale, *The Myth of Japanese Uniqueness* (New York, 1986), pp. 50–51.

9 See, for example, Christopher Driver, *The British at Table, 1940–1980* (London, 1983); Donna R. Gabaccia, *We Are What We Eat: Ethnic Food and the Making of Americans* (Cambridge, MA, 1998); Anneke van Otterloo, 'Chinese and Indonesian Restaurants and the Taste for Exotic Food in the Netherlands: A Global–Local Trend', in *Asian Food: The Global and the Local*, ed. K. J. Cwiertka with B.C.A. Walraven (Honolulu, HI, 2002), pp. 156–61.

10 These observations are inspired by the abundant literature on dietary globalization. See, for example, Alfred W. Crosby, *The Columbian Exchange: Biological and Cultural Consequences of 1492* (Westport, CT, 1972); Alan Davidson, *Food in Motion: The Migration of Foodstuffs and Cookery Techniques* (Leeds, 1983); Sidney W. Mintz, *Sweetness and Power: The Place of Sugar in Modern History* (New York, 1985); Henry Hobhouse, *Seeds of Change: Five Plants that Transformed Mankind*

(New York, 1986); Raymond Grew, ed., *Food in Global History* (Boulder, CO, 1999); Katarzyna J. Cwiertka with Boudewijn C. A. Walraven, eds, *Asian Food: The Global and the Local* (Honolulu, HI, 2002).

11 See, for example, Joseph J. Tobin, *Re-Made in Japan: Everyday Life and Consumer Taste in a Changing Society* (New Haven, CT, and London, 1992); John Clammer, *Contemporary Urban Japan: A Sociology of Consumption* (Oxford and Malden, MA, 1997); Michael Ashkenazi and John Clammer, eds, *Consumption and Material Culture in Contemporary Japan* (London and New York, 2000).

12 Emiko Ohnuki-Tierney, *Rice as Self: Japanese Identities through Time* (Princeton, NJ, 1993).

13 Theodore C. Bestor, *Tsukiji: The Fish Market at the Center of the World* (Berkeley, CA, 2004), p. 150.

14 Warren Belasco, 'Food and the Counterculture: A Story of Bread and Politics', in *Food in Global History*, ed. R. Grew (Boulder, CO, 1999), p. 276.

15 Jack Goody, *Cooking, Cuisine and Class: A Study in Comparative Sociology* (Cambridge, 1982), pp. 97–153.

16 Priscilla Parkhurst Ferguson, *Accounting for Taste: The Triumph of French Cuisine* (Chicago, IL, and London, 2004), pp. 3, 19.

17 Sidney W. Mintz, 'Eating Communities: The Mixed Appeals of Sodality', in *Eating Culture: The Poetics and Politics of Food Today*, ed. T. Döring, M. Heide and S. Mühleisen (Heidelberg, 2003), p. 27.

18 Sidney W. Mintz, *Tasting Food, Tasting Freedom: Excursions into Eating, Culture and the Past* (Boston, MA, 1996), p. 96.

19 Elizabeth Rozin, 'The Structure of Cuisine', in *Psychobiology of Human Food Selection*, ed. L.M. Barker (Westport, CT, 1982), pp. 189–203; Mary Douglas and Michael Nicod, 'Taking the Biscuit: The Structure of British Meals', *New Society*, 19 (1974), pp. 744–9; Peter Farb and George Armelagos, *Consuming Passions: The Anthropology of Eating* (Boston, MA, 1980), pp. 185–90.

20 Benedict Anderson, *Imagined Communities: Reflection on the Origin and Spread of Nationalism* (London, 1991).

One: Western Food, Politics and Fashion

1 Muraoka Minoru, *Nihonjin to seiyō shoku* (Tokyo, 1984), p. 174.

2 Takashi Fujitani, *Splendid Monarchy: Power and Pageantry in Modern Japan* (Berkeley, CA, 1996), pp. 32–42.

3 Ōhama Tetsuya and Yoshihara Ken'ichirō, *Edo, Tōkyō nenpyō* (Tokyo, 1993), pp. 154–6.

4 William W. Kelly, 'Incendiary Actions: Fires and Firefighting in the Shogun's Capital and the People's City', in *Edo and Paris: Urban Life and the State in the Early Modern Era*, ed. J. L. McClain, J. J. Merriman and Ugawa K. (Ithaca, NY, and London, 1994), pp. 310–13.

5 M. William Steele, *Alternative Narratives in Modern Japanese History* (London, 2003), pp. 120–21.

6 Ōhama and Yoshihara, *Edo, Tōkyō nenpyō*, pp. 156–9.
7 Steele, *Alternative Narratives*, pp. 116–18
8 Ibid., pp. 111, 126.
9 Fujitani, *Splendid Monarchy*, pp. 1–28.
10 For more details concerning the historical background, see Andrew Gordon, *A Modern History of Japan: From Tokugawa Times to the Present* (New York and Oxford, 2003).
11 See, Henry D. Smith II, 'Five Myths About Early Modern Japan', in *Asia in Western and World History: A Guide for Teaching*, ed. A. Embree and C. Gluck (Armonk, NY, 1997), pp. 520–21; Ronald P. Toby, *State and Diplomacy in Early Modern Japan: Asia in the Development of the Tokugawa Bakufu* (Princeton, NJ, 1984), pp. 3–22.
12 Gordon, *A Modern History of Japan*, pp. 46–59.
13 Peter Duus, *The Abacus and the Sword: The Japanese Penetration of Korea, 1895–1910* (Berkeley, CA, 1995), p. 3.
14 Harada Nobuo, *Konomi to hanbāgā: Nihon shokuseikatsushi no kokoromi* (Tokyo, 1995), p. 206.
15 Julia Meech-Pekarik, *The World of the Meiji Print: Impressions of a New Civilization* (New York and Tokyo, 1986), p. 65.
16 Ibid., pp. 133, 178.
17 Mary Crawford Fraser, *A Diplomat's Wife in Japan: Sketches at the Turn of the Century* (New York and Tokyo, 1982), p. 336.
18 Hugh Cortazzi, *Victorians in Japan: In and Around the Treaty Ports* (London and Atlantic Highlands, NJ, 1987), p. 135.
19 Selçuk Esenbel, 'The Anguish of Civilized Behaviour: The Use of Western Cultural Forms in the Everyday Lives of the Meiji Japanese and the Ottoman Turks during the Nineteenth Century', *Japan Review*, 5 (1994), pp. 145–85.
20 Fujitani, *Splendid Monarchy*, pp. 19–21.
21 Noguchi Hokugen, 'Shokumotsu chōri ron', *Fūzoku gahō*, 1 (1880), pp. 13–15.
22 Takie Sugiyama Lebra, *Above the Clouds: Status Culture of the Modern Japanese Nobility* (Berkeley, CA, 1993), pp. 187–9.
23 Fraser, *A Diplomat's Wife in Japan*, pp. 20–21.
24 Kumakura Isao, 'Kaisetsu (2)', in *Nihon kindai shisō taikei 23: Fūzoku, sei*, ed. Ogi S., Kumakura I. and Ueno C. (Tokyo, 1990), p. 483.
25 Ulf Hannerz, *Transnational Connections: Culture, People, Places* (London and New York, 1996), p. 24
26 Donald Keene, *Emperor of Japan: Meiji and his World, 1852–1912* (New York, 2002), pp. 194–213.
27 Fujitani, *Splendid Monarchy*, p. 4.
28 Harada Nobuo, *Rekishi no naka no kome to niku* (Tokyo, 2005), p. 22.
29 Naomichi Ishige, 'Japan', in *The Cambridge World History of Food*, ed. K. F. Kiple and K. C. Ornelas (Cambridge, 2000), vol. II, pp. 1176–82.
30 Naomichi Ishige, *The History and Culture of Japanese Food* (London, 2001), pp. 53–5. See also Harada, *Rekishi no naka no kome to niku*, pp. 72–95.

31 Okada Akio, 'Bunmei kaika to shokumotsu', in *Nihon no shokubunka 8: Ibunka to no sesshoku to juyō*, ed. Haga N. and Ishikawa H. (Tokyo, 1997), p. 57.

32 Ishige, *History and Culture of Japanese Food*, p. 55.

33 Ishikawa Hiroko, 'Nihon ni okeru sesshō kinrei to nikushoku no kihan', *Vesta*, 24 (1996), pp. 21–2.

34 Susan Hanley, *Everyday Things in Premodern Japan: The Hidden Legacy of Material Culture* (Berkeley, CA, 1997), pp. 65–6.

35 Harada, *Rekishi no naka no kome to niku*, pp. 146–7.

36 Michael Cooper, ed. and trans., *This Island of Japon: João Rodrigues' Account of 16th-century Japan* (Tokyo and New York, 1973), pp. 237–8.

37 Kumakura Isao, 'Enkyo to shite no shokutaku', in *Gendai Nihon bunka ni okeru dentō to hen'yō: Shōwa no sesōshi*, ed. Ishige N. (Tokyo, 1993), pp. 37–8.

38 Michael Cooper, ed., *They Came to Japan: An Anthology of European Reports on Japan, 1543–1640* (Berkeley, CA, 1965), p. 285.

39 Matsushita Michiko, *Zusetsu Edo ryōri jiten* (Tokyo, 1996), pp. 3–4.

40 Watanabe Minoru, *Nihon shokuseikatsu shi* (Tokyo, 1986), p. 53.

41 Okada, 'Bunmei kaika to shokumotsu', pp. 36–8.

42 Ishikawa, 'Nihon ni okeru sesshō kinrei to nikushoku no kihan', p. 25.

43 Nihon Fūzoku Gakkai, ed., *Zusetsu Edo jidai shokuseikatsu jiten* (Tokyo, 1989), p. 28

44 Eiichi Kiyooka, trans., *The Autobiography of Yukichi Fukuzawa* (New York and London, 1966), pp. 58–9.

45 Nihon Fūzoku Gakkai, *Zusetsu Edo ryōri jiten*, p. 379.

46 Emiko Ohnuki-Tierney, 'We Eat Each Other's Food to Nourish Our Body: The Global and the Local as Mutually Constituent Forces', in *Food in Global History*, ed. R. Grew (Boulder, CO, 1999), p. 252.

47 Ibid., pp. 252–4; Majima Ayu, 'Nikushoku to iu kindai: Meijiki Nihon ni okeru shokuniku gunji juyō to nikushokukan no tokuchō', *Ajia bunka kenkyū*, 11 (2002), pp. 214–15.

48 David Burton, *The Raj at Table* (London and Boston, MA, 1993); David Burton, *French Colonial Cookery: A Cook's Tour of the French Speaking World* (London, 2000); J.A.G. Roberts, *China to Chinatown: Chinese Food in the West* (London, 2002), pp. 66–70.

49 Harvey A. Levenstein, *Revolution at the Table: The Transformation of the American Diet* (New York and Oxford, 1988), pp. 4, 21; John Burnett, *Plenty and Want: A Social History of Food in England from 1815 to the Present Day* (London, 1989), p. 69; C. Anne Wilson, ed., *Eating with the Victorians* (Stroud, 2004).

50 Kusama Shunrō, *Yokohama yōshoku bunka kotohajime* (Tokyo, 1999), pp. 106–7; Okada, 'Bunmei kaika to shokomutso', pp. 51–6.

51 Wada Kunihei et al., ed., *Nihon no shokuseikatsu zenshū 28: Kikigaki Hyōgo no shokuji* (Tokyo, 1992), p. 28.

52 Ann Yonemura, *Yokohama: Prints from Nineteenth-century Japan* (Washington, DC, 1990).

53 Ishige, *The History and Culture of Japanese Food*, p. 150.

54 John Mertz, *Novel Japanese: Spaces of Nationhood in Early Meiji Narrative, 1870–1888* (Ann Arbor, MI, 2003), p. 4.

55 Donald Keene, ed., *Modern Japanese Literature: An Anthology* (New York, 1956), p. 32.

56 Watanabe Zenjirō, *Kyōdai toshi Edo ga washoku o tsukutta* (Tokyo, 1988), p. 190.

57 Ishige, *The History and Culture of Japanese Food*, p. 151; Ogi Shinzō et al., eds, *Edo, Tōkyō gaku jiten* (Tokyo, 1987), p. 502.

58 Majima, 'Nikushoku to iu kindai', p. 218.

59 Mark R. Finlay, 'Early Marketing of the Theory of Nutrition: The Science and Culture of Liebig's Extract of Meat', in *The Science and Culture of Nutrition*, ed. H. Kamminga and A. Cunningham (Amsterdam and Atlanta, GA, 1995), pp. 50–51.

60 Majima, 'Nikushoku to iu kindai', pp. 215–17.

61 Finlay, 'Early Marketing of the Theory of Nutrition', p. 48.

62 Gordon, *A Modern History of Japan*, pp. 78–9.

Two: The Road to Multicultural Gastronomy

1   James E. Hoare, *Japan's Treaty Ports and Foreign Settlements: The Uninvited Guests, 1858–1899* (Sandgate, 1994), pp. 6–7.

2   Hugh Cortazzi with I. Nish, P. Lowe and J. E. Hoare, eds, *British Envoys in Japan, 1859–1972* (Folkestone, 2004), pp. 9–52.

3   Hoare, *Japan's Treaty Ports and Foreign Settlements*, pp. 21–3.

4   James E. Hoare, *Embassies in the East: The Story of the British Embassies in Japan, China and Korea from 1859 to the Present* (Richmond, Surrey, 1999), p. 7.

5   Hoare, *Japan's Treaty Ports and Foreign Settlements*, p. 5. See also Susan Schoenbauer Thurin, *Victorian Travellers and the Opening of China, 1842–1907* (Athens, OH, 1999).

6   J.A.G. Roberts, *China to Chinatown: Chinese Food in the West* (London, 2002), pp. 66–70.

7   Basil Hall Chamberlain and W. B. Mason, *A Handbook for Travellers in Japan* (London, 1891), p. 10.

8   Major Henry Knollys, *Sketches of Life in Japan* (London, 1887), pp. 119–20.

9   Isabella L. Bird, *Unbeaten Tracks in Japan: An Account of Travels in the Interior, Including Visits to the Aborigines of Yezo and the Shrine of Nikko* (Rutland, VT, 1973), p. 19.

10 Roberts, *China to Chinatown*, p. 75.

11 Mario Emilio Cosenza, ed., *The Complete Journal of Townsend Harris: First American Consul and Minister to Japan* (Rutland, VT, and Tokyo, 1959), p. 377.

12 Ibid., p. 391.

13 Nagasaki Foreign Settlement Research Group, *Nagasaki: People, Places and Scenes of the Nagasaki Foreign Settlement 1859 to 1941*, www.nfs.nias.ac.jp (accessed 25 October 2005).

14 Kusama Shunrō, *Yokohama yōshoku bunka kotohajime* (Tokyo, 1999), pp. 183–7, 194.

15 Gregory Houston Bowden, *British Gastronomy: The Rise of Great Restaurants* (London, 1975); Beat Kümin, 'Eating Out Before the Restaurant: Dining Cultures in Early-Modern Inns', in *Eating Out in Europe: Picnics, Gourmet Dining and Snacks since the Late Eighteenth Century*, ed. M. Jacobs and P. Scholliers (Oxford and New York, 2003), pp. 71–87; John Burnett, *England Eats Out: A Social History of Eating Out in England from 1830 to the Present* (Harlow, 2004), pp. 70–79.

16 Hugh Cortazzi, *Victorians in Japan: In and Around the Treaty Ports* (London and Atlantic Highlands, NJ, 1987), pp. 166–7.

17 Kusama, *Yokohama yōshoku bunka kotohajime*, pp. 182, 187.

18 Nagasaki Foreign Settlement Research Group, *Nagasaki*.

19 Sakurai Miyoko, 'Meiji kōki no toshi no shokuseikatsu: Jōryū kaisō no shufu no nikki o chūshin ni', *Tōkyō kaseigakuin daigaku kiyō*, 36 (1996), pp. 25–34.

20 Cortazzi, *Victorians in Japan*, p. 119.

21 For a more elaborate account on the subject, see Harada Nobuo, *Edo no ryōri shi* (Tokyo, 1989), and Harada Nobuo, 'Edo no tabemonoya: Furiuri kara ryōri chaya e', in *Rakugo ni miru shoku bunka*, ed. Tabi no Bunka Kenkyūjo (Tokyo, 2000), pp. 105–27. A good account on pre-modern Japanese restaurant culture in English is provided by Naomichi Ishige, *The History and Culture of Japanese Food* (London, 2001), pp. 117–28, and Matsunosuke Nishiyama, *Edo Culture: Daily Life and Diversions in Urban Japan, 1600–1868* (Honolulu, HI, 1997), pp. 164–78.

22 Harada, *Edo no ryōri shi*, pp. 104–31.

23 Nihon Fūzokushi Gakkai, ed., *Zusetsu Edo jidai shokuseikatsu jiten* (Tokyo, 1989), pp. 216–17, 244, 279–80; Nishiyama Matsunosuke et al., eds, *Edogaku jiten* (Tokyo, 1984), pp. 257–67.

24 Etchū Tetsuya, 'Tēburu no shoku: Nagasaki o chūshin to shita nanban, kara, akahige no shoku', in *Gairai no shoku no bunka*, ed. Kumakura I. and Ishige N. (Tokyo, 1988), pp. 103–18; Tanaka Seiichi, *Ichii taisui: Chūgoku ryōri denrai shi* (Tokyo, 1987), pp. 138–42.

25 Kusama Shunrō, 'Seiyō no shokubunka juyō no katei to kyōiku: Meiji shoki no Yokohama mainichi shinbun no yakuwari', in *Nihon no shokubunka 8: Ibunka to no sesshoku to juyō*, ed. Haga N. and Ishikawa H. (Tokyo, 1997), p. 142.

26 Chamberlain and Mason, *A Handbook for Travellers in Japan*, pp. 4–7.

27 Yō Maenobō, *Meiji seiyō ryōri kigen* (Tokyo, 2000), p. 23.

28 Ibid., pp. 24–31.

29 Henry D. Smith II, 'The Edo–Tokyo Transition: In Search of Common Ground', in *Japan in Transition from Tokugawa to Meiji*, ed. M. B. Jansen and G. Rozman (Princeton, NJ, 1986), p. 354.

30 Stephen Mennell, *All Manners of Food: Eating and Taste in England and France from the Middle Ages to the Present* (Oxford, 1985), pp. 134–5.

31 Maenobō, *Meiji seiyō ryōri kigen*, pp. 88–9.

32 Shūkan Asahi, ed., *Meiji, Taishō, Shōwa nedan no fūzoku shi* (Tokyo, 1987), vol. I, pp. 11, 23, 35, 47, 121, 125, 157.

33 Maenobō, *Meiji seiyō ryōri kigen*, p. 85.

34 Sakurai, 'Meiji kōki no toshi no shokuseikatsu', p. 30; Maenobō, *Meiji seiyō ryōri*

kigen, pp. 74, 80.

35   Basil H. Chamberlain, *Japanese Things: Being Notes on Various Subjects Connected with Japan* (1904) (Tokyo, 1971), p. 181.

36   Taitō Kuritsu Shitamachi Fūzoku Shiryōkan, ed., *Rōjin ga tsuzuru Shitaya, Asakusa no Meiji, Taishō, Shōwa, daisankan* (Tokyo, 1988), vol. II, pp. 57–9.

37   Eliza Ruhamah Scidmore, *Westward to the Far East: A Guide to the Principal Cities of China and Japan with a Note on Korea* (n. p., 1894), p. 24.

38   Mennell, *All Manners of Food*, p. 206.

39   Tetsuka Kaneko, 'Seiyō ryōrihō', *Joshi daigaku kasei kōgi*, I/I (1911), pp. 1–2.

40   Maenobō, *Meiji seiyō ryōri kigen*, pp. 90–97.

41   Ben Rogers, *Beef and Liberty: Roast Beef, John Bull and the English Nation* (London, 2003), pp. 170–72; See also C. Anne Wilson, ed., *Eating with the Victorians* (Stroud, 2004).

42   Ishige, *The History and Culture of Japanese Food*, p. 155.

43   Maenobō, *Meiji seiyō ryōri kigen*, pp. 49–50.

44   Ishige, *The History and Culture of Japanese Food*, p. 155.

45   Brian Moeran, 'The Birth of the Japanese department Store', in *Asian Department Stores*, ed. K. L. MacPherson (Richmond, Surrey, 1998), pp. 141–76.

46   Kerrie L. MacPherson, 'Introduction: Asia's Universal Providers', in *Asian Department Stores*, pp. 1–33.

47   Hatsuda Tōru, *Hyakkaten no tanjō* (Tokyo, 1993), p. 118.

48   Clerk Tono, *Shokudō nisshi* (unpublished manuscript, 1933).

49   Hatsuda, *Hyakkaten no tanjō*, p. 121.

50   Watanabe Zenjirō, *Kyōdai toshi Edo ga washoku o tsukutta* (Tokyo, 1988), p. 222.

51   Shūkan Asahi, *Meiji, Taishō, Shōwa nedan no fūzoku shi*, vol. I, pp. 11, 23, 35, 47, 121, 125, 157.

52   Watanabe, *Kyōdai toshi Edo ga washaku o tsukutta*, pp. 221–4.

53   Kabushiki Gaisha Meidi-ya, *Meidi-ya hyakunen shi* (Tokyo, 1987), pp. 114–18.

54   Moeran, 'The Birth of the Japanese Department Store', p. 163.

55   Hatsuda, *Hyakkaten no tanjō*, p. 173.

56   For more information on *ekiben*, see Paul Noguchi, 'Savor Slowly: *Ekiben* – the Fast Food of High-Speed Japan', *Ethnology*, XXXIII/4 (1994), pp. 317–30.

Three: Strengthening the Military

1   Hugh Cortazzi, *Victorians in Japan: In and Around the Treaty Ports* (London and Atlantic Highlands, NJ, 1987), p. 76.

2   Aoba Takashi, *Yasai no Nihon shi* (Tokyo, 1991), pp. 189–200.

3   Kagome Hachijūnen Shi Hensan Iinkai, ed., *Kagome hachijūnen shi* (Nagoya, 1978), pp. 102–8.

4   Aoba, *Yasai no Nihon shi*, pp. 201–16.

5   Ōzawa Ichimori, *Chōki keizai tōkei VIII: Bukka* (Tokyo, 1973), p. 78.

6   'Yasai futsū sōba hyō' *Katei shūhō*, 77 (1906), p. 3.

7   Bruce F. Johnston with Mosaburo Hosoda and Yoshio Kusumi, *Japanese Food*

Management in World War II (Stanford, CA, 1953), p. 27.

8   Ogi Shinzō et al., eds, *Edo, Tōkyō gaku jiten* (Tokyo, 1987), p. 502; Aoba, *Yasai no Nihon shi*, pp. 213–16.

9   Andrew Gordon, *A Modern History of Japan: From Tokugawa Times to the Present* (New York and Oxford, 2003), pp. 66–76; See also Gotaro Ogawa, *The Conscription System in Japan* (New York, 1921), pp. 3–69.

10 Fukuda Kenji, *Kanie Ichitarō: Tomato kakō no senkusha* (Tokyo, 1974), pp. 18–32; Gordon, *A Modern History of Japan*, p. 95

11 Ibid., pp. 34–64, 73–117.

12 Ibid., pp. 151–5; Kagome Hachijūnen Shi Hensan Iinkai, ed., *Kagome hachijūnen shi* (Nagoya, 1978), p. 154.

13 Nihon Kanzume Kyōkai, *Kanzume raberu hakubutsukan* (Osaka, 2002), p. 2.

14 Yamanaka Shirō, *Nihon kanzume shi* (Tokyo, 1962), vol. I, pp. 62–7, 83–4; Fumiko Fujita, *American Pioneers and the Japanese Frontier: American Experts in Nineteenth-Century Japan* (Westport, CT, 1994), pp. 15–41; Bekkai-chō Kyōdo Shiryōkan, *Kaitakushi Bekkai kanzumejo* (Bekkai, 2004), www.betsukai.gr.jp/homepage/yakuba/510_kyoudo/kanzume (accessed 30 October 2005).

15 Shōwa Joshi Daigaku Shokumotsugaku Kenkyūshitsu, *Kindai Nihon shokumotsu shi* (Tokyo, 1971), p. 65.

16 Yamanaka, *Nihon kanzume shi*, pp. 657–71.

17 Katarzyna J. Cwiertka, 'From Yokohama to Amsterdam: Meidi-ya and Dietary Change in Modern Japan', in *Japanstudien 12: Essen und Ernährung im Modernen Japan*, ed. N. Liscutin and R. Haak (Munich, 2000), pp. 45–63.

18 R. W. Pilcher et al., ed., *The Canned Food Reference Manual* (New York, 1943), pp. 25–32; Jack Goody, *Cooking, Cuisine and Class: A Study in Comparative Sociology* (Cambridge, 1982), pp. 154–61; Mark William Wilde, 'Industrialization of Food Processing in the United States, 1860–1960' (PhD thesis, University of Delaware, 1988), pp. 1–27; Martin Bruegel, 'How the French Learned to Eat Canned Food, 1809–1930s', in *Food Nations: Selling Taste in Consumer Societies*, ed. W. Belasco and P. Scranton (New York and London, 2002), pp. 113–30.

19 Simon Naylor, 'Spacing the Can: Empire, Modernity and the Globalisation of Food', *Environment and Planning*, A, 32 (2000), pp. 1625–39; J.A.G. Roberts, *China to Chinatown: Chinese Food in the West* (London, 2002), pp. 69–70, 86; Richard R. Wilk, 'Food and Nationalism: The Origins of "Belizean Food"', in *Food Nations: Selling Taste in Consumer Societies*, ed. W. Belasco and P. Scranton (New York and London, 2002), pp. 71–5.

20 Mark R. Finlay, 'Early Marketing of the Theory of Nutrition: The Science and Culture of Liebig's Extract of Meat', in *The Science and Culture of Nutrition*, ed. H. Kamminga and A. Cunningham (Amsterdam and Atlanta, GA, 1995), p. 49.

21 Ōhama Tetsuya, *Meiji no bohyō: Shomin no mita nisshin, nichiro sensō* (Tokyo, 1990), pp. 26–8; Carl Mosk, *Making Health Work: Human Growth in Modern Japan* (Berkeley, CA, 1996), p. 54.

22 Adel P. den Hartog, 'Modern Nutritional Problems and Historical Nutrition Research, with Special Reference to the Netherlands', in *European Food History:*

A Research Review, ed. H. J. Teuteberg (London, 1992), p. 59; Mosk, *Making Health Work*, p. 19.

23 Major Henry Knollys, *Sketches of Life in Japan* (London, 1887), p. 243.

24 Fujita Masao, 'Senjō no shoku: Nichiro sensō ni okeru Nihon rikugun no ryōmatsu taikei', in *Tatakai no shosō to isan*, ed. Gunjishi Gakkai (Tokyo, 2005), p. 52; Yasuhara Miho, 'Nihon ni okeru shoku no kindaika ni kan suru kenkyū: Shōwa senzenki no shokuji no naiyō bunseki o chūshin to shite' (PhD thesis, Nara Women's University, 2004), p. 54.

25 Mosk, *Making Health Work*, p. 36.

26 Nakajima Tsuneo, ed., *Gendai Nihon sangyō hattatsu shi 18: Shokuhin* (Tokyo, 1967), pp. 399, 403; Fujita, 'Senjō no shoku', pp. 47–8.

27 Yasuhara Miho, '"Heishoku" no kindaika to sono hensen: Shokuryō kakuho, shokumotsu chishiki, chōri gijutsu o chūshin ni', in *Kindai no 'heishoku' to Ujina rikugun ryōmatsu shishō*, ed. Hiroshimashi Kyōdo Shiryōkan (Hiroshima, 2003), p. 13.

28 Richard John Bowring, *Mori Ōgai and the Modernization of Japanese Culture* (Cambridge, 1979), p. 13.

29 D. Eleanor Westney, 'The Military', in *Japan in Transition from Tokugawa to Meiji*, ed. M. B. Jansen and G. Rozman (Princeton, NJ, 1986), p. 176.

30 Yamashita Teruo, 'Shūdan kyūshoku katei e no eikyō: Hensen kara "tsukuru" o kangaeru', in *Shoku no bunka III: Chōri to tabemono*, ed. Sugita K. (Tokyo, 1999), p. 406.

31 Yamashita Teruo, 'Toshika to ryōshoku', in *Toshika to shoku*, ed. Takada M. and Ishige N. (Tokyo, 1995), pp. 124–9. Under the New Currency Regulation of 1871 a centralized monetary system was introduced in Japan, establishing yen as the basic unit of currency; 100 sen constituted 1 yen, and 1 rin was one tenth of a *sen*. The use of *shu*, *zeni* and other units that had been used during the pre-modern period was soon discontinued.

32 Ehara Ayako, 'Nichijō no shokuzai to ryōri', in *Rakugo ni miru Edo no shokubunka*, ed. Tabi no Bunka Kenkyūjo (Tokyo, 2000), p. 37; Ehara Ayako, 'Kindaika no ugoki to shokuseikatsu', in *Kingendai no shokubunka*, ed. Ishikawa H. and Ehara A. (Kawasaki, 2002), p. 28.

33 Knollys, *Sketches of Life in Japan*, p. 252.

34 Shunsaku Nishikawa, 'Grain Consumption: The Case of Chōshū', in *Japan in Transition from Tokugawa to Meiji*, ed. M. B. Jansen and G. Rozman (Princeton, NJ, 1986), p. 422.

35 Susan Hanley, *Everyday Things in Premodern Japan: The Hidden Legacy of Material Culture* (Berkeley, CA, 1997), pp. 78–9.

36 Ehara, 'Nichijō no shokuzai to ryōri', pp. 26–7; Ehara, 'Kindaika no ugoki to shokuseikatsu', pp. 26–9.

37 Emiko Ohnuki-Tierney, *Rice as Self: Japanese Identities through Time* (Princeton, NJ, 1993), pp. 36–40.

38 Matsunosuke Nishiyama, *Edo Culture: Daily Life and Diversions in Urban Japan, 1600–1868* (Honolulu, HI, 1997), p. 160.

39 Hanley, *Everyday Things in Premodern Japan*, pp. 159–64.
40 Simon Partner, *Toshié: A Story of Village Life in Twentieth Century Japan* (Berkeley, CA, 2004), p. 13.
41 Hanley, *Everyday Things in Premodern Japan*, pp. 163–4; Ehara, 'Nichijō no shokuzai', pp. 38–46.
42 Ehara, 'Kindaika no ugoki to shokuseikatsu', p. 26.
43 Naomichi Ishige, *The History and Culture of Japanese Food* (London, 2001), pp. 117–22; Nishiyama, *Edo Culture*, pp. 160–61. See also Akira Oshima, Patrick Faas and Katarzyna Cwiertka, *Kaiseki Cuisine: Hotel Okura Amsterdam* (Bruges, 2003).
44 Hagiwara Hiromichi, *Nihon eiyōgaku shi* (Tokyo, 1960), p. 16.
45 Hanley, *Everyday Things in Premodern Japan*, p. 79.
46 Sema Takashi, *Nihon kaigun shokuseikatsu shiwa* (Tokyo, 1985), pp. 15, 76–7; Kikuchi M., 'Kaigun heishoku ni tsuite', in *Ryōyū*, V/5 (1930), p. 24.
47 James R. Bartholomew, *The Formation of Science in Japan: Building a Research Tradition* (New Haven, CT, and London, 1989), pp. 78–9.
48 Sema, *Nihon kaigun shokuseikatsu shiwa*, pp.16–22.
49 Ibid., pp. 61–5, 76–7, 80.
50 Marui Eiji, 'Mori Ōgai ni miru shoku no shisō to sono konnichiteki igi', *Vesta*, 25 (1996), p. 63.
51 Hagiwara, *Nihon eiyōgaku shi*, pp. 23–5.
52 Yamashita, 'Toshika to ryōshoku', pp. 124–9; Sema, *Nihon kaigun shokuseikatsu shiwa*, pp. 15, 76–7; Fujita Masao, 'Heishi no shokutaku o sayū shita makanairyō', in *Teikoku rikugun senjō no ishokujū* (Tokyo, 2002), p. 137.
53 Fujiwara Akira, *Uejini shita eireitachi* (Tokyo, 2001), p. 3.
54 Stewart Lone, *Army, Empire and Politics in Meiji Japan* (Basingstoke, 2000), p. 16.
55 Yasuhara, '"Heishoku" no kindaika to sono hensen', p. 11.
56 Ishimoto Masaki, 'Rikugun ni okeru ryōmatsu chōtatsu, hokyū kikan', in *Kindai no 'heishoku' to Ujina rikugun ryōmatsu shishō*, ed. Hiroshimashi Kyōdo Shiryōkan (Hiroshima, 2003), p. 26; Kawai Masahiro, *Rikugun Ryōmatsushō*, unpublished research report, History Research Department, Japan Self-Defence Forces, pp. 4–9.
57 Ishimoto, 'Rikugun ni okeru ryōmatsu chōtatsu, hokyū kikan', p. 26.
58 Kikuchi, 'Kaigun heishoku ni tsuite', pp. 24–5.
59 Akiyama Teruko, 'Nisshin, nichiro sensō to shokuseikatsu', in *Kingendai no shokubunka*, ed. Ishikawa H. and Ehara A. (Kawasaki, 2002), p. 66.
60 Kaigunshō Kyōikukyoku, *Kaigun shukeihei chōrijutsu kyōkasho* (n.p., 1918), pp. 1–2.
61 'Odaidokoro gunkan', *Asahigurafu*, XXIII/11 (1937).
62 Sema, *Nihon kaigun shokuseikatsu shiwa*, pp. 61–2; Yamashita, 'Shūdan kyūshoku katei e no eikyō', p. 409.
63 Kaigun Shukeika, *Kenkyū kondateshū* (n. p., 1936).
64 Yamashita, 'Toshika to ryōshoku', p. 128.
65 David C. Evans and Mark R. Peattie, *Kaigun: Strategy, Tactics and Technology in the Imperial Japanese Navy, 1887–1941* (Annapolis, MD, 1997), p. 402; Yano Tsuneta

Kinenkai, ed., *Sūji de miru Nihon no 100 nen: 20 seiki ga wakaru dētā bukku* (Tokyo, 2000), p. 561.

66 Ōhama, *Meiji no bohyō*, p. 65.

67 Fujita, 'Senjō no shoku', p. 39.

68 Ibid., p. 49.

69 Yoshida Yutaka, *Nihon no guntai: Heishitachi no kindai shi* (Tokyo, 2002), p. 37.

70 Akiyama, 'Nisshin, nichiro sensō to shokuseikatsu', p. 66.

71 Yasuhara, '"Heishoku" no kindaika to sono hensen', p. 12.

72 Anonymous, *Guntai ryōrihō* (Tokyo, 1910), p. 1.

73 Yasuhara, *Nihon ni okeru shoku no kindaika ni kan suru kenkyū*, pp. 58–70.

74 Ishiguro Tadanori, 'Rikugun sōsetsu jidai no heishoku', *Ryōyū*, 1/9 (1926), pp. 68–71.

75 Yasuhara, '"Heishoku" no kindaika to sono hensen', p. 13.

76 Ogawa, *The Conscription System in Japan*, p. 212.

77 M. Olson Jr, *The Economics of the Wartime Shortage: A History of British Food Supplies in the Napoleonic War and in World Wars I and II* (Durham, NC, 1963); Mikuláš Teich, 'Science and Food during the Great War: Britain and Germany', in *The Science and Culture of Nutrition*, ed. H. Kamminga and A. Cunningham (Amsterdam and Atlanta, GA, 1995), pp. 213–34.

78 Yasuhara, *Nihon ni okeru shoku no kindaika ni kan suru kenkyū*, pp. 58–73.

79 Egawa Tsuneo, 'Rikugun no ryōshoku', in *Gendai shokuryō taikan*, ed. Ryōyūkai (Tokyo, 1929), p. 565.

80 Rikugun Ryōmatsu Honshō, 'Dai nikai guntai chōri kōshū kiji', *Ryōyū*, III/4 (1928), pp. 80–93.

81 Yasuhara, '"Heishoku" no kindaika to sono hensen', p. 15.

82 'Kakushidan kabō hoheitai ni okeru shō ninen ichigatsu kondate jisshi kaisū tōkei-hyō', unpublished manuscript, date unknown, Ajinomoto Foundation for Dietary Culture Library, Tokyo, pp. 139–46.

83 Ishige, *The History and Culture of Japanese Food*, pp. 114–15.

84 Hayashi Reiko and Masatoshi Amano, eds, *Nihon no aji: Shōyu no rekishi.* (Tokyo, 2005), pp. 146–9, 183; Nagatsuma Hiroshi, 'Kindai shōyu jōzōgyō to nōson', in *Shōyu jōzō gyōshi no kenkyū*, ed. Hayashi R. (Tokyo, 1990), pp. 430–32. See also William Shurtleff and Akiko Aoyagi, 'History of Soy Sauce, Shoyu and Tamari: A Special Report on the History of Traditional Fermented Soyfoods', in *History of Soybeans and Soyfoods: 1100 BC to the 1980s* (Lafayette, CA, 2004), www.thesoydaily.com/SFC/Fsoyfoods426.asp (accessed 10 January 2006).

85 W. Mark Fruin, *Kikkoman: Company, Clan and Community* (Cambridge, MA, 1983), pp. 72–5. See also William Shurtleff and Akiko Aoyagi, 'History of Soy Sauce, Shoyu and Tamari: A Special Report on the History of Traditional Fermented Soyfoods', in *History of Soybeans and Soyfoods*, www.thesoydaily.com/SFC/Fsoyfoods425.asp (accessed 10 January 2006).

86 Fruin, *Kikkoman*, p. 261.

87 Yamashita, 'Toshika to ryōshoku', p. 129; Egawa, 'Rikugun no ryōshoku', p. 565.

88 Konoe hohei daiichi rentai suiji bu, 'Heitai san no yorokobu heiei ryōri', *Shufu no*

tomo, XX/5 (1936), p. 508.

89 Kawashima Shirō, *Jippei 50 nin o motteseru gun'yō ryōshoku no eiyō jintai jikken no kenkyū* (Tokyo, 1980), p. 64.

90 Rikugun Ryōmatsu Honshō, *Shōwa nananen chōri kōshū haifu shorui*, unpublished manuscript, Ajinomoto Foundation for Dietary Culture Library, Tokyo, dated 1932, pp. 102–6.

91 Yoshida, *Nihon no guntai*, pp. 40, 109.

92 Sidney W. Mintz, *Tasting Food, Tasting Freedom: Excursions into Eating, Culture and the Past* (Boston, MA, 1996), pp. 25–8.

93 Yoshida, *Hihon no guntai*, p. 110.

Four: Reforming Home Meals

1 Kathleen S. Uno, 'One Day at a Time: Work and Domestic Activities of Urban Lower-class Women in Early Twentieth-century Japan', in *Japanese Women Working*, ed. J. Hunter (London, 1993), p. 53; Ochiai Emiko, *The Japanese Family System in Transition: A Sociological Analysis of Family Change in Postwar Japan* (Tokyo, 1994), p. 35; Jordan Sand, *House and Home in Modern Japan: Architecture, Domestic Space and Bourgeois Culture, 1880–1930* (Cambridge, MA, 2003), p. 372. See also Ronald P. Dore, *City Life in Japan: A Study of a Tokyo Ward* (London, 1958), Ezra F. Vogel, *Japan's New Middle Class: The Salary Man and His Family in a Tokyo Suburb* (Berkeley, CA, 1963), and Anne E. Imamura, *Urban Japanese Housewives: At Home and in the Community* (Honolulu, HI, 1987).

2 Bryan S. Turner, 'The Discourse of Diet', *Theory, Culture & Society*, 1 (1982), pp. 23–32.

3 Sand, *House and Home in Modern Japan*, p. 54.

4 Ibid., pp. 22–33.

5 Ibid., pp. 9–12; Minami Hiroshi, *Taishō bunka* (Tokyo, 1965), pp. 183–95.

6 David R. Ambaras, 'Social Knowledge, Cultural Capital and the New Middle Class in Japan, 1895–1912', *Journal of Japanese Studies*, XXIV/1(1998), p. 30.

7 Sakai Toshihiko, *Katei no shin fūmi* (Tokyo, 1901), quoted in Ambaras, 'Social Knowledge, Cultural Capital and the New Middle Class in Japan', p. 29.

8 Kathleen S. Uno, *Passages to Modernity: Motherhood, Childhood and Social Reform in Early Twentieth Century Japan* (Honolulu, HI, 1999), p. 5; Sand, *House and Home in Modern Japan*, p. 55; See also Kathleen S. Uno, 'The Death of "Good Wife, Wise Mother"?', in *Postwar Japan as History*, ed. A. Gordon (Berkeley, CA, 1993), pp. 293–322.

9 Kathleen S. Uno, 'Women and Changes in the Household Division of Labor', in *Recreating Japanese Women, 1600–1945*, ed. G. L. Bernstein (Berkeley, CA, 1991), pp. 26–35; Yasuko Tabata, 'Women's Work and Status in the Changing Medieval Economy', in *Women and Class in Japanese History*, ed. H. Tonomura, A. Walthall and H. Wakita (Ann Arbor, MI, 1999), pp. 99–118; Harald Fuess, 'A Golden Age of Fatherhood? Parent–Child Relations in Japanese Historiography', *Monumenta Nipponica*, LII/3 (1997), pp. 381–7; Sand, *House and Home in Modern*

Japan,, pp. 65, 93.

10 Sand, *House and Home in Modern Japan*, p. 61.

11 Ibid., pp. 62–3.

12 Chapter 2 in Sand's volume provides a comprehensive description of the house-wife and her laboratory; ibid., pp. 55–94.

13 Ueno Chizuko, 'Kaisetsu (3)', in *Nihon kindai shisō taikei 23: Fūzoku, sei*, ed. Ogi S., Kumakura I. and Ueno C. (Tokyo, 1990), p. 507.

14 Sonoda Hidehiro, ' Tomo o shitau kokoro no bunretsu', in *Gendai Nihon bunka ni okeru dentō to hen'yō: Shōwa no sesōshi*, ed. Ishige N. (Tokyo, 1993), pp. 229–42.

15 Sand, *House and Home in Modern Japan*, pp. 33–4.

16 Okumura Shigejirō, *Katei wayō ryōrihō* (Tokyo, 1905).

17 Sand, *House and Home in Modern Japan*, p. 36.

18 Ishige Naomichi and Inoue Tadashi, eds, 'Gendai Nihon ni okeru katei to shoku-taku: Meimeizen kara chabudai e', *Kokuritsu minzokugaku hakubutsukan kenkyū hōkoku*, XVI (1991), pp. 3–51.

19 Ehara Ayako, 'Katei ryōri no hatten', in *Kingendai no shokubunka*, ed. Ishikawa H. and Ehara A. (Kawasaki, 2002), p. 102.

20 Sand, *House and Home in Modern Japan*, p. 66; Matsunosuke Nishiyama, *Edo Culture: Daily Life and Diversions in Urban Japan, 1600–1868* (Honolulu, HI, 1997), pp. 161–2; 'Shogei ichiryū: Ima no meijin', *Yomiuri shinbun*, 25–6 September 1903.

21 Ehara Ayako, 'Nichijō no shokuzai to ryōri', in *Rakugo ni miru Edo no shokubunka*, ed. Tabi no Bunka Kenkyūjo (Tokyo, 2000), pp. 38–46.

22 'Shokumotsu no kairyō', *Fujin zasshi*, 5 (1916), p. 53.

23 Akabori Ryōri Gakuen, *Ryōri kyōiku hachijūnen no ayumi* (Tokyo, 1963). See also Katarzyna Cwiertka, 'Minekichi Akabori and his Role in the Development of Modern Japanese Cuisine', in *Cooks and Other People: Proceedings of the Oxford Symposium on Food and Cookery, 1995*, ed. H. Walker (Devon, 1996), pp. 68–80.

24 Ehara Ayako, *Kōtō jogakkō ni okeru shokumotsu kyōiku no keisei to tenkai* (Tokyo, 1998), p. 8.

25 Ibid., p. 266.

26 Sand, *House and Home in Modern Japan*, p. 164.

27 Ehara, *Kōtō jogakkō ni okeru shokumotsu kyōiku no keisei to tenkai*, pp. 356–7.

28 Ōhama Tetsuya, *Ōe Sumi sensei* (Tokyo, 1978), p. 213.

29 Sand, *House and Home in Modern Japan*, p. 14.

30 Kimura Ryōko, 'Fujin zasshi no jōhō kūkan to josei taishū dokushasō no seiritsu', *Shisō*, 2 (1992), pp. 231–52; See also Katarzyna Cwiertka, 'How Cooking Became a Hobby: Changes in Attitude toward Cooking in Early Twentieth Century Japan', in *The Culture of Japan as Seen through its Leisure*, ed. S. Linhart and S. Frühstück (Albany, NY, 1998), pp. 53–4.

31 Anne Murcott, 'Modes of Eating the Other: On the Analytic Utility of "Culinary Tourism"', unpublished manuscript.

32 Stephen Mennell, *All Manners of Food: Eating and Taste in England and France from the Middle Ages to the Present* (Oxford, 1985), p. 233.

33 Ehara, 'Katei ryōri no hatten', pp. 97–100.

34 Katarzyna Cwiertka, 'Wayō setchū ryōri no chōri bunkashiteki kōsatsu', in *21 seiki no chōrigaku I: Chōri bunka gaku*, ed. Ōtsuka S. and Kawabata A. (Tokyo, 1996), pp. 68–76.

35 'Kondate ni tsukite no chūi', *Katei shūhō*, 4 (1904), p. 2.

36 Sand, *House and Home in Modern Japan*, p. 63.

37 Alan Warde, 'Eating Globally: Cultural Flows and the Spread of Ethnic Restaurants', in *The Ends of Globalization: Bringing Society Back In*, ed. D. Kalb et al. (Lanham, MD, 2000), p. 306.

38 'Our Weekly Menu and Cookery Chat', *Home Chat*, XII/151 (1898), pp. 369–71.

39 Sasaki Sachiko, 'Nihon ryōrihō: Nichiyōbi no kondate', *Joshi daigaku kasei kōgi*, i/1 (1911), pp. 1–2.

40 Nihon Joshi Daigakkō Ōfūkai Ryōri Kenkyūbu, *Nihon joshi daigaku kōgi XIV: Ryōri* (Tokyo, 1909), pp. 1–4.

41 Kumakura Isao, 'Enkyo to shite no shokutaku', in *Gendai Nihon bunka ni okeru dentō to hen'yō: Shōwa no sesōshi*, ed. Ishige N. (Tokyo, 1993), pp. 29–30.

42 Sand, *House and Home in Modern Japan*, p. 163.

43 'Wagaya de jiman no osōzai', *Shufu no tomo*, V/8, 11, 12 (1921), V/11, 2, 5, 9, 12 (1922), VII/2–6 (1923). See also Cwiertka, 'How Cooking Became a Hobby', pp. 53–4.

44 Mizumachida Tsuruko, 'Keizaiteki na isshūkanbun no sōzai ryōri', *Shufu no tomo*, IV/7 (1920), p. 174.

45 'Jūgatsu no oryōri', *Fujin zasshi*, 4 (1915), p. 103.

46 'Natsumuki no wagaya no jiman ryōri', *Shufu no tomo*, V/8 (1921), pp. 186–7.

47 'Jūichigatsu no kondate', *Katei shūhō*, 12 (1904), p. 4.

48 'Bareisho ryōri', *Katei shūhō*, 150 (1908), p. 2.

49 Akabori Minekichi, Akabori Kikuko and Akabori Michiko, *Katei nichiyō ryōri, ge* (Tokyo, 1911), pp. 62–3.

50 'Jōshoku kenkyū: jagaimo no ryōri', *Katei shūhō*, 410 (1917), p. 4.

51 Akabori, *Katei nichiyō ryōri*, pp. 92–3.

52 Ōfūkai Ryōri Kenkyūbu, *Nihon joshi daigaku*, p. 180. In this recipe, onion substitutes for *daikon* radish from the recipe for radish *furofuki* which was a well-known winter dish. Other tubers were also cooked this way.

53 'Sōmen no seiyō ryōri', *Katei shūhō*, 115 (1908), p. 3.

54 Ōishi Rokutei, 'Shin'an ryōri sūhin', *Katei zasshi*, IV/4 (1906), p. 26.

55 Noguchi Hokugen, 'Shokumotsu chōri ron', *Fūzoku gahō*, 1 (1880), pp. 13–15.

56 Yoshimura Chizu, *Jitchi ōyō kaji kyōkasho* (Tokyo, 1919), p. 22.

57 Sand, *House and Home in Modern Japan*, pp. 50–51; Kumakura Isao, 'Chanoyu no taishūka', in *Chanoyu bunkashi* (Tokyo, 1995), pp. 126–41.

58 Kumakura Isao, *Nihon ryōri bunkashi: Kaiseki o chūshin ni* (Tokyo, 2002), p. 19.

59 Kumakura Isao, 'Sen no Rikyū: Inquiries into his Life and Tea', in *Tea in Japan: Essays on the History of Chanoyu*, ed. P. Varley and Kumakura I. (Honolulu, HI, 1989), pp. 57–8.

60 Kumakura, *Nihon ryōri bunkashi*, p. 20.

61 Kumakura Isao, 'Tea and Japan's Culinary Revolution', *Japan Echo*, XXVI/2 (1999), p. 43.

62 Murai Yasuhiko 'The Development of *Chanoyu*: Before Rikyū', in *Tea in Japan: Essays on the History of Chanoyu*, ed. P. Varley and Kumakura I. (Honolulu, HI, 1989), p. 28.

63 Kumakura, *Nihon ryōri bunkashi*, p. 20. For more details about restaurant *kaiseki*, see also Akira Oshima, Patrick Faas and Katarzyna Cwiertka, *Kaiseki Cuisine: Hotel Okura Amsterdam* (Bruges, 2003).

64 Kumakura, *Nihon ryōri bunkashi*, pp. 18–19. See also Kumakura, 'Sen no Rikyū', p. 56, and Kumakura Isao, 'Ryōri, chanoyu, fūryū: Yuki Teiichikou no sekai', in *Kitchō Yuki Teiichi no yume*, ed. Yuki Bijutsukan (Tokyo, 2002), pp. 72–3.

65 Okumura Ayao, 'Ryōriya no ryōri: Kindai o chūchin to shite', in *Washoku to Nihon bunka: Nihon ryōri no shakai shi*, ed. Takada Masatoshi (Tokyo, 2004), pp. 76–9. For more details about the life and work of Yuki Teiichi, see Suehiro Yukiyo, 'Yuki Teiichi no shōgai', in *Kitchō Yuki Teiichi no yume*, ed. Yuki Bijutsukan (Tokyo, 2002), pp. 170–273.

66 A typical example of this is the introduction to Elisabeth Andoh's *Washoku: Recipes from the Japanese Home Kitchen* (Berkeley, CA, and Toronto, 2005), pp. 1–6.

67 Yamao Mika, *Kyō mo ryōri: Oryōri bangumi to shufu kattō no rekishi* (Tokyo, 2004), pp. 92–163.

68 Kumakura, 'Enkyo to shite no shokutaku', pp. 44–5. See also Inoue Tadashi, 'Chanoma bunka ron', in *'Katei' to iu fūkei: Shakai shinri shi nōto* (Tokyo, 1988), pp. 147–65.

69 Masako Ishii-Kuntz, 'Are Japanese Families "Fatherless"?', *Sociology and Social Research*, LXXVI/3 (1992), pp. 105–10; Masako Ishii-Kuntz, 'Balancing Fatherhood and Work: Emergence of Diverse Masculinities in Contemporary Japan', in *Men and Masculinities in Contemporary Japan: Dislocating the Salaryman Doxa*, ed. J. E. Roberson and N. Suzuki (London and New York, 1992), pp. 199–201.

70 Ishikawa Naoko, 'Kōdo keizai seichōki ga umidashita shoku jijō', in *Kingendai no shokubunka*, ed. Ishikawa H. and Ehara A. (Kawasaki, 2002), p. 170.

71 Seikatsu Jōhō Sentā, ed., *Shokuseikatsu dēta sōgō tōkei nenpō* (Tokyo, 2003), p. 303.

72 Iwamura Nobuko, *Kawaru kazoku, kawaru shokutaku: Shinjitsu ni hakai sareru maaketingu jōshiki* (Tokyo, 2003).

73 T.J.M. Holden, '"And Now for the Main (Dis)course . . . ," or: Food as Entrée in Contemporary Japanese Television', *M/C: A Journal of Media and Culture*, II/7 (1999), www.uq.edu.au/mc/9910/entree.php (accessed 10 February 2006).

Five: Wartime Mobilization and Food Rationing

1 Roger Chickering and Stig Förster, 'Are we There Yet? World War II and the Theory of Total War', in *A World at Total War: Global Conflict and the Politics of Destruction, 1937–1947*, ed. R. Chickering et al. (Cambridge, 2005), pp. 1–16.

2 Quoted in Richard J. Smethurst, *A Social Basis for Prewar Japanese Militarism:*

The Army and the Rural Community (Berkeley, CA, 1974), p. 25.

3 Andrew Gordon, *A Modern History of Japan: From Tokugawa Times to the Present* (New York and Oxford, 2003), pp. 212–17.

4 Bruce F. Johnston with Mosaburo Hosoda and Yoshio Kusumi, *Japanese Food Management in World War II* (Stanford, CA, 1953), pp. 165–85; Erich Pauer, 'Neighbourhood Associations and Food Distribution in Japanese Cities in World War II , in *Agriculture and Food Supply in the Second World War*, ed. B. Martin and A. S. Milward (Ostfildern, 1985), p. 220.

5 Ruth F. Benedict, *The Chrysanthemum and the Sword: Patterns of Japanese Culture* (New York, 1967), p. 182. See also Sonia Ryang, 'Chrysanthemum's Strange Life: Ruth Benedict in Postwar Japan', *Asian Anthropology*, I/1 (2002), pp. 87–116.

6 Kosuge Keiko, *Kindai Nihon shokubunka nenpyō* (Tokyo, 1997), pp. 169, 178.

7 Ishikawa Naoko, 'Dainiji sekai taisen to kibishii shokuseikatsu', in *Kingendai no shokubunka*, ed. Ishikawa H. and Ehara A. (Kawasaki, 2002), p. 138.

8 Hagiwara Hiromichi, *Nihon eiyōgaku shi* (Tokyo, 1960), p. 155.

9 Sheldon Garon, *Molding Japanese Minds: The State in Everyday Life* (Princeton, NJ, 1997), pp. 3–22. See also Sabine Frühstück, *Colonizing Sex: Sexology and Social Control in Modern Japan* (Berkeley, CA, 2003).

10 Bryan S. Turner, 'The Discourse of Diet', *Theory, Culture & Society*, I (1982), p. 23.

11 John Coveney, *Food, Morals and Meaning: The Pleasure and Anxiety of Eating* (London and New York, 2000), pp. 26–7, 89. See also Michel Foucault, 'Governmentality', in *The Foucault Effect: Studies in Governmentality*, ed. G. Burchel, C. Gordon and P. Miller (Sydney, 1991), pp. 87–104.

12 E. N. Todhunter, 'Chronology of Some Events in the Development and Application of the Science of Nutrition', *Nutrition Reviews*, XXXIV/12 (1976), pp. 353–65.

13 Mikuláš Teich, 'Science and Food during the Great War: Britain and Germany', *The Science and Culture of Nutrition, 1840–1940*, ed. H. Kamminga, H. Cunningham and A. Cunningham (Amsterdam and Atlanta, GA, 1995), pp. 213–34; See also David F. Smith, ed., *Nutrition in Britain: Science, Scientists and Politics in the Twentieth Century* (London, 1997).

14 Lothar Burchardt, 'The Impact of the War Economy on the Civilian Population of Germany during the First and Second World War', in *The German Military in the Age of Total War*, ed. W. Deist (Oxford and New York, 1985), pp. 40–70; Belinda J. Davis, *Home Fires Burning: Food, Politics, and Everyday Life in World War I Berlin* (Chapel Hill, NC, 2000).

15 Harm Beukers et al., eds, *Red-Hair Medicine: Dutch–Japanese Medical Relations* (Amsterdam and Atlanta, GA, 1991); Sumio Ishida, 'The Utrecht Training College for Military Surgeons and the Introduction of its System to Japan', *Journal of the Japan-Netherlands Institute*, I (1989), pp. 39–57.

16 Hagiwara, *Nihon eiyōgaku shi*, pp. 279–80.

17 Shimazono Norio, *Eiyōgaku shi* (Tokyo, 1978), p. 146.

18 Toyokawa Hiroyuki and Kaneko Shun, *Nihon kindai no shokuji chōsa shiryō: Daiikkan, Meiji hen* (Tokyo, 1988), p. 22.

19 Imada Setsuko, 'Dainiji sekai taisen to kibishii shokuseikatsu', in *Kingendai no shokubunka*, ed. Ishikawa H. and Ehara A. (Kawasaki, 2002), p. 109.

20 Mark W. Weatherall, 'The Foundation and Early Years of the Dunn Nutritional Laboratory', in *Nutrition in Britain: Science, Scientists and Politics in the Twentieth Century*, ed. D. F. Smith (London, 1997), pp. 30–35; Annemarie De Knecht-van Eekelen, 'De doos van Pandora: Het Vitaminen-Laboratorium', *Gewina*, XIX/1 (1996), pp. 43–5.

21 The Imperial Government Institute for Nutrition, *A Brief Outline of The Imperial Government Institute for Nutrition* (Tokyo, 1924), pp. 6–14.

22 Saiki Yoshiko, *Eiyōgakusha Saiki Tadasu den* (Tokyo, 1986), pp. 20–27.

23 The Imperial Government Institute for Nutrition, *A Brief Outline*, p. 2; The Imperial Government Institute for Nutrition, *The Imperial Government Institute for Nutrition and Nutrition Experts* (Tokyo, 1935), p. 3; Hagiwara, *Nihon eiyōgaku shi*, p. 288.

24 Morikawa Kiku, *Nihongo eiyō: Sono naritachi to goi* (Tokyo, 1975), p. 54.

25 Yasuhara Miho, 'Nihon ni okeru shoku no kindaika ni kan suru kenkyū: Shōwa senzenki no shokuji no naiyō bunseki o chūshin to shite' (PhD thesis, Nara Women's University, 2004), p. 81.

26 Shimazono, *Eiyōgaku shi*, pp. 169–72; Hagiwara, *Nihon eiyōgaku shi*, pp. 79–81.

27 'Zaidan hōjin Ryōyūkai shokuryō gakkō Shōwa 16 nendo seito bōshū', *Ryōyū*, XVI/2 (1941).

28 Yasuhara, *Nihon ni okeru shoku no kindaika ni kan suru kenkyū*, pp. 78–103.

29 Kisara Shūsuke, ' Bisuketto', in *Shōwa no shokuhin sangyō shi*, ed. Nihon Shokuryō Shinbunsha (Tokyo, 1990), pp. 581–3.

30 *Asahigurafu*, XXXI/15 (1938), back cover.

31 *Asahigurafu*, XXXII/10 (1939), back cover.

32 Ann Waswo, *Modern Japanese Society, 1868–1994* (Oxford, 1996), pp. 88–9. See also Smethurst, *A Social Basis for Prewar Japanese Militarism*.

33 'Shin shūzōhin ten', exhibition at Edo Tokyo Museum, 16 August–21 September 2002: blog.mag2.com/m/log/0000081891/75526437?page=2 (accessed 30 March 2005). See also www.city.kawasaki.jp/28/28kikaku/home/isan/lb/lb0520.htm (accessed 11 January 2006).

34 Shimokawa Kōshi and Katei Sōgō Kenkyūkai, ed., *Shōwa, heisei kateishi nenpyō, 1926–1995* (Tokyo, 1997), p. 121.

35 Imada, 'Dainiji sekai taisen', p. 139.

36 Johnston with Hosoda and Kusumi, *Japanese Food Management in World War II*, p. 152.

37 Ibid., pp. 198–201; Pauer, 'Neighbourhood Associations', pp. 226–7.

38 Simon Partner, *Toshié: A Story of Village Life in Twentieth Century Japan* (Berkeley, CA, 2004), p. 85.

39 Nihon Shokuryō Shinbunsha, ed., *Gendai shokuhin sangyō jiten* (Tokyo, 1987), p. 89.

40 'Daiyōshoku kenshō kyōgikai', *Kaihō*, 10 (1940), pp. 39–55.

41 Johnston with Hosoda and Kusumi, *Japanese Food Management in World War II*, pp. 154, 201–3.

42 Bernd Martin, 'Agriculture and Food Supply in Japan during the Second World War', in *Agriculture and Food Supply in the Second World War*, ed. B. Martin and A. S. Milward (Ostfildern, 1985), p. 188; Tsutomu Ouchi, 'Occupational Change in the Agricultural Population of Japan during Wartime: The Formation of "Worker-Peasants"', in *Agriculture and Food Supply in the Second World War*, pp. 209–11.

43 Martin, 'Agriculture and Food Supply in Japan during the Second World War', p. 203. See also Johnston with Hosoda and Kusumi, *Japanese Food Management in World War II*, p. 169.

44 Partner, *Toshié*, pp. 81–7.

45 Ehara Ayako, 'Taishō, Shōwa shoki no shokuseikatsu: Chiiki ni yoru nichijōshoku no chigai o chūshin ni', *Tōkyō kaseigakuin daigaku kiyō*, 36 (1996), p. 12; Imada, 'Dainiji sekai taisen', p. 140. See also Emiko Ohnuki-Tierney, *Rice as Self: Japanese Identities through* Time (Princeton, nj, 1993), pp. 15–17.

46 Pauer, 'Neighbourhood Associations', pp. 220–31.

47 Fujiwara Akira, *Ueijini shita eireitachi* (Tokyo, 2001), p. 3.

48 Advertisements in *Ryōyū*, XIX/3 (1944), *Asahigurafu*, XLII/7, 10, 17 (1944).

49 John W. Dower, *Embracing Defeat: Japan in the Wake of World War II* (New York, 1999), pp. 93–5. See also Johnston with Hosoda and Kusumi, *Japanese Food Management in World War II*, pp. 213–30.

50 Ehara Ayako, 'Nihon ni okeru gakkō chōri kyōiku no shiteki kiten ni kan suru kenkyū: Chūtō gakkō rei (1943) kōfu no zengo o chūshin ni,' *Kyōikushi gakkai kiyō*, 36 (1993), pp. 146–50

51 Arthur Marwick, *War and Social Change in the Twentieth Century: A Comparative Study of Britain, France, Germany, Russia and the United States* (London and Basingstoke, 1974), p. 12.

52 Hagiwara, *Nihon eiyōgaku shi*, pp. 155, 296.

53 Yamashita Tamiki, *Kawashima Shirō: 90sai no kaiseinen* (Tokyo, 1983), p. 254.

Six: The Culinary Consequences of Japanese Imperialism

1 Miriam Silverberg, 'Constructing a New Cultural History of Prewar Japan', in *Japan in the World*, ed. M. Miyoshi and H. D. Harootunian (Durham, NC, and London, 1993), p. 141. See also Miriam Silverberg, 'Constructing the Japanese Ethnography of Modernity', *Journal of Asian Studies*, LI/1 (1992), pp. 30–54; Joseph J. Tobin, ed., *Re-made in Japan: Everyday Life and Consumer Taste in Changing Society* (New Haven, CT, and London, 1992); Stephen Vlastos, ed., *Mirror of Modernity: Invented Traditions of Modern Japan* (Berkeley, CA, 1998).

2 See, for example, Michael Weiner, ed., *Japan's Minorities: The Illusion of Homogeneity* (London and New York, 1997), and Andre Schmid, 'Colonialism and the "Korea Problem" in the Historiography of Modern Japan: A Review Article', *Journal of Asian Studies*, LIX/4 (2000), pp. 951–76.

3 John Lie, *Multiethnic Japan* (Cambridge, MA, 2001), p. 1.

4 Ibid., p. 4.

5   Noguchi Hokugen, 'Shokumotsu chōri ron', *Fūzoku gahō*, 1 (1880), pp. 13–15.
6   Naomichi Ishige, *The History and Culture of Japanese Food* (London, 2001),
    pp. 113–15; H. T. Huang, *Part v: Fermentations and Food Science* in *Science and
    Civilisation in China: Volume vi* (Cambridge, 2000), pp. 375–8.
7   Etchū Tetsuya, 'Tōburu no shoku: Nagasaki o chūshin to shita nanban, kara,
    akahige no shoku' in *Gairai no shoku no bunka*, ed. Kumakura I. and Ishige N.
    (Tokyo, 1988), pp. 103–18; Harada Nobuo, *Edo no ryōri shi* (Tokyo, 1989), p. 181.
    For the Chinese influences in Japanese food history, see Ishige, *The History and
    Culture of Japanese Food*, pp. 46–52, 67–79.
8   Andrew Gordon, *A Modern History of Japan: From Tokugawa Times to the Present*
    (New York and Oxford, 2003), pp. 115–23, 173–81. See also Raymon H. Myers
    and Mark R. Peattie, eds, *The Japanese Colonial Empire, 1895–1945* (Princeton, NJ,
    1984), and Louise Young, *Japan's Total Empire: Manchuria and the Culture of
    Wartime Imperialism* (Berkeley, CA, 1998).
9   Tanaka Seiichi, *Ichii taisui: Chūgoku ryōri denrai shi* (Tokyo, 1987), p. 224.
10 Seikatsu Jōhō Sentā, ed., *Shokuseikatsu dētā sōgō tōkei nenpō* (Tokyo, 2003), p. 254.
    For more details about the history of *gyōza* in Japan, see Kusano Miho, 'Zai Riben
    de Zhongguo liaoli (san): Jiaozi de puji ji jiaozi rechao de xingqi', in *Zhongguo
    yinshi wenhua: jinjihui huixun*, x / 3 (2004), pp. 56–9.
11 James E. Hoare, 'The Chinese in the Japanese Treaty Ports, 1858–1899: The
    Unknown Majority', *Proceedings of the British Association for Japanese Studies*,
    2 (1977), pp. 19–22; Andrea Vasishth, 'The Chinese Community: A Model
    Minority', in *Japan's Minorities: The Illusion of Homogeneity*, ed. M. Weiner
    (London and New York, 1997), pp. 118–22.
12 Isabella L. Bird, *Unbeaten Tracks in Japan: An Account of Travels in the Interior,
    Including Visits to the Aborigines of Yezo and the Shrine of Nikko* (Rutland, VT,
    1973), p. 15.
13 Major Henry Knollys, *Sketches of Life in Japan* (London, 1887), pp. 226–7.
14 Noriko Kamachi, 'The Chinese in Meiji Japan: Their Interactions with the
    Japanese before the Sino-Japanese War', in *The Chinese and the Japanese:
    Essays in Political and Cultural Interactions*, ed. A. Iriye (Princeton, NJ, 1980),
    pp. 64–6.
15 Hoare, 'The Chinese in the Japanese Treaty Ports', pp. 30–31; Timothy Y. Tsu,
    'From Ethnic Ghetto to "Gourmet Republic": The Changing Image of Kobe's
    Chinatown in Modern Japan', *Japanese Studies*, XIX / 1 (1999), pp. 19–22. See also
    J.A.G. Roberts, *China to Chinatown: Chinese Food in the West* (London, 2002),
    pp. 136–7, 144–6.
16 Kosuge Keiko, *Nippon rāmen monogatari* (Tokyo, 1998), pp. 240–44; Hirade
    Kōjiro, *Tōkyō fūzoku shi* (Tokyo, 1901), vol. II, p. 159; Sakurai Miyoko, 'Meiji kōki
    no toshi no shoku seikatsu: Jōryū kaisō no shufu no nikki o chūshin ni', *Tōkyō
    kaseigakuin daigaku kiyō*, 36 (1996), pp. 25–34.
17 Gennifer Weisenfeld, 'Guest Editor's Introduction', *Positions: East Asia Cultures
    Critique*, VIII / 3 (2000), p. 596.
18 Harada Nobuo, *Washoku to Nihon bunka: Nihon ryōri no shakai shi* (Tokyo, 2005),

p. 173; Kinoshita Kenjirō, *Bimi tankyū: Aji to ryōri no genten* (Tokyo, 1997), vol. I, p. 98.

19 Kosuge, *Nippon rāmen monogatari*, pp. 66–98.

20 Okumura Ayao, *Shinka suru men shokubunka: Rāmen no rūtsu o saguru* (Tokyo, 1998), p. 150

21 Kosuge, *Nippon rāmen monogatari*, pp. 34–48.

22 Okumura Ayao, 'Rāmen', in *Gaikokugo ni natta Nihongo no jiten*, ed. Katō H. and Kumakura I. (Tokyo, 1999), pp. 255–6.

23 www.instantramen.or.jp/data/data01.html (accessed 19 January 2006) and www.nissinfoods.co.jp/english/inv/pdf/ar04_01.pdf (accessed 19 January 2006).

24 Kosuge, *Nippon rāmen monogatari*, pp. 75, 95.

25 Ishige, *The History and Culture of Japanese Food*, pp. 251–2.

26 Kosuge, *Nippon rāmen*, pp. 267–9.

27 *Shikō*, XXVIII/12 (1935), p. 19; XXIX/4 (1936), p. 17.

28 Tanaka, *Ichii taisui*, p. 207.

29 'Meishi no gokatei de otoku no osōzai ryōri kurabe', in *Shufu no tomo*, XIII/3 (1929), pp. 340–41.

30 Tanaka, *Ichii taisui*, p. 203.

31 Harada, *Washoku to Nihon bunka*, pp. 193–5; Miyatsuka Toshio, *Nippon yakiniku monogatari* (Tokyo, 1999), p. 53.

32 George De Vos and Changsoo Lee, 'The Colonial Experience, 1910–1945', in *Koreans in Japan: Ethnic Conflict and Accommodation*, ed. C. Lee and G. De Vos (Berkeley, CA, 1981), p. 37; Michael Weiner, *Race and Migration in Imperial Japan* (London and New York, 1994), p. 198.

33 Sonia Ryang, 'Japan's Ethnic Minority: Koreans', in *A Companion to the Anthropology of Japan*, ed. J. Robertson (Malden, MA, 2005), pp. 89–103. See also Changsoo Lee, 'The Politics of Repatriation', in *Koreans in Japan: Ethnic Conflict and Accommodation*, ed. C. Lee and G. De Vos (Berkeley, CA, 1981), pp. 91–109.

34 Matsudaira Makoto, *Yamiichi maboroshi no gaido bukku* (Tokyo, 1995), pp. 95–7, 187–91.

35 John W. Dower, *Embracing Defeat: Japan in the Wake of World War II* (New York, 1999), pp. 140–43.

36 Miyatsuka, *Nippon yakiniku monogatari*, pp. 163–5.

37 Chong Dae Sung, *Yakiniku, kimuchi to Nihonjin* (Tokyo, 2004), pp. 62–3; Miyatsuka, *Nippon yakiniku monogatari*, pp. 154–8; Asakura Toshio, *Nihon no yakiniku, Kankoku no sashimi: Shokubunka ga 'naizu' sareru toki* (Tokyo, 1994), pp. 68–9.

38 Miyatsuka, *Nippon yakiniku monogatari*, pp. 242–3; Asakura, *Nihon no yakiniku*, pp. 44–6.

39 Miyatsuka, *Nippon yakiniku monogatari*, pp. 209–15; Chong, *Yakiniku, kimuchi to Nihonjin*, pp. 74–8.

40 Asakura, *Nihon no yakiniku, kankoku no sashimi*, pp. 18–39.

41 Majima Ayu, 'Nikushoku to iu kindai: Meijiki Nihon ni okeru shokuniku gunji juyō to nikushokukan no tokuchō', *Ajia bunka kenkyū*, 11 (2002), pp. 218–25. See

also Chōsen Sōtokufu Shokusankyoku, *Chōsen no chikusan* (Keijō, 1930).

42 Niino Yutaka, 'An Introduction to Sources: The Agriculture and Forestry Bureau of the Government-General of Chōsen's General Plan of the Project to Increase Korean Beef, March 1938', paper presented at Chōsen kindai chiikishika kenkyūkai, Tokyo, 27 March 2006.

43 Boudewijn Walraven, 'Bardot Soup and Confucians' Meat: Food and Korean Identity in Global Context', in *Asian Food: The Global and the Local*, ed. K. J. Cwiertka with B.C.A. Walraven (Honolulu, HI, 2002), pp. 97–101. See also Chun Ja Lee, Hye Won Park and Kwi Young Kim, *The Book of Kimchi* (Seoul, 1998); Han Pong-nyŏ, *Kimuchi no hyakka: Kankoku dentō kimuchi 100* (Tokyo, 2005).

44 Chong, *Yakiniku, kimuchi to Nihonjin*, pp. 127, 135.

45 Ibid., p. 127.

46 Sasaki Michio, 'Nihon no kimuchi 6: Kimuchi būmu no bunseki, sono 2', *Mukuge Tsūshin*, 209 (2005), p. 18.

47 Sasaki Michio, 'Nihon no kimuchi 5: Kimuchi būmu no bunseki, sono 1', *Mukuge Tsūshin*, 208 (2005), pp. 16–8.

48 Hirata Yukie, 'Manazasu mono to shite no Nihon josei kan(kō)kyaku: "Fuyu no Sonata" rokechi meguri ni miru toransunashonaru na tekusuto dokkai', in *Nisshiki kanryū: 'Fuyu no sonata' to nikkan taishū bunka no genzai*, ed. Mōri Yoshitaka (Tokyo, 2004), pp. 60–62; Sasaki, 'Nihon no kimuchi 6', pp. 16–17.

49 See John Horne and Wolfram Manzenreiter, eds, *Japan, Korea and the 2002 World Cup* (London and New York, 2002), and Wolfram Manzenreiter and John Horne, eds, *Football Goes East: Business, Culture and the People's Game in China, Japan and South Korea* (New York and London, 2004).

50 Roald Maliangkay, 'When the Korean Wave Ripples', *IIAS Newsletter*, 42 (2006), p. 15. See also Mōri Yoshitaka, '"Fuyu no Sonata" to nōdōteki fan no bunka jissen', in *Nisshiki kanryū: 'Fuyu no sonata' to nikkan taishū bunka no genzai*, ed. Mōri Yoshitaka (Tokyo, 2004), pp. 14–50.

Seven: Multiple Circuits of Affluence

1 John W. Dower, *Embracing Defeat: Japan in the Wake of World War II* (New York, 1999), p. 73.

2 Bruce Cumings, 'Japan in the World System', in *Postwar Japan as History*, ed. A. Gordon (Berkeley, CA, 1993), p. 39. For an overview of US–Japan relations since 1951, see Steven K. Vogel, ed., *US–Japan Relations in a Changing World* (Washington, DC, 2002).

3 Tessa Morris-Suzuki, 'Introduction: Japanese Economic Growth, Images and Ideologies', in *Japanese Capitalism since 1945: Critical Perspectives*, ed. T. Morris-Suzuki and T. Seiyama (Armonk, NY, and London, 1989), pp. 7–10.

4 Michael Schaller, 'The Korean War: The Economic and Strategic Impact on Japan, 1950–53', in *The Korean War in World History*, ed. W. Stueck (Lexington, KY, 2004), p. 148.

5 Bruce F. Johnston, with Mosaburo Hosoda and Yoshio Kusumi, *Japanese Food*

Management in World War II (Stanford, CA, 1953), p. 233.

6   Ibid., pp. 215–16.

7   Ehara Ayako, 'School Meals and Japan's Changing Diet', *Japan Echo*, XXVI/4 (1999), p. 57; Gen Itasaka, 'LARA , in *Kodansha Encyclopedia of Japan* (Tokyo, 1983), vol. IV, p. 368.

8   Ehara, 'School Meals and Japan's Changing Diet', p. 57.

9   Ibid., pp. 58, 60. See also Emiko Ohnuki-Tierney, *Rice as Self: Japanese Identities through* Time (Princeton, NJ, 1993), pp. 16–17.

10 Hiromitsu Kaneda, 'Long-term Changes in Food Consumption Patterns in Japan', in *Agriculture and Economic Growth: Japan's Experience*, ed. K. Ohkawa, B. F. Johnston and H. Kaneda (Princeton, NJ, 1970), p. 417.

11 Akira Ishida, *Food Processing Industry in Japan* (Tokyo, 1978), p. 9.

12 Kaneda, 'Long-term Changes in Food Consumption Patterns in Japan', p. 421.

13 Simon Partner, *Assembled in Japan: Electrical Goods and the Making of the Japanese Consumer* (Berkeley, CA, 1999), p. 51.

14 See also Takafusa Nakamura, *The Postwar Japanese Economy: Its Development and Structure* (Tokyo, 1981), and Chalmers Johnson, *MITI and the Japanese Miracle: The Growth of Industrial Policy, 1925–1975* (Stanford, CA, 1982).

15 Partner, *Assembled in Japan*, pp. 142–50.

16 Akira Ishida, *Food Processing Industry in Japan*, pp. 9–10.

17 Partner, *Assembled in Japan*, p. 191.

18 Yano Tsuneta Kinenkai, ed., *Sūji de miru Nihon no 100 nen: 20 seiki ga wakaru dētā bukku* (Tokyo, 2000), p. 294.

19 Ishikawa Naoko, 'Kōdo keizai seichōki ga umidashita shoku jijō', in *Kingendai no shokubunka*, ed. Ishikawa H. and Ehara A. (Kawasaki, 2002), p. 170.

20 Ehara, 'School Meals and Japan's Changing Diet', p. 57; 'Gakkō de ninki no aru kyūshoku ryōri', *Shufu no tomo*, XXXIX/4 (1955), pp. 412–15.

21 Ehara Ayako, 'Sōkatsu: Shoku no denshō, kyōiku, jōhō', in *Shoku to kyōiku*, ed. Ehara A. (Tokyo, 2001), p. 237.

22 Katja Schmidtpott, 'Heilmittel, Genussmittel, Erfrischungsgetränk: Milchkonsum in Japan 1920–1970', in *Japanstudien 12: Essen und Ernährung im Modernen Japan*, ed. N. Liscutin and R. Haak (Munich, 2000), pp. 117–56.

23 Iwamura Nobuko, *Kawaru kazoku, kawaru shokutaku: Shinjitsu ni hakai sareru maaketingu jōshiki* (Tokyo, 2003), pp. 60, 95, 114, 119, 154, 193.

24 Ehara, 'School Meals and Japan's Changing Diet', p. 58.

25 Emiko Ohnuki-Tierney, 'McDonald's in Japan: Changing Manners and Etiquette', in *Golden Arches East: McDonald's in East Asia*, ed. J. L. Watson (Stanford, CA, 1997), p. 162; 'McDonald's Japan Expects Net Loss', electronic document www.mcspotlight.org/media/press/mcds/yahoonews200212.html (accessed 5 May 2006).

26 Ohnuki-Tierney, 'McDonald's in Japan', pp. 172–3. In fact, the information provided here is slightly incorrect. The first McDonald's outlet, which opened in July 1971, was located in the Mitsukoshi Department Store on Ginza, see Higashi Masahiro, 'Gaishoku Sangyō', in *Shōwa no shokuhin sangyō shi*, ed. Nihon

Shokuryō Shinbunsha (Tokyo, 1990), p. 786. See also www.mcdonalds.co.jp.

27 Yano, *Sūji de miru Nihon no 100 nen*, p. 337.

28 Asahi Shinbunsha, *The Asahi Shimbun Japan Almanac 2006* (Tokyo, 2005), pp. 195, 200; Ishikawa, 'Kōdo keizai seichōki ga umidashita shoku jijō', p. 170.

29 Asahi, *The Asahi Shimbun Japan Almanac 2006*, p. 254.

30 John Clammer, *Contemporary Urban Japan: A Sociology of Consumption* (Oxford, 1997), pp. 40–41. See also John L. McCreery, *Japanese Consumer Behavior: From Worker Bees to Wary Shoppers* (Richmond, Surrey, 2000), and Joseph J. Tobin, ed., *Re-made in Japan: Everyday Life and Consumer Taste in a Changing Society* (New Haven, CT, and London, 1992).

31 See Japan-related press articles in www.licenseenews.com and www.mcspotlight.org.

32 'Trouble Brewing for Starbucks in Japan', electronic document, www.siamfuture. com/asiannews/asiannewstxt.asp?aid=2471 (accessed 10 May 2006).

33 Koishihara Haruka, *Sutābakkusu maniakkusu* (Tokyo, 2001), p. 39. See also www.starbucks.co.jp.

34 'Starbucks Discoveries Milano (Espresso) Coffee Beverage Relaunched in Japan', electronic document www.foodingredientsfirst.com/newsmaker_article.asp? idNewsMaker=10586&fSite=AO545&next=5 (accessed 10 May 2006). See also www.starbucks.co.jp/rtd.

35 Inge Maria Daniels, *The Fame of Miyajima: Spirituality, Commodification and the Tourist Trade of Souvenirs in Japan*, PhD thesis, University College London, 2001, pp. 141, 219. See also Kanzaki Noritake, *Omiyage: Zōtō to tabi no Nihon bunka* (Tokyo, 1997).

36 Theodore C. Bestor, *Tsukiji: The Fish Market at the Center of the World* (Berkeley, CA, 2004), pp. 146–7, 159–60.

37 Jennifer Robertson, 'It Takes a Village: Internationalization and Nostalgia in Postwar Japan', in *Mirror of Modernity: Invented Traditions of Modern Japan*, ed. S. Vlastos (Berkeley, CA, 1998), pp. 110–29; See also Marilyn Ivy, *Discourses of the Vanishing: Modernity, Phantasm, Japan* (Chicago, IL, and London, 1995).

38 Erik C. Rath, 'How Does a Vegetable Become "Traditional" in Kyoto?', paper presented at the Annual Meeting of the American Anthropological Association, Washington, DC, 29 November 2001. See also www.pref.kyoto.jp/nosan/yasai/.

39 Raymond A. Jussaume Jr, Hisano Shūji and Taniguchi Yoshimitsu, 'Food Safety in Modern Japan', in *Japanstudien 12: Essen und Ernährung im Modernen Japan*, ed. N. Liscutin and R. Haak (Munich, 2000), pp. 217–18.

40 Darrell Gene Moen, 'Grassroots-based Organic Food Distributors, Retailers and Consumer Cooperatives in Japan: Broadening the Organic Farming Movement', *Hitotsubashi Journal of Social Studies*, 32 (2000), p. 56.

41 Ibid., pp. 57–8.

42 Darrell Gene Moen, 'The Japanese Organic Farming Movement: Consumers and Farmers United', *Bulletin of Concerned Asian Scholars*, XXIX/3 (1997), p. 14. See also Moen, 'Grassroots-based Organic Food', pp. 60–73.

43 Moen, 'Grassroots-based Organic Food', p. 74.

44 Seikatsu Jōhō Sentā Henshūbu, ed., *Mosu no kokoro: Mosu bāgā hātofuru bukku* (Tokyo, 2006), p. 135.

45 Jussaume, Hisano and Taniguchi, 'Food Safety in Modern Japan', p. 221.

46 Seikatsu Jōhō Sentā Henshūbu, *Mosu no kokoro*, pp. 34–61.

47 Ibid., pp. 12–25.

48 Jane Cobbi, '*Sonaemono*: Ritual Gifts to the Deities', in *Ceremony and Ritual in Japan*, ed. J. van Bremen and D. P. Martinez (Richmond, Surrey, 1995), pp. 201–9.

49 Robert J. Smith, *Ancestor Worship in Contemporary Japan* (Stanford, CA, 1974), pp. 90–91, 105, 133–4.

Conclusion: The Making of a National Cuisine

1 Harada Nobuo, *Washoku to Nihon bunka: Nihon ryōri no shakai shi* (Tokyo, 2005), p. 10.

2 Ernest Gellner, *Nationalism* (London, 1997), p. 94.

3 John Tomlinson, *Globalization and Culture* (Cambridge, 1999), pp. 20–31, 43.

4 Gellner, *Nationalism*, p. 26, 51.

5 Rupert Emerson quoted in John Hutchinson, *Modern Nationalism* (London, 1994), p. 13.

6 Benedict Anderson, *Imagined Communities* (London, 1991), p. 6.

7 Gellner, *Nationalism*, pp. 20, 45.

8 Catherine Palmer, 'From Theory to Practice: Experiencing the Nation in Everyday Life', *Journal of Material Culture*, III/2 (1998), p. 182.

9 Anne Murcott, 'Food as an Expression of Identity', in *The Future of the Nation State: Essays on Cultural Pluralism and Political Integration*, ed. S. Gustavsson and L. Lewin (London, 1996), pp. 50–51

10 Ibid., p. 69.

11 Lewis M. Barker, 'Building Memories for Foods', in *Psychobiology of Human Food Selection*, ed. L. M. Barker (Westport, CT, 1982), pp. 85–99; David E. Sutton, *Remembrance of Repasts: An Anthropology of Food and Memory* (Oxford and New York, 2001), pp. 159–71; Efrat Ben-Ze'ev, 'The Politics of Taste and Smell: Palestinian Rites of Return', in *The Politics of Food*, ed. M. E. Lien and B. Nerlich (Oxford and New York, 2004), pp. 142–6.

12 Eric Hobsbawm, 'Introduction: Inventing Traditions', in *The Invention of Tradition*, ed. E. Hobsbawm and T. Ranger (Cambridge, 1983), pp. 1–14.

13 Richard Wilk, 'Food and Nationalism: The Origins of "Belizean Food"', in *Food Nations: Selling Taste in Consumer Societies*, ed. W. Belasco and P. Scranton (New York and London, 2002), p. 70.

14 Igor Cusack, 'African Cuisines: Recipes for Nation-Building?', *Journal of African Cultural Studies*, XIII/2 (2000), pp. 207–25; Arjun Appadurai, 'How to Make a National Cuisine: Cookbooks in Contemporary India', *Comparative Study of Society and History*, XXX/1 (1988), pp. 3–24; Jeffrey Pilcher, *Que Vivan los Tamales! Food and the Making of Mexican Identity* (Albuquerque, NM, 1998).

15 Katarzyna J. Cwiertka, 'Introduction', in *Asian Food: The Global and the Local*,

ed. K. J. Cwiertka with B.C.A. Walraven (Honolulu, HI, 2002), pp. 1–15.

16 Alan Warde, 'Eating Globally: Cultural Flows and the Spread of Ethnic Restaurants', in *The Ends of Globalization: Bringing Society Back In*, ed. D. Kalb et al. (Lanham, MD, 2000), pp. 306–9. See also Ian Cook and Philip Crang, 'The World on a Plate: Displacement and Geographical Knowledge', *Journal of Material Culture*, 1/2 (1996), pp. 131–53.

17 See Christopher Driver, *The British at Table, 1940–1980* (London, 1983), and Susanne Mühleisen, 'Globalized Tongues: The Cultural Semantics of Food Names', in *Eating Culture: The Poetics and Politics of Food Today*, ed. T. Döring, M. Heide and S. Mühleisen (Heidelberg, 2003), pp. 71–88.

18 Sidney W. Mintz, 'Eating Communities: The Mixed Appeals of Sodality', in *Eating Culture: The Poetics and Politics of Food Today*, p. 26. See also Lisa M. Heldke, *Exotic Appetites: Ruminations of a Food Adventurer* (New York and London, 2003).

19 Susan J. Terrio, 'Crafting *Grand Cru* Chocolates in Contemporary France', in *The Cultural Politics of Food and Eating: A Reader*, ed. J. L. Watson and M. L. Caldwell (New York and London, 2005), p. 149.

Postscript: Japanese Cuisine Goes Global

1 The following database is a reliable resource on Japanese restaurants operating outside Japan: www.sushi.infogate.de (accessed 5 January 2006). For a more elaborate account of the Japanese food boom in Europe, see Katarzyna J. Cwiertka, 'From Ethnic to Hip: Circuits of Japanese Cuisine in Europe', *Food and Foodways*, XIII/4 (2005), pp. 241–72.

2 Stewart Lone, *The Japanese Community in Brazil, 1908–1940: Between Samurai and Carnival* (Basingstoke and New York, 2001), pp. 13–16.

3 Louise Young, *Japan's Total Empire: Manchuria and the Culture of Wartime Imperialism* (Berkeley, CA, 1998), p. 314; Peter Duus, *The Abacus and the Sword: The Japanese Penetration of Korea, 1895–1910* (Berkeley, CA, 1995), p. 290; Roger Daniels, *Asian America: Chinese and Japanese in the United States since 1850* (Seattle, WA, and London, 1988), pp. 115, 127.

4 Daniels, *Asian America*, pp. 214–17.

5 Koyama Shūzō, 'Nihon ryōriten no seiritsu to tenkai', in *Los Angeles no Nihon ryōriten: Sono bunka jinruigaku kenkyū*, ed. N. Ishige et al. (Tokyo, 1985), p. 37.

6 Warren Belasco, *Appetite for Change: How the Counterculture Took on the Food Industry* (Ithaca, NY, 1989), pp. 43–67.

7 Theodore C. Bestor, 'How Sushi Went Global', in *The Cultural Politics of Food and Eating: A Reader*, ed. J. L. Watson and M. L. Caldwell (New York and London, 2005), pp. 14–15.

8 Theodore C. Bestor, 'Main Street Sushi: The Americanization of Japanese Cuisine', paper presented at the symposium *Japanese Cuisine in the West*, Leiden University, 20 June 2001.

9 Nobuyuki Matsuhisa, *Nobu: The Cookbook* (London, 2001). See also

www.noburestaurants.com.
10 'Sukiyaki Hausu San Furanshisuko', *Asahigurafu*, IV/6 (1955), p. 8.
11 Yano Tsuneta Kinenkai, ed., *Sūji de miru Nihon no 100 nen: 20 seiki ga wakaru dētā bukku* (Tokyo, 2000), pp. 376–7. See also Fujiwara Sadao, 'Foreign Trade, Investment and Industrial Imperialism in Postwar Japan', in *Japanese Capitalism since 1945: Critical Perspectives*, ed. T. Morris-Suzuki and T. Seiyama (Armonk, NY, and London, 1989), pp. 166–206.
12 Merry White, *The Japanese Overseas: Can They Go Home Again?* (Princeton, NJ, 1988), p. 17.
13 Asahi Shinbunsha, *The Asahi Shimbun Japan Almanac 2006* (Tokyo, 2005), p. 90.
14 Harumi Befu, 'Globalization as Human Dispersal: From the Perspective of Japan', in *Globalization and Social Change in Contemporary Japan*, ed. J. S. Eades, T. Gill, and H. Befu (Melbourne, 2000), pp. 29–33.
15 For details about the enterprise, see www.benihana.com.
16 Ishige Naomichi, 'Guriru Misono: Teppanyaki no genso to shite no hatten', in *Gurume City Kobe: Oishisa no haikei* (Kobe, 1997), pp. 136–9.
17 Ishige Naomichi, 'Seihō yūshoku: Teppanyaki sutēki Kōbe ga genso', *Keizai Shinbun*, 22 November 1993.
18 Eugene Fodor and Robert C. Fisher, *Fodor's Guide to Japan and East Asia* (New York, 1963), p. 179.
19 *Japan Illustrated*, 3 (1965), p. 36; Boye De Mente, *International Business Man's Afterhours Guide to Japan* (Tokyo, 1968), pp. 131–2, 138, 145.
20 Japan National Tourist Organization, *The New Official Guide: Japan* (Tokyo, 1966), p. 547.
21 John Klug, *Benihana of Tokyo*, Harvard Business School Research Paper no. 9–673–057 (1995), pp. 1–2.
22 Ibid., p. 18.
23 Ibid., p. 16.
24 Personal Communication, Kikkoman Trading Europe, June 2001. See also www.daitokai.de.
25 Frank N. Pieke, 'De Chinese gemeenschap in verstarring', *Sociologische Gids*, XXXI/5 (1984), pp. 427–41.
26 Bestor, 'How Sushi Went Global', p. 18.
27 Keiko Itoh, *The Japanese Community in Pre-War Britain: From Integration to Disintegration* (Richmond, Surrey, 2001), pp. 2, 17; Young, *Japan's Total Empire*, p. 315.
28 Paul White, 'The Japanese in London: From Transience to Settlement?', in *Global Japan: The Experience of Japan's New Immigrants and Overseas Communities*, ed. Roger Goodman et al. (London, 2003), p. 80.
29 Asahi, *Asahi Shimbun Japan Almanac 2006*, p. 90.
30 Sanda Ionescu, 'Soka Gakkai in Germany: The Story of a Qualified Success', in *Globalizing Japan: Ethnography of the Japanese Presence in Asia*, ed. H. Befu and S. Guichard-Anguis (London, 2001), p. 103. See also Günter Glebe, 'Segregation and the Ethnoscape: The Japanese Business Community in Düsseldorf', in *Global*

Japan: The Experience of Japan's New immigrants and Overseas Communities, ed. Roger Goodman et al. (London, 2003), pp. 98–115.

31 Akira Oshima, Patrick Faas and Katarzyna Cwiertka, *Kaiseki Cuisine: Hotel Okura Amsterdam* (Bruges, 2003).

32 Hidemine Takahashi, 'It Started in Japan: Conveyor-Belt Sushi', *Nipponia*, 15 (2000), p. 18. See also Theodore C. Bestor, *Tsukiji: The Fish Market at the Center of the World* (Berkeley, CA, 2004), pp. 161–3.

33 Shinoda Osamu, *Sushi no hon* (Tokyo, 2002), pp. 7–11, 82–5; Shūkan Asahi, ed., *Meiji, Taishō, Shōwa nedan no fūzoku shi* (Tokyo, 1987), vol. 1, pp. 11, 35.

34 Emiko Ohnuki-Tierney, "McDonald's in Japan', in *Golden Arches East: McDonald's in East Asia*, ed. J. Watson (Stanford, CA, 1997), pp. 178–9.

35 Masahiro Ota, 'Focus Japan: Bring on the Sushi!', *Pacific Friend*, XXIX/5 (2001), p. 12.

36 Ota, 'Focus Japan', pp. 11–12; John Broe, 'Endless Sushi', electronic document www.mainichi.co.jp/edu/weekly/essay/99/1106/ (accessed 21 January 2004).

37 Jonathan Goff, 'Putting a New Spin on Sushi', electronic document www.mainichi.co.jp/english/food/archives/food/990727.html (accessed 21 January 2004).

38 See, for example, www.k10.net, www.sushiogko.dk, www.sushitime.nl, www.zushi.nl, www.sushi-circle.de, www.sakura-leipzig.de, www.sachikosushi.com, www.zenworld.it, www.matsuri.fr, www.divan.com.tr/gastronomi/haisushi. This is just a tip of an iceberg, since there are many rotating bars that do not operate their own websites: Aya in Dublin, Aya Bistro in Lisbon, Bando in Bochum, Ginza Kaiten Sushi in Madrid, Lô Sushi in Paris, Nippon-kan in Warsaw, Sushi No.1 and Sushi En in Cologne.

39 Tamamura Toyoo, *Kaitenzushi sekai isshū* (Tokyo, 2000), p. 110. See also www.moshimoshi.co.uk.

40 See www.noto.co.uk.

41 Dominic Walsh, 'Yo! Sushi Rolls through Europe with US in Sight', in *Times online* 16 April 2005, electronic document business.timesonline.co.uk/article/0,,9070–1571191,00.html (accessed 22 April 2006). See also www.yosushi.com and www.brilliantstages.com/Latest%20News/Yo%20Sushi/Yo%20Sushi%20Athens.htm.

42 London Business Forum, 'Simon Woodroffe', electronic document www.londonbusinessforum.com/woodroffe.html (accessed 19 June 2002).

43 Kate Crockett, 'Sushi: What Goes Around Comes Around', electronic document www.metropolis.co.jp/tokyominifeaturestories/285/tokyominifeaturestoriesinc.htm (accessed 21 January 2004).

44 Ibid.

45 Wagamama Limited, *Way of the Noodle* (London, 1994), p. 84.

46 Ibid., p. 6.

47 Cahal Milmo, 'Chinese Restaurant Takes Away Michelin Star', electronic document enjoyment.independent.co.uk/food_and_drink/news/story.jsp?story=370017 (accessed 22 January 2004).

48 Mark Stretton, 'American Dream: Wagamama and YO! Sushi Head for the US,
    M&C Report, 72 (2006), pp. 1–2. See also www.wagamama.co.uk.
49 Sholto Douglas-Home and Susan Kessler, eds, *Zagat Survey: 2006 London Restaurants* (New York, 2005), p. 6.
50 Nick Lander, 'Alan Yau – London Miracle Man', *Nick's Food News*,
    www.jancisrobinson.com/nick/2004/nick0320.html (accessed 3 August 2004).

Glossary

agemono	'deep-fried dish'
agepan	a deep-fried bread
amazake	a hot drink made by letting a mixture of cooked rice, water and rice, barley or soybeans infected with the mould *Aspergillus oryzae* to ferment for 12–24 hours; sweetened and often flavoured with ginger
asazuke	fresh pickle. Cucumbers, carrots, cabbage and other vegetables are salted and left for three to four days to ferment
azuki beans	small red beans, *Vigna angularis*
buta kimuchi	pork pan-fried with *kimuchi*
chāhan	cooked rice pan-fried with various ingredients; also known under the name *yakimeshi*
Chikuzenni	soy-stewed chicken with vegetables; a *nimono* that originated in Chikuzen province (currently Fukuoka prefecture on the island of Kyushu)
Chirashizushi	seafood and vegetables scattered over rice flavoured with vinegar, salt and sugar; the kind of sushi most often prepared at home
chūka soba	'Chinese noodles', a former name of *rāmen*
daikon	giant white radish, *Raphanus sativus*
dashi	stock, usually taken from dried, smoked and mould-cured bonito, dried kelp or little dried anchovies
Edomaezushi	'sushi from Edo', an alternative name for *nigirizushi*
ekiben	*obentō* sold on trains and train stations, usually containing a local speciality
fukujinzuke	a mixture of thinly sliced vegetables, salted and then pickled in soy sauce and *mirin*
furai	fish or prawns (and occasionally other ingredients) dipped in egg, coated with breadcrumbs and deep-fried; see also *tonkatsu*
furofuki	well-boiled white radish or turnip served with a topping of flavoured *miso*
gobō	the root of great burdock, *Arctium lappa*

gyōza	a kind of Chinese dumpling (*jiaozi*), usually filled with a mixture of minced pork, cabbage and Chinese chives (*Allium tuberosum*), and steam-fried
gyūnabe	beef and other ingredients cooked in a cast-iron pan, flavoured with *miso* or soy sauce; a predecessor of *sukiyaki*
hagate	a meagre peasant dish consisting of rice, millet and barley cooked with chopped *daikon* leaves
hishio	an ancient category of fermented food products, with three major types – vegetable-based, fish or meat-based, and grain-based; the last is the prototype for today's soy sauce and *miso*
honzen ryōri	a formal, opulent banquet with a large number of dishes served simultaneously at several small tables
horumonyaki	grilled tripe and offal; a wartime dish of Korean origin and a predecessor of *yakiniku*
kabu	turnip, *Brassica campestris* var. *glabra*
kaiseki	short for *kaiseki ryōri* (*kaiseki* cuisine), a refined meal consisting of several courses served in sequence; two styles of *kaiseki* are distinguished: the tranquil and minimalist 'tea *kaiseki*' (*chakaiseki*) and the more flamboyant 'restaurant kaiseki' or 'banqueting *kaiseki*' (*enkaiseki*)
kaitenzushi	'rotary sushi': sushi served on a conveyor belt
kanpan	ship's biscuits
Kantōni	'*nimono* from the Kantō region', an alternative name for *oden*
karintō	one of the oldest Japanese sweets: pieces of dough made of flour, water and egg, deep-fried and coated with brown sugar
katemeshi	a meagre peasant dish consisting of rice, millet and barley cooked with chopped *daikon*
katsu karē	breaded cutlet in curry sauce on rice
kimuchi	a Japanese name of a Korean-style pickle (*kimch'i*), made of salted vegetables fermented with red chilli pepper, garlic, green onions, ginger, seafood and other ingredients, very popular in Japan
kimuchi nabe	a variety of ingredients simmered directly at the table in a large earthenware pot, flavoured with *kimuchi*
kishimen	wide and flat wheat noodles, a speciality of Nagoya
Konbu	kelp, *Laminaria* spp., customarily used dried for making stock
konnyaku	a gelatinous paste made from the root of devil's tongue, *Amorphophallus rivieri* var. *konjac*, formed into bricks
kuchitori	assorted appetizers; the first course in the 'restaurant *kaiseki*' menu
kuromame	small black beans, *Glycine max*
mabodōfu	a dish of Sichuan origin (*mapo doufu*): minced pork stir-fried with *tōfu* in hot chilli sauce
makizushi	*sushi* roll: rice flavoured with vinegar, salt and sugar, stuffed

	with a variety of fillings and rolled in a sheet of *nori*; also known as *norimaki*
mirin	a sweet liquid flavouring made by mixing steamed glutinous rice, on which the mould *Aspergillus oryzae* has developed, with distilled spirit and fermenting for 40–60 days; commonly known as 'sweet cooking *sake*'
miso	fermented paste of soybeans and either rice or barley, with salt; hundreds of different varieties can be found. Consumed chiefly in the form of *miso* soup, which is made by dissolving a small amount of *miso* in *dashi* and adding one or two ingredients; one of the classics is *wakame* with *tōfu*
mochi	glutinous rice steamed, pounded into a dough and shaped into cakes, either by cutting the dough into rectangular shapes with a knife or by shaping into circles by hand; the major component of *zōni*
mukōzuke	a dish served with rice and soup as the first course in the 'tea *kaiseki*' menu
mushimono	'steamed dish'
myōga	myoga ginger, *Zingiber mioga*; only the buds and stems, not the root, are eaten
Narazuke	a famous vegetable pickle from Nara; radishes, aubergines (eggplants) and cucumbers are salted and pickled in sake lees
nattō	soaked and steamed soybeans inoculated with *Bacillus natto* and fermented for about a day; the end-product has a thready stickiness and a very strong aroma and flavour
nigirizushi	'squeezed' or 'hand-moulded' morsels of rice flavoured with vinegar, salt and sugar, topped with a slice of (raw) seafood; now the best-known and preferred type of sushi both inside and outside Japan
nikujaga	soy-simmered beef, potatoes, carrots, onions and (often) green peas; a *nimono* made with Western ingredients
nimono	'simmered-dish', flavoured with soy sauce or *miso*; sake, *mirin* and ginger may also be added
nori	laver *Porphyra* spp. The best-known and most widely used variety is *asakusa nori* (red alga *Porphyra tenera*), which grows in bays; after collecting, it is dried into sheets of 22.5 × 17.5 cm and toasted, sometimes coated with a flavouring. *Aonori* (green laver, *Enteromorpha* spp.), which grows in rivers, is dried in flakes and sprinkled on *okonomiyaki, yakisoba* and other dishes
obentō	or *bentō*; a boxed meal containing rice, pickles and several small side dishes
oden	short for *nikomi dengaku*, a variety of ingredients simmered in a large container of hot *dashi*; also known as *Kantōni*

ohagi	balls of steamed rice coated with a paste made of *azuki* beans boiled with sugar; the cake is named after *hagi* (bush clover), the flowers of which it vaguely resembles
okonomiyaki	a savoury pancake made of flour-and-egg batter mixed with shredded cabbage and a choice of other ingredients, which may include chunks of squid, prawns, slices of bacon and cheese. When ready, the pancake is brushed with thick brown sauce resembling Worcester sauce (see *sōsu*), sprinkled with *aonori* (see *nori*) and *katsuobushi*, and topped with mayonnaise
rāmen	Chinese-style wheat-noodles in broth; the classic version is flavoured with black pepper and contains roast pork, pickled bamboo shoots (*shinachiku*) and a few slices of fish-paste loaf (*kamaboko*)
sashimi	slices of raw seafood eaten with a dip of soy sauce and grated *wasabi*
satoimo	taro, dasheen *Colocasia esculenta*
Satsumajiru	a hearty soup that originated in Satsuma province (now Kagoshima prefecture on the island of Kyushu), containing chicken on the bone with lots of vegetables and flavoured with *miso*
shiizakana	a course in the *kaiseki* menu (both styles); it is a dish that the cook prepared with particular attention
Shina soba	'Chinese noodles', a former name for *rāmen*
shiruko	or *oshiruko*; a sweet soup made of *azuki* beans boiled with sugar and served with small pieces of *mochi* or with rice dumplings (*dango*)
shiso	beefsteak plant, *Perilla frutescens* var. *crispa*
shōyu	soy sauce, a liquid flavouring acquired through the fermentation of soybeans, wheat and the mould *Aspergillus oryzae* in brine
soba	noodles made from buckwheat flour, usually with some wheat flour added; served either cold, with a dipping broth, or in hot *dashi*, sometimes with a topping such as raw egg, tempura or deep-fried *tōfu*
sōmen	thin wheat noodles, customarily served in summer in icy cold water, with a dipping broth
sōsu	short for *usutā sōsu*; the Japanese version of Worcester sauce, but less pungent and much thicker than the original: a classic accompaniment to *tonkatsu*, *furai* and *okonomiyaki*
soy sauce	see *shōyu*; the English word 'soy' or 'soya' probably originated from the Japanese word *shoyu*, referring initially to soy sauce and not soy beans
suimono	'clear soup'; it is considered more elegant than the everyday *miso* soup and is made from the best stock
sukiyaki	thin slices of beef cooked in a shallow cast-iron pan with vegetables and other ingredients, flavoured with soy sauce,

	mirin and sugar: before being eaten, the ingredients are dipped in beaten raw eggs
sunomono	'vinegared dish'; a variety of ingredients – usually greens and slices of seafood – dressed in flavoured vinegar
takuan	short for *takuanzuke*, *daikon* pickled in rice bran
tamari shōyu	or *tamari*, soy sauce brewed without the addition of wheat
tenpura	seafood and vegetables deep-fried in batter; usually served with dipping broth or with salt and lemon
teppanyaki	slices of meat, seafood and vegetables grilled on an iron hot plate and served with a dipping sauce
teriyaki	'luster grilling'; fish, chicken and vegetables are basted with soy sauce enriched with *mirin* and sugar while being grilled
tonkatsu	a slice of pork dipped in egg, coated with breadcrumbs and deep-fried, served with finely shredded raw cabbage and *sōsu*
tōfu	soybean curd
tōgan	wax gourd, *Benincasa hispida*
tsukudani	salt-sweet preserve; fish, shellfish, seaweed and vegetables simmered in a mixture of soy sauce, *mirin* and sugar until almost dry
udo	Japanese spikenard (*Aralia cordata*), a plant reminiscent of asparagus
udon	soft, thick wheat noodles served in hot broth, often with a topping of *tenpura* or deep-fried *tōfu*
umeboshi	dried, salt-pickled Japanese apricot, *Prunus mume*
wakame	brown seaweed, *Undaria pinnitifida*
wasabi	wasabi plant, *Wasabia japonica*, commonly known as Japanese horseradish
yakimono	'grilled dish'; in practice synonymous with 'grilled fish'
yakiniku	thin slices of meat cooked on a griddle or a hot plate, served with lettuce and dipping sauces; a dish of Korean origin
yakisoba	Chinese-style wheat noodles stir-fried with pork, onions, carrots and cabbage, flavoured with *sōsu* and topped with *aonori* (see *nori*) and strips of red-colour pickled ginger (*benishōga*)
yakitori	bite-sized pieces of chicken and chicken giblets grilled on a skewer
Yamatoni	meat (originally beef) simmered in soy sauce with ginger and sugar; originated as canned food
yūgao	white flowered gourd, *Lagenaria siceraria*
zōni	or *ozōni*, a special New Year dish of *mochi* in vegetable soup; the recipe varies considerably throughout the country

Acknowledgements

The work on this book began in 1992, when I started gathering material for my MA thesis, which I submitted at Tsukuba University two years later. I will always be grateful to Kumakura Isao, my supervisor at the time, for opening my eyes to the excitement of scholarship. My research has since been financially supported by the Japanese Ministry of Education, Ajinomoto Foundation for Dietary Culture, Asahi Beer Foundation, Canon Foundation Europe and Isaac Alfred Ailion Foundation. The fieldwork on which the Postscript is based was part of the international research project 'Model of Global Japan and Globalization' coordinated by Harumi Befu and sponsored by the Japanese Ministry of Education (grant no: 10041094). The Glossary is largely based on Richard Hosking, *A Dictionary of Japanese Food: Ingredients and Culture* (Rutland, VT, and Tokyo, 1996).

I am very grateful to all friends, colleagues and mentors from whose advice I have benefited over the years. I owe particular gratitude to Jennifer Robertson and Sidney Mintz, who proved very generous teachers and friends, in their own, very different ways providing me with inspiration and encouragement. I must also mention Paul Wijsman – in my opinion the best librarian in the world – who never failed to help with my queries, even if they involved such unusual activities as searching for an early Meiji drawing of a tomato (we managed to find an eggplant in the end). Most of the illustrations in this book were generously made available to me by the library of Tokyo Kaseigakuin University, and the help of Ehara Ayako in this respect was crucial. I am also grateful to Inge Daniels, Niek Ijzinga, Sidney Mintz, Rachel Laudan, Jennifer Robertson, Jordan Sand and Brigitte Steger, along with the Reaktion Books publisher Michael Leaman, for their valuable comments on earlier versions of the manuscript. Of course, all the failings of this book are my own doing.

Parts of chapters Two, Three and the Postscript first saw the light of day as my articles 'Eating the World: Restaurant Culture in Early Twentieth-Century Japan', *European Journal of East Asian Studies*, II/1 (2003), pp. 89–116; 'Popularising a Military Diet in Wartime and Postwar Japan', *Asian Anthropology*, I/1 (2002), pp. 1–30; and 'From Ethnic to Hip: Circuits of Japanese Cuisine in Europe', *Food and Foodways*, XIII/4 (2005), pp. 241–72. The manuscript is a substantially reworked and expanded version of my contributions to *The Politics of Food* (Oxford: Berg, 2004), edited by

Marianne Lien and Brigitte Nerlich, and *A Companion to the Anthropology of Japan* (Oxford: Blackwell, 2005), edited by Jennifer Robertson.

I dedicate this work to my big brother, who has watched over me since the day I was born, and to my husband, who assumed this task much later, but approached it with even more devotion.

Photo Acknowledgements

The author and publishers wish to express their thanks to the below sources of illustrative material and/or permission to reproduce it.

Photos author's collection: pp. 15, 25, 40, 43, 55, 61, 73, 94, 97 foot, 99, 102, 123, 127, 128, 129, 131, 133, 158, 168, 184, 185, 186, 192 top, 195; photo courtesy of Chong Dae Sung: p. 150; photos courtesy of Inge Daniels: pp. 173, 174; photo courtesy of Earl Kinmonth: p. 196; photo courtesy of Ehara Ayako: p. 118; photos courtesy of Fujita Institute for Research into Military Equipment: pp. 78, 81, 86; photo courtesy of Hokkaidōritsu Bunshokan: p. 62; photos courtesy of Isetan Co.: p. 52, 53; photos courtesy of Ishige Naomichi: pp. 187, 193; photos from *Japan Pictorial*: pp. 137, 141; photos courtesy of Kagome Co.: pp. 58, 60; photos Mainichi Shinbunsha: pp. 71, 84; photos courtesy of Morinaga Co.: pp. 125, 126; photo courtesy of Mos Burger Co.: p. 172; photos courtesy of the National Science Museum, Tokyo: pp. 90, 91, 92; photo from *Shufu no tomo*: p. 160; photo courtesy of Tanaka Naomi, The Society for Research in Food Culture Design: p. 8; photos courtesy of Tokyo Kaseigakuin University: pp. 19, 22, 30, 32, 36, 38, 39, 47, 67, 93, 95, 97 top, 142; photo: Wagamama London p. 198; photos courtesy of www.oldTokyo.com: pp. 50, 51; photos courtesy of Yasuhara Miho: pp. 145, 146, 151, 153, 161, 164, 166, 171; photo Yomiuri News: p. 116; photo Zushi Amsterdam: p. 192 foot.

Index